SCHOOL DEVELOPMENT SERIES

General Editors: David Hopkins and David Reynolds

SCHOOL MANAGEMENT AND EFFECTIVENESS IN DEVELOPING COUNTRIES

OTHER TITLES IN THE SCHOOL DEVELOPMENT SERIES

SCHOOL MANAGEMENT AND EFFECTIVENESS IN DEVELOPING COUNTRIES

The Post-Bureaucratic School

Clive Harber and Lynn Davies

CASSELL

Cassell
Wellington House
125 Strand
London WC2R 0BB

PO Box 605
Herndon
VA 20172

First published 1997

British Library Cataloguing-in-Publication Data
A catalogue record for this book is available from the British Library.

ISBN 0-304-70064-9

Typeset by SetSystems Ltd, Saffron Walden, Essex
Printed and bound in Great Britain by J. W. Arrowsmith Ltd, Bristol.

Contents

Series Editors' Foreword

School effectiveness research is now two decades old. It has performed a valuable service in alerting policy-makers and practitioners, together with researchers, to the potential that schools have to transform children's life chances, and to the characteristics of those schools which add value. However, the research base has been almost exclusively taken from a small number of developed societies.

The importance of this well-written, meticulously researched and trenchantly argued book is that it demonstrates that such ethnocentrism is unfortunate. The authors combine a critique of the 'bureaucratic paradigm' within which effectiveness research operates with a powerful argument for the development of context-specific, non-bureaucratic forms of school that will suit the needs of developing societies. Schools in developing societies may not be ineffective because they lack something found in effective schools in industrialized settings, they argue – they are ineffective because of their context-specific fragility.

This book will repay reading by all those who feel that school effectiveness needs to advance from further celebration of the general towards a contingency perspective that celebrates difference. In its criticisms of effectiveness research, it is doing more than celebrate the needs of developing societies for relevant knowledge to enhance practice. It is developing a critique of what many of us have been engaged upon that has major importance for the field. This is, clearly, a very important book indeed.

David Hopkins
David Reynolds

Abbreviations

AIDS	Acquired Immunodeficiency Syndrome
ANC	African National Congress
BRAC	Bangladesh Rural Advancement Committee
CFA	Central African franc
CIEP	Integrated Centres of Public Education
CINEP	Colombian Research Centre in Popular Education
DEO	District Education Officer
EN	Escuela Nueva
EO	Education Officer; Equal Opportunities
GDP	gross domestic product
HGSCE	Higher General Certificate of Education
HIV	Human Immunodeficiency Virus
IGCSE	International General Certificate of Education
IMF	International Monetary Fund
IMPACT	Instructional Management by Parents, Community and Teachers
NFE	non-formal education
OECD	Organisation for Economic Co-operation and Development
PAMONG	Indonesian version of IMPACT
PTA	Parent–Teacher Association
SADCC	Southern African Development Coordination Conference
SAP	structural adjustment programme
UNDP	United Nations Development Programme
UNESCO	United Nations Educational, Scientific and Cultural Organization
USAID	United States Agency for International Development

Introduction

Heading South: Internationalizing Educational Management and School Effectiveness

We believe that this book is a new contribution to the literature on school management and school effectiveness. This is the case for three reasons.

1. This book is the first to attempt to theorize educational management and school effectiveness in developing countries. It not only describes and analyses the way in which schools operate in developing countries but, more significantly, tries to explain why they are as they are. We do this at three levels – the macro, meso and micro – and employ what we term transformational, prismatic and script theories respectively. The whole is embedded in a theoretical framework which we have termed 'post-bureaucracy'.

This endeavour originated in 1989 when the two authors began to work with each other on a full-time basis at the University of Birmingham and were drawing up new courses on educational management that were relevant to students who came predominantly from Africa, Asia and the Caribbean, with occasional students from Latin America. Both authors had lived and worked in developing countries and had travelled widely in them, continuing to do so for purposes of research, consultation and teaching over the next seven years.

It was clear that existing courses on educational management in the School of Education in which we worked – and in other institutions which we visited – were inadequate for teachers and managers from developing countries. This was because either they were so general and context-free that they did not address relevant issues or use relevant examples or, more commonly – and especially after the Education Reform Act of 1988 – they were entirely specific to the English and Welsh context. Courses entitled 'The Management of the Secondary School', for example, should really have been called 'The Management of the British Secondary School'. Increasingly, educational management courses in the UK have become concerned with markets, marketing, school league tables, implementing a central-ized curriculum, school-level control of budgets, 'opting out' of local government control, staff appraisal or assessment, 'kitemark' quality controls, performance indicators and corporate identity. This is not to say that some of these issues are not of interest to international educationists; but their presentation has increasingly been within the context of the enormous upheavals within the UK which heads and teachers are having to cope with on a daily basis.

Yet, as Hughes (1990, p. 9) has noted, the uncritical transportation of theories and tools of educational management across the world without regard to the qualities and circumstances of different communities can no longer be regarded as acceptable. As Lungu (1983, p. 90), writing on Africa, put it:

Most theorizing in administrative sciences has been based on the experiences of European and North American organizations, and almost nothing has been done in African settings, let alone African organizations. What these gaps portend for training programmes in Africa is that new and original thinking and research will be required.

So far, this original thinking and research on educational management in developing areas such as Africa has, with some important exceptions, been rather thin on the ground and piecemeal in nature. Indeed, if a recent book on theories of educational management is anything to go by (Bush, 1995), it does not exist at all. This book therefore should help fill a conspicuous gap in the literature.

2. In explaining how schools in developing countries presently operate, this book reconceptualizes the relationships between structure and agency (see Chapter 7). It uses essentially *contextual theory* and stands the contingency theory of educational management on its head. Contingency theory is largely a prescriptive one, about consciously planning and designing organizations that are suitable for, and do not conflict with, the environment in which they operate (Morgan, 1986, p. 48). Schools in developing countries often do not have this luxury. They are essentially contextually driven, ambient organizations, shaped by colonial history, global economic relationships, local cultural interaction and post-independence political needs. The result in the majority of cases is an ineffective mixture of authoritarianism and bureaucratic malfunction.

However, judging school effectiveness in terms of contextual relevance is fraught with difficulties, especially in developing countries. One major problem is the question of outcomes and goals, further discussed below. A second is the contextual nature of 'successful' operation. Judging the effectiveness of schools in developing countries may well involve substantially different criteria, given their contextual realities. The pressing questions are likely to be, for example: Have the teachers actually been there most of the year, and been paid? Are the majority of children sufficiently fed and healthy to benefit from being there? Do the children manage to attend regularly, or do they take large periods of time out for domestic or agricultural support to the family? Has the school managed to educate about avoiding malaria, HIV/AIDS or bilharzia? Has the school managed to get hold of a spirit duplicator? These issues are not usually priority questions in Western books on school effectiveness.

3. Creating the management environment that is best able to raise, discuss and cope with such issues in the future is the eventual concern of this book. Although in Chapter 8 we discuss some possible strategies for school improvement in developing countries, 'solutions' that might be quite different from those in so-called developed ones, all these solutions might be useful in some contexts and none in others. What is required, therefore, is not a particular management design in the sense of a more refined contingency theory, but rather a set of operating principles which allow for effective decision-making: flexibility, transparency, innovation, informed choice and localized consultation. This is why we have argued for a democratization of school management involving teachers, students, parents and other relevant partners. Although consciously based on one ideology, demo-cratic styles of management paradoxically allow for and encourage wide-ranging

participation from all those concerned prior to decisions being taken. They therefore build in maximum consultation and take into account a variety of viewpoints or interests, enhancing the quality of decision-making.

We have also argued for democratization because, in discussing school effectiveness, it is – or should be – impossible to ignore the issue of goals or the purposes for which schools exist. Of vital importance is the potential role that schools can play in sustaining democratic political systems. Without the peaceful conflict resolution made possible by genuine democracy, developing countries will be consigned to living under authoritarian regimes in which the violent suppression of human rights is a daily occurrence and in which civil and other forms of war are a regular possibility. Schools which contribute to such conditions, at present probably the majority, cannot be said to be effective.

Such a direct concern with broad politics and democratic forms of school management is also strangely absent from the conventional literature on school administration. As Ball (1987, p. 280) pointed out at the end of his book on the micro-politics of the school,

> Beyond the attempt at theorizing school organization, another
> fundamental question is begged. Is the form of organizational life
> presented here the only possible way of running schools? The answer
> must be 'no', and as I see it the alternative lies in the direction of school
> democracy. But that, as they say, is another story.

While there is a recent Western literature on democratic forms of school organ-ization and management (for example, Harber and Meighan, 1989; Jensen and Walker, 1989; Harber, 1992; Trafford, 1993; Davies, 1994; Chapman, Froumin and Aspin, 1995; Harber, 1995, 1996), its genesis outside conventional school manage-ment circles and its critique of existing authoritarian models seem so far to have rendered it largely invisible in the 'standard' texts. Even a very recent book on theories of educational management (Bush, 1995) deals only with 'collegial' theories of management which concern staff but tend to ignore student participation. The original contribution of our book to democratic theories of management is that it focuses on the context and experiences of developing countries to indicate how democratic forms of school management can significantly enhance school effective-ness in such countries.

Our focus in talking of 'schools' is mainly the formal school rather than non-formal education. Many interesting developments and initiatives are emerging from the non-formal sector. Yet non-formal education continues to be a small part of education spending, and in spite of the enormous issues of anachronism and irrelevance in the formal sector, it is likely that this style of collectivized education is here to stay – at least for the next twenty years or so. The reasons for its persistence will be analysed in Chapter 5. Given people's current acceptance of the inevitability of schooling, it is crucial, therefore, that the massive expenditure on this sector be used in a way that can aid rather than hinder a country's progress towards social justice, peace and the eradication of poverty. We argue that the 'post-bureaucratic school' is the mark of the future – from which the West could profitably learn.

'DEVELOPING COUNTRIES' – A BRIEF NOTE

In the post-World War II discussions of 'development', this was originally conceived of primarily in terms of levels of wealth and output measured by gross national product. The main division was therefore between the rich, predominantly industrialized countries of the North and the poor, predominantly agricultural countries of the South. More recently, as attempts to measure development become increasingly sophisticated, other indicators have been added. Social indicators concerned, for example, with levels of health, education, the environment and gender equity have also been used, as have economic indicators that include the *spread* of wealth, rather than just the total of wealth. Most recently of all, political indicators of human rights, freedom and political choice have been discussed, although these are often more difficult to quantify.

Perhaps the most authoritative statement on this debate is the annual *Human Development Report* produced by the UNDP (United National Development Programme). Each year its measurements of human progress become more complex and refined. However, it still divides up the world into 'developing countries' and 'industrialized countries'. The 1995 edition, for example, includes the whole of Africa, Latin America, the Arab states of the Middle East, the Caribbean, Asia (minus Australia, New Zealand and Japan) and Cyprus and Turkey from Southern Europe under developing countries. Industrialized countries are North America, Western and the rest of Southern Europe, the countries of the former Soviet Union and Warsaw Pact, and Japan, Australia and New Zealand. We are very aware that development is not an either/or, and that not only might there be a continuum of development but that there are indeed a number of different continua and interpretations. However, while recognizing the difficulties and imperfections involved in such gross classifications and measurements, we have also used the UNDP language and broad divide when we talk of 'developing countries'. Immediately we realize that this causes problems when thinking of countries we know well, such as Malaysia or South Korea, where at least on the 'wealth' dimension they might be classified as something like 'newly emergent industrialized economies'. Yet we have had to use a shorthand of some sort, otherwise the writing would have become unmanageable. We fully recognize that there are fashions in these terms (backward; underdeveloped; less developed; Third World; emergent; North–South and so on), and that 'developing' carries the (false) implication that the contrasting 'industrialized' countries have somehow arrived. We pondered on finding another term altogether, but expected that whatever was used this would be offensive or inaccurate for someone or some country. Given that 'developing' appears to be the currently least unacceptable word, we have decided to stay with that.

It will nonetheless be clear, as the book progresses, that from our particular research and teaching interests we have been concerned with countries under particular economic stringency. Our use of the term 'developing countries' therefore mostly refers to those countries which have undergone and continue to experience economic and political problems at the 'stringency' end of the continuum. Similarly, when we use the term 'Western', we are using this as a shorthand for literature and thinking which has emerged from industrialized areas such as the USA, the UK and Northern Europe as well as Australasia. It refers to an economic and ideological reality rather than a geographical one.

THE STRUCTURE OF THE BOOK

The book has four interlinked sections, which build towards our final arguments. In the first part, 'The State of the Field', we examine the existing economic and theoretical contexts around school effectiveness. Chapter 1 provides an analysis of the causes of economic crisis in developing countries and the impact of this crisis on the management of schools; Chapter 2 is an overview and critique of existing literature on school effectiveness and its relevance to the contexts described in the first chapter.

The second part, 'Contextual Realities for School Management', again has two chapters. The first begins the essential analysis of existing schools as bureaucracies – or, more precisely, as bureaucratic façades. The second provides an account, from ethnographic research, of the actual job of the headteacher in developing countries. The aim of this section is to demonstrate the realities of school life, organization and culture from which any theory of school effectiveness must derive.

The third part, 'Explaining School Management: Levels of Understanding', explores different ways to understand the realities described in the previous section. Our claim is that school effectiveness literature has been under-theorized, and that, particularly in a developing country context, we need to locate the management of schools within broad parameters of the international and local economy, of the local culture, and of the way that social actors make sense of these worlds. The section has three chapters. The first explores the 'macro' level of global relationships, and the theories which explain development and underdevelopment, with their implications for interpretations of the 'effective school'. The second moves to the 'meso' level, which we conceptualize as the particular national and community cultures which form the backdrop for ways in which 'traditional' and 'modern' intersect in a school. The third, 'micro', level uses contemporary theories around discourse, scripts, structure and agency to locate how individual actors position themselves within the various discursive fields of 'effectiveness', and use knowledge and power either to reproduce or to challenge existing forms of school organization.

The final part, 'Towards Post-Bureaucracy', draws together these realities and levels to argue for forms of schooling which can genuinely contribute to development. The first chapter of the section looks at the need for flexible schools which are more in tune with the imperatives of economic, social and political progress. Using examples from those developing countries which have challenged outdated bureaucratized and formalized modes of organization, it provides a range of initiatives which demonstrate that schools do not have to resemble prisons or factories in order to achieve 'outputs'. The final chapter sets such initiatives within an argument for the democratic school. Here, we argue that 'democracy' is not an endpoint, a Western imposition or an ideal state, but a term for a *process* – and for us the only process which can enable schools and their participants effectively to debate and meet the international challenges which the twenty-first century will generate.

PART ONE

The State of the Field

Chapter 1

Education in the Context of Developing Countries

Students at Nginda Girls High School in Murang'a are consuming water that has been declared to be unfit for human consumption by a government chemist. The school's headmistress, Mrs C. W. Gitu, said that this had led to a marked increase in waterborne diseases among the students. However, the students have to continue using the water from a nearby stream because the school did not have a water treatment plant, she said. Whenever the water pump broke down, Gitu said, students were forced to fetch water from the stream two kilometres away. . . . She said lack of teachers' houses forced the school to spend Ksh18,000 annually to ferry them to and from Maragua town where they lived. She also said that the school urgently needed laboratory equipment which was vital in the teaching of science. It also requires a school bus and electricity so as to reduce fuel bills. The headmistress said that if the teachers lived in the school they would have enough time to prepare their lessons which would improve the performance of the school in national examinations.

(Kenya, *Daily Nation*, 11 April 1992)

'The children learn nothing that is of use to them in that school. All the teachers do is to stop them from doing useful work.' There is not enough water in the village and it has to be brought in. It takes three hours to walk to their fields and they often have to stay overnight. They cannot leave their children in the village. Who would look after them? The teachers? Once, long ago, the old man recalls, his grandson came home and showed him how to make compost. That was the only time either of them had profited from school.

(Zimmer, 1992, p. 240, recounting discussions in a Mong village in northern Thailand)

Every day we are awoken at 5.00 am, when we wash our faces. After this we take machetes and go to weed the farm for 15 minutes. We then collect buckets and walk to the borehole to pump water for bathing. After assembly and regular daily academic classes, broken by an hour's sleep, we are divided into groups. Some of the boys then go the school farm to tend peppers, tomatoes, potatoes and cassava, while others go to the piggery to clean and feed the pigs. The girls help with the cooking, carry fire wood or pump water.

(Report by five students aged 12–14 at John Teye School, Ghana. *Focus on Africa*, October–December 1994)

INTRODUCTION

The purpose of this chapter is to explore different dimensions of the context in which schools in developing countries operate. The main argument of the chapter is that often this context is very different from that pertaining in most schools in developed countries. It would be very unusual, for example, for a teacher in Britain or America to work in the circumstances described in the quotations above. Inevitably, the need to generalize about 'developing countries' means that there is a risk that contrasts between individual developing countries and the existence of similarities with developed countries are not sufficiently highlighted in what is a broad continuum rather than an absolute divide. However, what is certainly the case is that most of the literature on school management and school effectiveness has been written in developed, industrialized countries and describes educational conditions and realities as they exist in those countries. As this chapter will demonstrate, it would be very mistaken to assume automatically that these conditions prevail in developing countries. There is, nevertheless, a danger that in stressing the problematic context of education in developing countries, too negative a picture will be painted. It is therefore important to bear in mind that considerable progress has been made in developing countries in a whole range of fields over the past two to three decades. The UNDP's 'balance sheet' of human development for developing countries, for example, records significant progress in life expectancy, access to safe water, primary school enrolment, per capita food production, agricultural and food production, declines in fertility rates, increased female access to education, decreased infant mortality and the extension of democracy. However, as will be discussed in this chapter, the 'deprivation' side of the balance sheet is another story (UNDP, 1995, p. 16) and it remains true that the everyday contexts in which children grow up and educational institutions function in some developing countries can differ markedly from those predominant in developed, industrialized countries. In this chapter we look at six contexts – demographic, economic, resources, violence, health and cultural – and then provide a case study (Mozambique) which exemplifies all these contexts.

THE DEMOGRAPHIC CONTEXT

> According to recent projections the world's primary school age population will increase from 652 million in 1990 to 760 million in the year 2000. Rapid population growth in some developing regions accounts primarily for this expected additional 100 million people. The number of out of school children in this age group is projected to rise from 129 million in 1990 to 144 million in 2000 unless major efforts are made to increase schooling capacity.
>
> (UNESCO, 1995, p. 2)

One glaring difference between developed and developing countries is in terms of their effectiveness at getting children educated in the light of rapidly expanding school-age populations. Whereas in developed countries primary and secondary education is universally available, only about 75 per cent of eligible children on average attend primary schools in developing countries. In 1987 59 per cent of 6- to 11-year-olds were enrolled in primary schools in Africa, and the equivalent figures for Asia and Latin America and the Caribbean were 80 per cent and 86 per cent. At the secondary level the enrolment figures taper off sharply: in 1987 they were 31 per cent in Africa, 42 per cent in Asia and 54 per cent in Latin America (Colclough with Lewin, 1993, pp. 1, 16, 18). The main reasons for this are that the state cannot afford education for all, that parents cannot afford fees, that the labour of the children is required elsewhere, or that education is not seen as worthwhile. This last factor particularly affects the education of girls. Despite widespread agreement in educational circles that the education of girls is one of the most important investments that any developing country can make, the traditional view that a girl does not need an education to be a wife and mother still persists. The majority of out-of-school children are therefore girls, and this is particularly the case in South Asia, the Middle East and North Africa and in sub-Saharan Africa (UNICEF, 1994a, pp. 20–1).

One further feature of enrolment confronting educational managers in developing countries is that there is often a high drop-out rate, caused by such factors as the inability to pay fees and teenage pregnancy. Students therefore tend to come in and out of education and, as a result, many are much older than their equivalents in industrialized nations. For example, in the mid-1980s over half those attending primary schools in Mozambique, Haiti, Lesotho and Colombia were outside the official age range, though at the other end of the scale the figure was less than 5 per cent in Korea, Sri Lanka and Rwanda (Colclough with Lewin, 1993, p. 40). In Mali Hough (1989, p. 81) reported that some 3000 'children' in primary schools were aged 20 and over. Moreover, in urban areas poor children not enrolled in school, or dropped out of school, whose families cannot support them increasingly end up as street children making a meagre living from selling, unskilled labour, begging or petty theft. Often these children would like to be educated but need to keep earning money and schools are not available at the times that suit their needs (Agnelli, 1986; Williams, 1992). However, not only do students drop out, sometimes schools do also. The following describes rural north-eastern Brazil:

> One of the most striking aspects of the rural schooling environment is the rate of demise of entire schools. Fully one third of our original sample of schools in 1981 no longer existed by 1983. The experiences in 1983 may have been atypical because of the severe drought that hit the northeast and caused substantial economic dislocation. Nevertheless, another 17 per cent of sampled schools disappeared between 1983 and 1985, suggesting that the stability of the schooling system in these rural areas is open to question.
>
> (Harbison and Hanushek, 1992, p. 192)

Exacerbating these demographic trends is rural–urban migration. In developing countries the urban population is expanding almost twice as fast as the total population, though in low-income Asian and African countries the rural population continues to grow at an average annual rate of 2 per cent or more. Part of the urban increase is due to rural–urban migration. Those who migrate from the countryside in search of a better quality of life are generally the better educated. As a result, the rural areas are deprived of a source of young, educated labour, a trend that increases their development problems. The effects of such migration are many: overcrowded schools, high repetition and drop-out rates, together with a deterioration in the quality of teaching in the urban areas and at the same time declining enrolments and the closing down of schools in rural areas (UNESCO, 1994, pp. 29–30).

THE ECONOMIC CONTEXT

For those in schools there are serious questions concerning the quality of education that can be provided. In 1990 recurrent expenditure per student in OECD countries was US$3000 – forty times that of countries in sub-Saharan Africa, thirty times that of countries in eastern Asia, twenty times that of countries in south Asia, ten times greater than that of the Arab states of the Middle East and seven times greater than that of Latin America and the Caribbean (UNESCO, 1994, p. 19). While already very much poorer than developed countries, the economies of developing countries are also particularly fragile and exposed to global economic changes. In July 1989, for example, the price of coffee on world markets dropped from $1.20 to 65 cents. While this may or may not eventually cause a small reduction in the price of coffee in developed countries, in Colombia some 800,000 families are dependent on coffee for their livelihood. If the coffee price is high they have schools, if it falls they starve (Graham-Brown, 1991, p. 13)

The rapid rise of the price of oil in the early 1970s had a major impact on many developing economies and consequently on their ability to pay for education. Surplus money in the Middle Eastern oil-producing nations was invested in banks in Western Europe and North America. This money was then recycled in the form of loans to developing countries, particularly in Africa and Latin America. However, the economic slow-down in Western economies following the oil crisis led to a reduction in the demand for, and hence a fall in the price of, the primary products that constitute the main exports of developing countries. This was coupled with a rise in the price of manufactured products imported into the same countries. On top of this the maintenance of a strong dollar meant that debt repayment became increasingly expensive. Between 1970 and 1987 the public debt service as a percentage of exports in Africa rose from 3.5 to 14.7 per cent (World Bank, 1989, Table 24). By 1991 debt in sub-Saharan Africa was 110 per cent of gross national product (London, *Guardian*, 20 July 1994). A study covering 107 developing countries, of which forty-one were categorized as 'least developed' found the following trends since 1980:

- Debt service (the amount of money paid in interest and other charges on loans) had increased to claim a greater share of export earnings in 87 per cent of the least developed countries and in 84 per cent of the other developing countries.

- Gross domestic product per capita had fallen in 54 per cent of the least developed countries and 64 per cent of the other developing countries.

- Private consumption per capita had decreased in 81 per cent of the least developed countries and in 64 per cent of other developing countries.

- Public expenditure per capita had fallen in 58 per cent of the least developed countries and in 64 per cent of other developing countries (Graham-Brown, 1991, pp. 13–14).

The decrease in money available for public expenditure has affected spending on education in many countries. In sub-Saharan Africa and Latin America public expenditure per inhabitant fell between 1980 and 1987 though it increased in Arab and Asian countries (Colclough with Lewin, 1993, p. 20). In terms of individual countries the proportion of public expenditure devoted to education between 1972 and 1986 fell, for example, in Bangladesh, Burkina Faso, Kenya, Malawi, Sri Lanka, Tanzania, Bolivia, Chile, El Salvador, Morocco, Tunisia, Mexico and Uruguay. In the case of Zaire it nearly disappeared from view, falling from 15.2 per cent to 0.8 per cent. Interestingly in twelve out of these fourteen countries the proportion of public expenditure devoted to defence actually increased (UNICEF, 1989, p. 17).

Illustrative of the vulnerability of developing economies to decisions made elsewhere is the French government's uncoupling of the French franc from the Central African franc, the currency of francophone central and west Africa, in 1994. This immediately resulted in a major devaluation of the CFA. Any devaluation has two consequences: it makes imported goods more expensive and it generates internal inflation thereby reducing the purchasing power of wages. These are exactly the two major components of every education budget in Africa: the major share of the budget is spent on teachers' salaries and the rest on the purchase of learning materials, in particular textbooks – most of which are imported. In reality, this simply worsened the economic difficulties caused by the persistent recession of the 1980s and the impact of structural adjustment policies, further discussed below. Public expenditure on education in the francophone zone had already dropped by 35.6 per cent between 1985 and 1990 (Donors to African Education, 1994).

Many developing countries, in order to get loans from the IMF and the World Bank, have had to agree to structural adjustment programmes which deliberately cut back on state funding for health, welfare and educational provision. One recent study of the educational effects of structural adjustment programmes in Latin America and Africa (Reimers, 1994) concluded that, in those countries with structural adjustment programmes, expenditure on education declined more than in those without, that private households were less able to make up the shortfall by contributing to education because of the sharply increased austerity created by the negative multiplier effects of SAP public expenditure cuts and that drops in enrolment rates were much more marked in countries with SAPs than without. Reimers (1994, p. 128) concludes:

> In sum, adjustment either directly via the effects on public financing of education or indirectly, via the incentives facing households, reduced educational opportunity. But it reduced it particularly for the disadvantaged ... If we assess the impact of adjustment programmes on education with the standards proposed earlier, that is in terms of whether the countries that adjusted are doing *better* than those that are not, it is clear that adjustment has fallen short of these targets.

THE RESOURCE CONTEXT

What is the effect of these low (and in some cases declining) levels of expenditure on human and material resources in schools in the light of ever-increasing levels of demand for education? One Zambian writer bleakly describes the conditions in schools in developing countries as 'wholesale systemic decay':

> Classrooms are overcrowded; teachers are overworked and underpaid, sometimes not paid at all for months on end; the books used in classrooms are often long out of date, and not enough to go round (it is not uncommon in rural African and Latin American schools to see a single textbook for a given subject shared by a whole class); and the school equipment and buildings are in such a state of neglect, due to lack of funds for maintenance and repair, that even the most basic functions, such as keeping out inclement weather, have been severely compromised. For long periods of time students and teachers have to go without the most rudimentary of classroom learning tools such as paper, pencils and chalk, let alone such equipment as stencil duplicating machines, and not to mention photocopiers and personal computers that have now become part of the standard equipment for schools in the Western industrialised nations. Midday school meals for children is a luxury that is unheard of. Lack of housing for teachers in some of the more remote schools has at times meant that classrooms have had to be converted into living quarters. That any kind of learning is taking place in such circumstances is a miracle in itself.
>
> (Lulat, 1988, p. 318)

The rest of this section will examine some of these conditions in more detail. In terms of class size, the average number of students per teacher in the world's primary schools varies from about a dozen in Norway to over 90 in the Central African Republic. These averages also conceal huge disparities within countries. In Malawi primary schools can have classes of 200 and secondary schools 65 (Scott, 1995, p. 41). Generally, class sizes in the developing world are at least two or three times larger than equivalent classes in industrialized nations. Moreover, if this was looked at in terms of providing education for all, the relevant figure would not be the teacher:student ratio but school-age children per teacher. This would produce a figure of 175 per teacher in Afghanistan, 188 in Mali and 145 in Bhutan (UNICEF, 1994a, p. 22). However, teacher:student ratios are not the only factor in overcrowding. A study by Moll (1995) in rural South Africa found that while the staff complement was correct for an official ratio of 1:43, there were too many teachers for the actual numbers of classrooms available so that teachers had to double up in the same classroom. On top of this, the principal revealed that another reason for the overcrowding was that, while the officially registered complement for the school was 420, the actual number at the school was 563. His explanation was simple: 'How can I turn children who come to school away?' A 1985 study of classroom conditions in urban schools in twelve African countries showed that nearly half were inadequate. Classrooms designed for 40 were accommodating 70 (Hallak, 1990, p. 43).

In terms of expenditure on teaching resources, in 1980 a study of 34 low-income countries revealed that they spent an average of $1.69 per head on instructional materials for primary schools. In 32 middle-income countries the figure was $6.14. In 16 industrialized countries the figure was $92.32. The figures ranged from $0.11 in the Philippines to $250 in Canada (World Bank, 1986). Moreover, expenditure on teaching materials actually declined as a proportion of expenditure on education in developing countries throughout the 1980s (Heyneman, 1990). In Guatemala, in the 1980s, 75 to 100 per cent of students had no textbooks at all. In Nigeria the figure was 98 per cent, in Paraguay and Peru 67 per cent and Pakistan 50 per cent (Hallak, 1990, p. 35). One study, in the Parish of St Thomas in Jamaica, found that 13 per cent of the students had neither pens nor pencils and 45 per cent had no textbooks (IIEP, 1983). A study in India found that 61 per cent of schools do not have enough blackboards, 49 per cent do not have enough maps and charts, and 49 per cent do not have any desks and chairs for students (Singhal, 1988).

The maintenance of school buildings is often the first to suffer in the context of budgetary cuts. In the early 1980s some 20 per cent of schools in the Ed Duneim district in Sudan had no water and 57 per cent had no latrines. In the Kilosa district of Tanzania 42 per cent of schools were without water and 10 per cent without latrines. In Nigeria many schools in the north lack roofs and have collapsed walls, and in some parts of the south children can be seen carrying their own desks to schools every day (Graham-Brown, 1991, p. 38). Similarly in north-eastern Brazil,

> most [schools] lack many or all the attributes of primary schools taken for granted in more prosperous settings. There is not even a guarantee of a building, however modest and minimally maintained, built to serve as a school. Existing buildings are often missing water service and sanitary facilities or desks and chairs for the students and teachers.
>
> (Harbison and Hanushek, 1992, p. 190)

A study in the Seti region of Nepal found that 80 per cent of schools had leaking roofs, only 28 per cent had toilets and 20 per cent were in a state of collapse (Caillods and Postlethwaite, 1989, p. 172). The following describes the position in Sierra Leone (Banya, 1991, p. 133):

> Many schools in the country are crumbling because of lack of repairs, building materials and money to pay contractors. This is especially true of primary schools. Many of the buildings were erected in the late 1950s and early 1960s with mud blocks and, in some instances, sticks. Today they are not only a health hazard but potential death traps. Indeed, in many areas, particularly in rural Sierra Leone, classes are now regularly held in the open during the dry season. During the rainy season from April till October, the children are crowded into the few buildings that are still standing. Makeshift buildings have been put up, with all the attendant health hazards. Typical of the comments of the teachers interviewed are the following:
> 'Since the building on the far corner of the football field collapsed, I have been using this makeshift room as a classroom. When it rains, I move the children to join those in Class III. There is not enough space for

everyone, so most of the children stand up till the rain ceases. In the dry season the dust from the floor makes the children cough a lot.'

Needless to say many schools in developing countries, probably the majority in rural areas, do not have electricity and, even if they are connected to the national grid, power supplies are often erratic and unpredictable.

As regards teachers themselves, in developing countries schools often have to function with either unqualified or underqualified staff. This is particularly so in rural areas where it is difficult to send qualified teachers. In Brazil in 1982, for example, whereas unqualified teachers represented 25 per cent of the whole teaching force in first-level schools at the national level, they constituted 73 per cent of rural teachers (Caillods and Postlethwaite, 1989, p. 169). In 1980 70 per cent of all teachers in Nicaragua were underqualified, as were 46 per cent in Bangladesh, 40 per cent in Cuba and 30 per cent in Guyana. In 10 out of 33 sub-Saharan African countries for which data were available in 1988, the majority of primary teachers had not even completed secondary education (Hallak, 1990, pp. 36–7). The need to rely on unqualified and underqualified teachers will probably become worse, as the teacher requirement for primary education in all developing countries was 16.3 million in 1990 but is expected to jump to 21.5 million in the year 2000 (UNESCO, 1994, p. 17).

Moreover, teachers' salaries in developing countries have declined in real terms. Mexican teachers lost about 40 per cent of their purchasing power between 1979 and 1984, Peruvian teachers lost 35 per cent of theirs between 1974 and 1980 and Bolivian teachers 65 per cent between 1980 and 1985. In the Philippines, the government doubled teachers' salaries at the end of the 1980s but they still remain below the official poverty line. In Tanzania salaries were fixed for teachers in 1974 and not revised until 1981. By 1987 most teachers had a purchasing power of only about 40–75 per cent that of the lowest-paid teacher in 1977 (Caillods and Postlethwaite, 1989, p. 171). A World Bank study of primary teachers' salaries in eighteen countries of sub-Saharan Africa found that real salaries had declined in all but two between 1980 and 1985. In eleven countries, including Kenya, Zambia, Zimbabwe and Senegal, the falls were 10 per cent or more (Graham-Brown, 1991, p. 39).

On top of this, salaries in more and more countries are paid late. In Sierra Leone in 1989, for example, teachers had not been paid for three months (Banya, 1991, p. 131). Late and irregular payment of salaries has also been recorded as a problem in, for example, Nigeria (Harber, 1989, pp. 120–1) and in Haiti, Liberia and Yemen (World Bank, 1990, p. 25). The result of these problems with inadequate and irregular salaries is low morale and work effort, departure of skilled teachers and increased absenteeism. Teachers take up second and third jobs, or spend more time farming, which interferes with their ability to function effectively as a teacher. They are also increasingly forced into illicit and corrupt practices in order to survive.

THE CONTEXT OF VIOLENCE

In the past thirty years developing countries have been plagued by war and violent unrest. In this violence it is increasingly the civilian population that is affected rather than soldiers. In World War I civilians accounted for only 14 per cent of those killed. The figure had reached 90 per cent in Africa by the 1990s (UNICEF; Johannesburg, *The Star*, 11 December 1995). A glance at a world map might, for example, produce the following list of developing countries where war has taken place since 1945: Afghanistan, Angola, Bangladesh, Burundi, Cambodia, Chad, East Timor, El Salvador, Ethiopia, Eritrea, Grenada, Guatemala, Guinea-Bissau, Haiti, Iran, Iraq, Kenya, Korea, Kuwait, Lao, Lebanon, Liberia, Mali, Mozambique, Namibia, Nicaragua, Nigeria, Rwanda, Sierra Leone, Somalia, South Africa, Spanish Sahara, Sri Lanka, Sudan, Uganda, Vietnam, Yemen, Zaire, Zimbabwe. In a number of other countries, such as Chile, Argentina and Myanmar (Burma), military dictatorships have carried out violent acts against their own people. The huge reduction in global military expenditure that took place between 1987 and 1994 because of the end of the cold war was money saved by developed countries (from whom the developing countries continue to buy large quantities of arms) and went towards reducing their budget deficits (UNDP, 1994). The following statement from UNICEF there-fore applies largely to developing countries:

> In the last decade alone an estimated 1.5 million children have been killed in armed conflicts. A further 4 million have been disabled, maimed, blinded, brain-damaged. At least five million have become refugees and 12 million more uprooted from their communities. Much larger numbers have seen their health, nutrition, and education suffer as conflicts have destroyed crops, infrastructure, clinics, schools . . . And in many parts of the world, children have been tortured and forced to watch or participate in atrocities. Hundreds and thousands have been crippled by landmines. Many more have been recruited into armies, given drugs and weapons and desensitized to others' pain. Uncounted millions of these young people are suffering from post-traumatic stress disorders, a new and chilling term in the international lexicon.
>
> (UNICEF, 1994b, p. 4)

In Africa, for example, women and children account for 92 per cent of war-related deaths. In Rwanda alone more than 200,000 children have been orphaned or separated from their families. In the early 1990s more children were dying in Mozambique every day than in all of the countries of the former Soviet Union (UNICEF, quoted in *Focus on Africa*, October–December 1994). Moreover, UNICEF has noted that there has been a frightening increase in the use of children as soldiers. In the same decade boys and girls under 16 had taken part in conflicts in 25 countries, notably in Cambodia and Liberia. In 1988 alone they numbered 200,000. Many children joined armed groups to survive, notably in Cambodia, Liberia and Burma. Others joined up to avenge the deaths of their relatives (Johannesburg, *The Star*, 11 December 1995). In the Philippines in 1990 there were over 2500 direct and indirect violations against children. By far the greatest number of violations were arrest and detention, with over 800 cases of physical and mental assault. At least 150 children were killed through assassination or by being caught in a crossfire in a military operation or by what is called 'salvaging', a military euphemism for extra-judicial execution (Marcelino, 1992, p. 164).

War has directly affected schools. During the 1980s the war in Mozambique caused the destruction or closure of 60 per cent of the country's schools (World University Service, 1994). In Liberia, where there is a bloody civil war in progress, 25 teachers have been murdered and, although 3000 teachers are officially working, an estimated 5000 teachers are in exile. Not surprisingly,

> The conditions of work are appalling in the aftermath of the war. Furniture and equipment have been stolen or broken, leaving very little in the way of facilities. Children are obliged to sit on the concrete floors in dark classrooms as even if there was lighting, electricity is rarely available. Due to a number of school buildings having been totally destroyed in the shelling, teachers can expect to face classes of up to 70 students. Due to the lack of material, children usually have to bring their own paper and pencils to school.
>
> (Danish Union of Teachers, 1994)

Schools have been sites of violence during these wars and periods of violent unrest. The following newspaper report describes a school in Afghanistan.

> The headmistress looked up quizzically at the crest of the hill overlooking the Zarghuma high school in eastern Kabul. The big guns had opened up again and the machine guns began to chatter. They were firing in the opposite direction but 'We might as well move to the yard on the other side of the school', she said. 'We're pretty used to it and we've never been hit but it is a nuisance. Bullets started whistling over us last Thursday when the local commander of Hisbe Wahadat (a Shi'ite mojahedin coalition) had a skirmish over a kilo of meat' . . . She (the headmistress) earns less than 6 pounds sterling a month and her 180 staff, all women, earn less than 2 pounds . . . The school is home to 650 refugees from the vicious fighting in Kabul earlier this year. They live in the classrooms and corridors, squeezing out the pupils . . . Behind a door marked English Department was a classroom filled with smoke. Three women were cooking over a wood fire on the stone flags . . . The headteacher was sympathetic but wanted her school for teaching. 'It's really unfair to move them out unless a proper place is found for them, but it's very hard for us to teach the children if the refugees don't go. We're having to use the library, laboratories and even the corridors and school yard.' With a staggering 4757 registered pupils – although in the present chaos only 2100 actually attend school – class sizes average 45–50. Pupils' ages range from 5 to 18, though some have stayed on until 22 because schools closed after the collapse of the government in the previous year . . . there are only three blackboards, the library has been looted of all but 1000 of its 7000 books and the simple science equipment is locked up.
>
> (London, *Guardian*, 24 August 1993)

Moreover, thousands of children are being killed and disabled by the anti-personnel mines that are waiting in their tens of millions in the earth of many developing countries. Afghanistan's war has left a legacy of 9–10 million mines, Angola 9 million (as many mines as people), Iraq 5–10 million, Kuwait 5–7 million, Cambodia 4–7 million and Mozambique 2 million. Another 10 million mines a year are being manufactured annually, primarily in the West, to feed the £200 million a year trade (UNICEF, 1994a, p. 39). For those children who survive the walk to school, lifelong disability can be the price paid.

Long-term violence in a society can create a culture of violence which it is difficult to eradicate overnight. In South Africa apartheid, which only finally disappeared in 1994, was both a violent system of repression in itself and spawned violent resistance. In the aftermath of the Soweto uprisings the police shot and killed some 1000 students during 1976/77, many more were injured and countless more arrested. In 1985 school and university students became increasingly militant and, with the South African army being used against its own people, they not only organized widespread boycotts, strikes, rallies and pickets but also barricaded streets and waged street battles with the police and army. They burnt property and attacked people they saw as collaborators. Their slogan became 'Liberation Now, Education Later' (Christie, 1991, ch. 8).

Inequality, poverty, too many weapons in the wrong hands and the willingness to use them are the legacy of apartheid. There is much discussion in South Africa about restoring a culture of learning in schools to replace the culture of violence that exists, particularly in the African townships. In a school in KwaMashu, for example, a township just outside Durban, a reporter and a photographer doing a piece on 'back to school' were attacked by youths wielding knives who stole their cameras. 100 KwaMashu residents demonstrated at the ANC regional offices in Durban, protesting that schools were like a war zone, especially early in the year when criminals know that schools are collecting fees. Intimidated by gangsters, many of the children have begun to carry knives and guns themselves – writing on the wall of one of two primary schools closed by the violence reads 'Sangena Ngesbhamu', 'We enter with a gun'. Some teachers are leaving the schools or simply not turning up. One teacher picked up his pay cheque at the end of the month after reporting to school only three times. Their reluctance is perhaps not surprising given that a teacher at one school was held hostage by students who were upset at being failed. Moreover, the general level of violence in rural KwaZulu/Natal resulting from clashes between supporters of the African National Congress and the Inkatha Freedom Party has also had its impact on education. At Ndwedwe, inland from Verulam, an already overcrowded primary school has had to pack in another 200 children from two neighbouring schools closed because of the violence (Durban, *Mercury*, 30 January, 1 and 2 February 1996).

THE HEALTH CONTEXT

For many of their citizens the economic context of developing countries is one of poverty. Of Africa's 500 million people, for example, 300 million are living in absolute poverty and the situation is getting worse. Incomes dropped from $570 per capita in 1980 to $350 in 1992 (Brittain, 1994). Poverty means hunger, and children cannot learn effectively if they are weak from hunger. Moreover, children who are malnourished will suffer other health problems which, in turn, will affect their education negatively. Though significant progress is being made in a number of countries, the following quotation from a UNICEF report indicates the difficulties.

> One third of the developing world's children suffer from protein-energy malnutrition. An estimated 250,000 children a year lose their eyesight because they lack vitamin A. At least 50 million children have impaired development because they lack iodine. Over half the pregnant women in the developing world suffer iron-deficiency anaemia. Millions of infants are exposed to illness, poor growth, and early death by the decline in breastfeeding. Approximately one third of the developing world's children are underweight.
>
> (UNICEF, 1994a, pp. 6–7)

Again, despite progress in their reduction, five diseases (pneumonia, diarrhoea, measles, tetanus and whooping cough) kill 8 million children a year in the developing countries (UNICEF, 1994b, p. 1). Many more children suffer from these and other diseases which hamper their education. The rural north-east region of Brazil faces multiple deprivations, of which poor health and nutrition rank high. A study in the region in 1987 found that short-term malnutrition, measured by skinfold thickness-for-age, was associated with poorer school performance. Moreover, the lowest achieving strata of students had the largest nutritional defects (Harbison and Hanushek, 1992, p. 200).

AIDS is also now a major health problem in developing countries. According to the World Health Organization, approximately 14 to 15 million people have been infected with the HIV virus worldwide, and the figure will rise to 40–50 million by the year 2000. Of these cases 90 per cent will be in developing countries. This particularly affects sub-Saharan Africa but there are also regions in Latin America, the Caribbean and Asia, especially Thailand, where the position is very serious. This not only affects health directly but, as the United Nations has warned, also causes labour shortages and places enormous economic burdens on poor societies because it threatens to hurt agricultural production and lead to food shortages and undernourishment (London, *Guardian*, 17 November 1994). This inevitably affects small children and young people, the former through maternal transmission during pregnancy and the latter through at-risk sexual behaviour. In 1994 the American Bureau of Statistics estimated the impact of AIDS on the under-5 mortality rate by the year 2010 in a selection of thirteen African countries and in Thailand, Brazil and Haiti. They estimated that without AIDS the mortality rate would be 1,234,000 and with AIDS 2,082,000 – a difference of 850,000 AIDS-related deaths (UNICEF, 1994a, p. 5). Schools in the regions seriously affected will be increasingly confronted with the management of large numbers of HIV- and AIDS-infected children and children whose close relatives are suffering from AIDS-related disorders. It also poses important curriculum challenges to schools in terms combating the spread of the disease.

> The spread of AIDS amongst children, their education and their life chances are also not helped by the increase in child prostitution in developing countries. Poverty and western sexual tourism means that the sexual exploitation of children is now a feature of economic life in several countries in Asia and Latin America. Recent estimates suggest that at least one million children are involved in eight Asian countries alone. There are now as many as 300,000 thousand child prostitutes in India,

100,000 in Thailand, 100,000 in Taiwan, 100,000 in the Philippines,
40,000 in Viet Nam, 30,000 in Sri Lanka and many thousands in China.
Nepali girls under 16 are to be found in Indian brothels and as many as
40,000 Bengali children are being prostituted in Pakistan.

(UNICEF, 1994a, p. 39)

Finally, in many African countries in arid regions there is always the threat of
drought and thus crop failure and famine. In recent years, for example, the rains
have failed in Zimbabwe and the drought has affected education, with record
numbers of students dropping out because they cannot afford the fees. In some
areas teachers reported that children were too hungry to learn effectively, and even
that they collapsed in class (London, *Guardian*, 2 February 1993). In other areas
it has been even worse. Famine in Ethiopia captured the attention of the world in
1984/85 and the Sahel region has suffered long periods of drought. The following
(from Biddlecombe, 1993, p. 54) describes the effect of severe drought in Burkina
Faso in the Sahel, one of the poorest nations in the world – ranked 169 out of 174
in the UNDP's Human Development Index (UNDP, 1995, p. 157).

> After the major drought in the early 1970s, the children all had those
> swollen bellies and matchstick legs. Men and women were wasting away
> on pavements, on street corners, in groups under the trees. I saw a fight
> over a crust of bread somebody had thrown into the gutter . . . Many
> children were so hungry they could no longer eat. They actually refused
> the food they needed to survive as if they had forgotten what eating and
> drinking was about. The extremest form of anorexia, it begins by the time
> a baby is six months old. If by then they have not received enough
> goodness and minerals and vitamins either naturally or artificially they
> are vulnerable. There is nothing anybody can do. They just wither away
> and die.

THE CULTURAL CONTEXT

In developing societies the values, beliefs and behaviours of traditional cultures
coexist, not always harmoniously, with imported Western ones. To illustrate this,
Hoogvelt (1978, p. 115) uses the example of an African student who is uncertain
about his or her examination results and so both consults a magician and at the
same time revises diligently until the early hours. Another example provided by
Hoogvelt (ibid., p. 126) is of Western doctors in a West African hospital who tried
to teach the local nursing staff to apply the ethical standards and requirements of
the nursing profession to all patients, regardless of ethnic background. Unsuccessful, the doctors finally decided to entrust even medical aspects of hospital treatment
to members of patients' families. (It is customary for hospitals in Africa to allow the
families of patients to attend and feed the patients inside hospitals all day and
sometimes during the night.)

Schools are also affected by the coexistence of the imported cultural values of
the Western school and the values of the surrounding society. In northern Kenya,
for example, Meru boys, especially adolescents, are not allowed to enter the kitchen
or serve food, yet local mission schools encourage such practices as a way of
training them to be responsible for their future life. Moreover, in the local Samburu

culture hair should be scattered after being cut, a situation which makes the school compound untidy and thus, in the eyes of the mission teachers, makes it difficult for the school to achieve its aim of making the students 'responsible members of the community' (Bala, 1994, pp. 67–8).

The relationship between schools and culture will be more fully explored in Chapter 6. However, it is also important to bear in mind that, especially in secondary schools, there may well exist a series of cultures each with different interpretations of the way in which a school should operate. This is not only because staff may be recruited from ethnically diverse parts of the state but also because expatriates, themselves possibly from different countries, may make up a substantial proportion of the staff. Schatzberg (1979), for example, provides a case study of cultural conflict over authority patterns in a Cameroonian lycée. He concludes that the 'rules of the game' are culturally relative. The principal, the other expatriates and the local Bamileke teachers acted on different conceptions of how authority relations should take place, with the result that social relations between the staff and the principal were often disrupted and the organization ran 'less than smoothly'.

A CASE STUDY

Mozambique in south-eastern Africa is a useful illustration of how many of the problems outlined above can come together in one, very poor, developing country. This account is based on work done in Mozambique by the World University Service (1994).

At independence, in 1975, Mozambique inherited a very fragile economy and a very weak educational system. Both were heavily dependent on, and geared to, the needs of the expatriate Portuguese. The mass exodus of the Portuguese at independence caused an enormous shock to the economy and the education system and simultaneously removed the country's capacity to adjust to that shock. Initial success with health and education was seriously undermined by the early 1980s as a result of economic decline caused by a combination of weaknesses in economic policy, adverse external circumstances and extreme weather conditions. The education system was further weakened during the 1980s as the security situation deteriorated with fighting between the FRELIMO government and the South Africa-backed RENAMO guerrillas. As a result, 60 per cent of the country's schools were destroyed or closed between 1983 and 1991; some 10 per cent of the population fled to neighbouring countries and a further 25 per cent were displaced within Mozambique. Despite the adoption of a World Bank/IMF-supported structural adjustment programme in 1987, economic growth has been negative since 1990. In 1991 the total foreign debt was equivalent to over 350 per cent of gross domestic product.

The combined effect of economic decline, external debt and adjustment has been to severely constrain the resources available for government recurrent expenditure. Overall recurrent expenditure per capita fell by 37 per cent between 1983 and 1993. The education sector has been particularly badly affected: recurrent expenditure per capita fell by over 40 per cent between 1982 and 1993. The combination of these factors has seriously affected both the quantity and quality of education:

- the gross primary enrolment ratio fell from 76 per cent in 1981 to 44 per cent in 1992;

- the rate of students repeating years in school is 27 per cent;

- over 80 per cent of children entering primary school do not successfully complete five years;

- whilst boys obtain a mean of 2.1 years of primary education, girls obtain only half of this;

- the national student:teacher ratio is 57:1, though in the first years of school it is probably nearer to 80:1;

- most schools run a two- or three-shift system;

- spending on teaching and learning materials is about US$1 per student per year. Only 50 per cent of textbooks produced actually reach schoolchildren, suggesting that US$1 is an overestimate;

- most classes therefore have only one textbook and some have none at all. Education is therefore little more than rote memorization of unsophisticated and poorly interpreted information;

- generally low levels of education affect the quality of the teachers' own education and hence their performance;

- teacher performance is also seriously constrained by exceedingly low salary levels of about US$80 per year.

ACHIEVEMENT

What are the outcomes of such schooling in developing countries? Caillods and Postlethwaite (1989, pp. 175–7) have summarized the evidence that exists, though they acknowledge difficulties caused by the paucity of data, the shortage of longitudinal studies and the norm-based nature of most examination systems in developing countries. They nevertheless note that there is some evidence that cognitive achievements in many, though not all, developing countries are low and, in general, the achievement is lower than that observed in developing countries. Using data from the International Association for the Evaluation of Educational Achievement, Heyneman and Loxley (1983), for example, concluded that school-children in low- and middle-income countries have learned less science after the same, or approximately the same, length of time in school as in wealthy countries. In the United States the average mean achievement score is 32.8 and in Japan 40.9. However, in India it is 20.6, in Colombia 24.0 and Thailand 28.2. In an IEA mathematics study in 1981 13- to 14-year-olds in the OECD countries scored an average of 52.9 per cent and the same age group in Nigeria and Swaziland scored 34.5 per cent. In a study of countries with very similar science curricula in the period 1984–86, the 14-year-olds in the OECD countries scored 60 per cent while Ghana, Nigeria, Zimbabwe and the Philippines scored 46, 41, 41 and 38 respectively. On the other hand students in China and Papua New Guinea scored 59 per cent and 55 per cent, though the Chinese sample was less reliable as it did not include all of China but only the three provinces around Beijing itself.

It is also important to stress, however, that the differences in achievement between schools seem much higher in developing countries than in industrialized ones. In Scandinavian countries the between-school variance accounts for as little as 2 per cent whereas in developing countries the difference can be as much as 30–40 per cent between primary schools and 60–70 per cent between secondary schools. It is important to note that in many cases these between-school differences are associated with urban–rural differences (Caillods and Postlethwaite, 1989, p. 179), and hence with resource and cultural factors outlined in this chapter, and that the rural context of the majority of schools in developing countries is an important consideration in debates about their management and effectiveness.

CONCLUSION

In 1988 one of the authors accompanied a young Kenyan friend to the primary school in the remote arid north of Kenya where he had begun working as an untrained teacher. The turnoff to the school was some sixty kilometres along a bad, untarred road. The turnoff was simply a gap between two trees and unrecognizable to the untutored eye and the school was ten kilometres down a track in an area where the bush was a little less dense. The 'school' consisted of one small mud building with a corrugated roof, and one round thatched building made out of branches. The other teachers and the children did not know we would be arriving that day. As we arrived, clusters of children were being taught English and maths under trees around the school area and rushed to greet their teacher. We watched part of a lesson where the children from nomadic ethnic groups showed off what they had learned in maths. The teachers were extremely poorly and unreliably paid, miles from any town and with no transport of their own. There seemed little incentive to do much at all. Yet, however basic, and despite the unpromising working conditions, education was taking place and the pupils seemed to be interested and to have learned something. The school seemed to be functioning reasonably effectively for its circumstances, but would need to be judged according to very different criteria from a school in Britain or America. That the school had managed to attract and hold children from nomadic groups traditionally hostile or indifferent to Western education was, for example, a significant mark of success.

Not all schools in developing countries experience the contexts outlined in this chapter. Many schools in the more prosperous areas of large cities function similarly to those in developed countries; other schools, in poorer regions, may face some of the problems described. The fact remains, however, that the populations of developing countries are still overwhelmingly poor and live mainly in rural areas. The majority of schools working in such a context may well have different criteria from Western schools for what counts as success in terms of academic achievement. Their goals may not be academic at all. Involvement in agricultural production, for example, seems a deliberate aim of the John Teye School in Ghana, described in the extract on page 9. To the writers of this book, for example, it seems that in addition to basic literacy and numeracy, peace education and health education should be high on any list of educational goals in developing countries. The management issues schools face in achieving their goals, and the inputs they have to achieve them, can also be very different from schools in developed countries. The issue may often seem to be one of making such schools less ineffective rather than more effective, though this too may be to judge such schools by Western standards of what is possible and achievable – which is especially ironic, as most Western teachers would not survive for long in these contexts.

Perhaps the puzzle, given the often very difficult circumstances, is why anything happens at all. The fact that it does is a salient reminder of the importance of human agency and the danger of fatalistic over-emphasis on the power of political and economic structures to completely determine behaviour:

> In a remote school in Matabele land there was a young student teacher *whose working conditions and social background were just as poor as that of any other student teacher and as that of the fifth grade children he was teaching* [writer's italics]. The children were busy doing different things. They seemed interested in what they were doing and smiled friendly to us, the intruders. Often children in these remote areas used to stare at foreigners with a frightened look. Not so with these children. In one corner of the classroom there was a bookshelf made of old bricks and planks wrapped up in newspaper. There were a few booklets and some magazines which the teacher had collected together with the children. In the windows, some with broken panes, big seeds had been threaded on strings and were waving happily as decoration in the light breeze from the window. In one corner the organization of SADCC was illustrated by means of empty coke tins and stones. Newspaper pictures were glued to the boxes, symbolizing different SADCC departments. On the floor maps of different countries were shaped with pebbles. There was hardly an empty space on the mud floor. But children stepped carefully around the creations so as not to destroy them. In another corner was a 'spelling tree' – just a few branches with cards hanging on strings like a Christmas tree. Children worked in pairs, asking each other to spell the difficult words. In another group some children were playing with a set of home-made maths cards. To honour the guests the children picked up their self-made costumes from the hooks on the wall, one drummed and the others performed a joyful and very rhythmic dance. To teach children about traditional handicraft techniques, like how to build a proper hut or how to make a hob-kerry, elderly people from the village were invited to the school to share their wisdom and knowledge with the children.
>
> (Nagel, 1992, p. xviii)

Chapter 2

School Effectiveness and Ineffectiveness

INTRODUCTION

This chapter examines the implications and problems of existing research on school effectiveness, especially as it relates to the twin concerns of this book: school management and developing countries. The effectiveness literature is now huge, and frequently contradictory. It is a growing movement and industry, as evidenced by new journals, the spread of international conferences and proliferating research reports. The intention of this chapter is not to embark on an exhaustive overview of the field, but to provide a framework in which the exploration of 'effectiveness' can be discussed. The deep problems surrounding the effectiveness discourse must be surfaced before attempting any new models or research designs.

The quantitative tradition within effectiveness research uses a methodology which is statistically complex but conceptually easy. One or more 'outcomes' of schooling are established and schools are compared on their results. Conventionally, these outcomes will be in terms of examination or test results, less often in terms of social behaviour or the employability of students. From the ranking that emerges, common features associated with the 'good' schools are extracted. The underlying justification for the research is that these associated factors may be *causal* or *contributory* ones, and not accidental, or indeed a *product* of the successful outcomes. Taking into account the initial intake of the students, the research seeks to establish how much of the 'variance' between schools in something like achievement can be attributed directly to the individual school. Whereas 'league tables' (as in football scores) rank schools only on results, school effectiveness research uses a 'value-added' approach: it looks at the intake of students (that is, their ability and background) and explores how much individual schools manage to 'add value' to their intake. If schools do indeed vary on this 'input–output' measure, then the implication is that there must be something which characterizes the more 'successful' school. Isolating these relevant organizational features will enable less successful schools to 'borrow' such ideas and strategies. Alternatively, if success appears primarily to be associated with more resources or more qualified teachers, then governments or agencies funding schools can be encouraged to equalize the provision, and to upgrade the resource input to the poorer schools. It sounds appealing, and relatively uncontroversial. Yet the whole process and ideology is fraught with difficulty, as we shall discuss shortly.

Chapter 1 identified degrees of variance between schools in developing countries, even under similar conditions of stringency. The Western research has found only a small proportion of the variance in student achievement to be linked to school and classroom factors: the studies range from 8 per cent to 14 per cent unaccounted for by social background and 'ability' factors concerning students

(Reynolds, 1992). Nonetheless, these 'school effects' can be identified and translated into factorial lists. Levine and Lazotte's (1990) review of a large number of American studies, for example, generated a list of the 'characteristics of unusually effective schools' under the headings of:

- productive school climate and culture
- focus on student acquisition of central learning skills
- appropriate monitoring of student progress
- practice-oriented staff development at the school site
- outstanding leadership
- salient parental involvement
- effective instructional arrangements and implementation
- high operationalized expectations and requirements for teachers

These sound relatively incontrovertible, and transferable without difficulty to developing countries. Yet one problem is immediately apparent; are these independent factors, or do they all interact and contribute to each other? Is parental involvement inevitably tied to students' acquisition of central learning skills? Dutch studies of this question have lent support to the case for the independence of individual factors, finding that, for example, 'orderly climate' *or* 'high expectations' are present. But the findings are not consistent. A remarkable conclusion of some Dutch school effectiveness research was that 'instructional leadership' does not contribute to school effectiveness (Creemers, 1992). This has profound implications for discussions of the contribution of school management.

The qualitative tradition of research on school effectiveness tends to exemplify an 'illuminative evaluation' approach, using case studies of projects to review whether schools have indeed made a difference to students' expected trajectories in the school, and identifying what factors have helped or hindered an innovation. In this chapter we shall be extracting those features for developing countries which are specifically linked to the internal management of the school. First, however, it is crucial to surface the general problems associated with the school effectiveness 'movement', whether in industrialized or developing country research.

PROBLEMS IN SCHOOL EFFECTIVENESS RESEARCH AND WRITING

There are a number of reasons why translating school effectiveness research into school improvement has proved so elusive. The problems appear at different stages and levels of investigation.

(a) Outcome measures

The first decision to be made in effectiveness research is the outcome on which schools will be measured and compared. This selection is not a neutral activity. A tendency to choose the 'measurable' leads to a focus on examination and test results; the implication of this is that we all agree that the school's main task is to get as many children through examinations as possible. All the other possible goals of the school – related to citizenship, workplace preparation, family life preparation, political awareness, self-esteem, social responsibility, caring for others, solidarity and co-operation, lifelong learning, even happiness – are implicitly secondary to competitive testing. Clearly, it is more difficult to evaluate such longer-term effects, which is why they are discarded as outcomes to be measured. The problem is that after a while in the discussion of an 'effective school' we begin to forget that variables were identified on a vary narrow range of outcome indicators. Alternatively, there may be the (unproven) assumption that what is good for competitive or individualized learning will also be good for co-operative or social learning. Is the factor for learning how to pass examinations the same as that required for the workplace realities of the year 2000? It may or may not be; but it is highly dangerous to embark on school improvement programmes based on effectiveness research unless the agreed goals of the school and the nation exactly match the measured outcomes in the studies.

There is the argument that standardized test results are a good proxy for entry into employment and later productivity at work; the latter assumption is particularly questionable. There are a few studies which show that more educated and achieving students in vocational schools show higher productivity in agricultural activities (Harbison and Hanushek, 1992); but other areas of work and life (such as the Civil Service, or industrial management) have not demonstrated such connections between test results and on-the-job productivity. Skills at passing examinations are not directly translatable into skills used in entrepreneurial activities, in the management of people, in family survival and health or in contribution to the workplace – sometimes quite the reverse. Hence the goals of the school and their link to national development goals need to be carefully formulated before research is embarked on to assess a school's possible effectiveness in achieving them. Clear cultural differences will ensue. A country such as Tanzania might have as its prime goal for education that of self-reliance; for Papua New Guinea it might be practical use of school curriculum to help the community. Now it *may* be that (as per the list above) 'outstanding leadership' or 'appropriate monitoring' are helpful both to academic orientations and to self-reliant ones; but this needs to be established empirically from research, especially research in cultures with markedly different outcome goals.

It is not impossible to draw up a list of indicators of success for supposedly abstract goals such as equity or democracy, as one of the authors has outlined (Davies, 1994). We shall look more at this in the final chapter. At present our concern is the irrelevance of the indicator of examination achievement to many developing countries. In Zimbabwe, for example, all secondary students take O level as part of their 'equality' programme. The current pass rate is between 20 and 25 per cent (unsurprising, as O level was designed for the top percentiles anyway). When one of the authors was interviewing inspectors and headteachers about what they would see as an indicator of school improvement, they all cited an increase in the O-level pass rate; few were able to think of anything else. Yet, as Ministry officials conceded, it might be possible to increase the pass rate from 22 to 23 or even 25 per cent, but not much more; and, anyway, a greater pass rate would undermine the function of O level as a selection device for further education or employment. An indicator of the successful school for the 75 per cent of children who are never going to pass O level would seem to be crucial; yet this has not been systematically addressed (Davies, 1995b). Similarly, Edwards and Fisher's (1995) study of 'Effective and ineffective secondary schools in Zimbabwe' compared schools on their O-level results and then proceeded to make comparisons only between the 55 (out of 344) 'highly successful' schools, in which 50 per cent of pupils had achieved five or more O levels. Nothing was said about whether the remaining 289 schools might have been effective for the majority of their pupils in giving them skills and competencies other than O levels. Such research only reinforces the notion that academic selective examinations are the only true benchmark of being 'highly successful', and that teachers' efforts in other directions are not worth researching. The collection and usage of results can be profoundly undemocratic.

(b) Technical problems

Effectiveness researchers themselves will be the first to point out the technical and statistical difficulties in drawing firm conclusions about an 'ideal' school. They have found that there can be differences in the effects for different geographical areas; for different subjects in the curriculum; for different ages of students; for girls and for boys; for high-achieving students and low-achieving students; and for different types of pupil learning. A management practice associated with good scores for rote memory in science by 'bright' 11-year-old boys in Kenya might be ineffective or even counterproductive for conceptual learning of mathematics by adult illiterate women in Pakistan.

One reason for such inconsistency is the way a particular school interprets a factor and how factors interact in a unique school setting. No one would *not* want to have 'a pleasant climate conducive to learning', as appears in some of the lists. It is when we start to break down 'conducive to learning' that contradictions appear. For an older student, conducive may mean the opportunity for self-directed study; for a younger child conducive may mean very firm structuring by the teacher. Even then, whether self-directed learning is effective will depend on other variables, such as library provision, flexible timetabling or the way that feedback is given by teachers or by the materials themselves. It comes as no surprise that the same achievements can be arrived at by contrasting methods, or conversely that a school trying to emulate another's 'successful factors' may achieve disappointing results.

The fundamental technical question is the *causal* one. A good school may be found to have high expectations of its students; but those high expectations may be a *result* of having a 'good' student intake over a number of years who are likely to produce commendable results – as in a selective or elite school. It would be difficult *not* to have high expectations; nor are those expectations the result of a deliberate management policy. A school in which students are found to be 'low-achieving' on some test measure and which suddenly decides to raise expectations on the basis of research evidence could meet with disappointment and see no dramatic improvement, and may also encounter a degree of cynicism from students and staff alike. Some studies undertaken in the UK showed effective schools to be housed in older, more cramped buildings (Reynolds *et al.*, 1987); this does not, of course, mean that the buildings *contributed* to the effectiveness, still less that government should stop spending money on capital expenditure for school build-ings. In this instance, the buildings were associated with other factors – longer traditions and loyalties which inspired a sense of ownership. Elsewhere, and particularly in some developing countries, the state of the buildings is a factor critical to student achievement, as it can represent the difference between learning under a roof and learning in the open air, subject to the heat of the sun or intrusions by local cattle.

(c) Confusion over factors and goals

Perusal of the effectiveness literature and its translation into school policy will evidence some very varied uses of language. An 'indicator' of effectiveness, for example, is sometimes used to mean a causal factor, sometimes just a sign of something happening, and sometimes a goal in its own right. Some areas might indeed be all three – for example, community participation – but others are not. 'Firm leadership' may be a *contributory* factor to the main goal of the school, that is, to pupil learning, but it is not one of the primary desired *outcomes* of the school. Also, for the abstract notion of 'leadership' to be translated into real indicators, decisions would have to be made about how leadership might be manifested – for example, through the production of a school mission statement, or the number of meetings held, or the way teachers or students are disciplined. The identification of precise indicators thus needs yet another set of value judgements about what 'leadership' might comprise, and what might be 'firm' about it.

What happens, however, is that because 'good management' is identified in all the school effectiveness research as a factor in the end-goal of pupil achievement, there is a tendency to focus on that alone, without continuously evaluating how management might be implicated in student learning. 'Management' starts to take on a life of its own, and managers assume vastly more importance than is advisable. The indicators of 'successful' management start to become goals in their own right, so that a school may feel satisfied that it has produced the school development plan, or delegated responsibility, or instigated a staff development programme.

A form of 'goal displacement' may occur, whereby running a smooth organization, and controlling the work of principals and teachers, becomes more important than the needs of pupils and their families. Management training also becomes a goal in itself, without always evaluating the impact. The 'Better Schools' head-teacher training modules developed by the Commonwealth Secretariat, which are currently in use in many countries of Africa, do not have a systematic long-term evaluation built in to see whether and how they might be impacting on student learning (Jeng, 1995). It appears sufficient that heads are now 'trained'. This is not to deny the importance and strength of these modules; but the point being made is that the problem is conceived of as a lack of management training rather than direct and continuous links being made between the proposed outcomes of the school and the way management might be organized to achieve them.

Over-quick interpretation of the often very cautious effectiveness research can lead to the assumption that if we focus on the factors, the goals will take care of themselves. This is obviously not the case, because the relationship between factor and goal is a dynamic one, subject to constant shifts and contradictions. As we shall explore in Chapter 9, on democracy, if a school goal is 'preparation of all students for active citizenship', then this has very different management implications than if the goal is 'winning the Lagos State French Competition'.

(d) Individual investment in school ineffectiveness

One of the fatal flaws in school effectiveness and improvement programmes is the assumption that everyone – teachers, principals, governments – would like total school effectiveness but that they are merely prevented from achieving this through lack of resources or know-how. The reality is quite different. There may be vested interests in maintaining school ineffectiveness (Davies, 1992). For example, in communities where teachers make an important second living from private tuition, it is actually beneficial to them for formal schooling – or even their own classroom teaching – to be ineffective, so that parents must buy costly private lessons from them. As we shall examine with regard to 'prismatic' societies (Chapter 6), managerial ineffectiveness may be *essential* for the preservation of individual power or status.

One of the more interesting related theoretical fields developed in Scheeren's (1992) book *Effective Schooling: Research, Theory and Practice* is public choice theory. The inherent tendency of bureaucracies towards inefficiency is explained by 'methodological individualism' (Van Mierlo, 1984), whereby individuals and sub-groups within larger organizations have their own preferences and goals which do not necessarily coincide with overall organizational aims. The inefficiencies of bureaucracies will be explained more fully in the next chapter; here our point is that people within them may *choose* whether to be efficient or inefficient. Their selective behaviour is the outcome of a trading process within the informal structure of organizations, with 'subordinates' purposely behaving counterproductively, for instance as a signal of discontent to 'superiors'.

In one school in Pakistan, known to the authors, the new principal was puzzled by the way the timetabling was handled. There were complaints from students that the curriculum was overloaded and that they could not get through all the syllabus. He found that in spite of the school day officially being 8.30am–4pm, senior members of staff uniformly taught only in the mornings. They all had private businesses which they ran in the afternoons, and had used their seniority to commandeer the favourite timetable slots. Attempts to make the timetabling both more equitable and efficient met with strong resistance, with outside political connections being brought in to put pressure on the principal to maintain the status quo. School effectiveness was not uppermost in the minds of the staff.

This notion of 'methodological individualism' fits well with that of 'maximiza-tion' (Davies, 1994) – that actors in educational institutions will seek to maximize the benefits to themselves of opportunities and changes in the organizational context. They will seek rewards – whether recognition, professional pride, money, or self-esteem – not all of which are consonant with the expressed goals of the organization. Chapter 7 will look more closely at the way in which actors legitimize such maximization. Unless innovators attempt to work out what rewards everyone will extract from a change, and indeed whether suitable rewards are actually available to all participants, the project is likely to fail. From the smallest child to the oldest serving teacher, everyone is able to act constructively in what they see as their own interests.

In theory, effective schools programmes should be rewarding to most partici-pants: children gain by achieving more, teachers gain professional pride and respect, managers see a purposeful institution, which reflects well on the leadership. Public choice theories and maximization theories nonetheless provide understandings of the subversion of these programmes. There is firstly the 'goal displacement' problem mentioned above, of managers simply being concerned to maintain 'smooth' administration in the interests of control rather than of student learning; and secondly there is the diverse interpretation of what the factors might mean. 'Firm leadership' may produce *weaker* power for other members of the organization. 'Imaginative teaching' requires thought, effort and risk on the part of (already stressed) teachers; an 'orderly environment' has little appeal for children seeking excitement or relief from boredom. The trade-offs, exchanges and bargains people seek in educational institutions are not always predictable; individual rationality is not the same as collective or national rationality.

(e) State investment in school ineffectiveness

A deeper motivational myth is that all governments want or need school effectiveness. The failure of improvement programmes often stems from a failure to recognize the need for a political analysis of the function of mass schooling – particularly in what Fuller terms 'fragile states' (1991). In most countries, formal schooling acts as a gate-keeping mechanism, controlling access to the elite, to higher education, or to prestigious jobs. It legitimizes the inevitable inequalities in a society by attributing a person's occupational low status to failure in previous educational performance. What happens in societies with pyramidal social structures is that if mass schooling becomes too effective in the sense of raising overall attainment and examination pass rates, there is increased pressure for the next level of education, there is qualification inflation, there is graduate unemployment and there is increased social dissatisfaction and unrest. The last thing a fragile state wants is too many articulate, well-qualified, demanding students.

We will explore fragile state theory more fully in Chapter 5. But it is not only in developing countries that governments are wary of too much achievement. In England and Wales, for example, every time the examination results show a rise in results, powerful elements within the Department for Education and Employment claim that standards of assessment must be falling and that more means worse. A switch to continuous course work assessment rather than one-off examinations meant a dramatic rise in achievement – particularly for girls. This frightened the traditionalists who insisted that assessment had become too easy or that it lent itself to cheating. With heightened attainment at A level, universities simply raise the entrance requirements. If graduates cannot get jobs, they are told that they have chosen the wrong subjects. Rarely is it acknowledged that schools and teachers have become more and more effective in educating children according to current goals. The immediate response by government when the system appears too successful is to instigate immediate 'reforms', sidetracking schools and teachers into other activities (inspections, or compulsory Christianity) to diminish their efficiency. One ploy is to engineer a 'moral panic' about, say, standards of literacy or numeracy, and wheel in employers to complain about the skills of their new entrants. Teachers, of course, cannot win: if exam results go up, it is because exams are now too easy; if they go down it is the fault of the teaching.

Developing countries are often the focus for school improvement programmes because their education systems appear very inefficient. Children do not all attend what education is provided; there are high repetition and drop-out rates; there are high levels of teacher and student absenteeism; and teaching materials are scarce, with teachers untrained to use them positively. Yet, taking the deeply cynical view, schooling in such countries may be highly effective in what it is at base intended for. It provides avenues for the few to gain specialized knowledge, while containing the mass in the myth of opportunity and promise. To maintain the system of power and privilege, it may be *essential* to have untrained teachers, inadequate buildings, high attrition rates and a strong emphasis on examinations but a low pass rate. The presence of a few high-achieving schools is indeed important to indicate the possibility of success, but it is crucial not to have too many of these, or the shaky pyramid of selection starts to bulge and crack. As Bennett (1993, p. 51) argued with reference to research in Thailand:

> If we are to provide effective schooling for poor and disadvantaged
> children, we must first show how this advances the political interests of
> those with power, or at least, how it benefits at least one powerful group.

(f) The seductions of effectiveness research

It is, therefore, unfortunate that effectiveness research can be used and abused by different vested interests in their pursuit of rewards or legitimacy. Governments often love conventional quantitative effectiveness research which compares individual schools or regions. They would welcome the idea that schools receiving similar funds, or with similar intakes of children, could produce markedly different results. The focus on 'whole school development' or on 'school climate' draws attention away from the effects of levels of poverty in the surrounding community, or from the effects of levels of state funding itself. The government message is, if one school can be effective with limited resources, why can you not all be? Teachers and principals can be blamed for anything, from unemployment to teenage pregnancy.

This is not to say that there are no differences between schools, nor that we do not want to improve them. The question returns to the outcomes on which they are compared, and the uses to which such comparisons are put. If, for example, schools are ranked on success in competitive, selective examinations, with only a limited number of future places available at the next level, then improving one school's success rate only depresses the results of the neighbouring school. By definition, not all schools can be 'good'. Such comparisons and rankings do nothing to question the whole system of selection or social exclusion. If effective schooling research is used to provide 'league tables' of schools in order to supposedly assist parental choice of school for their child, then good schools get better and poor schools get worse. This is what governments working within a market ideology want, of course, but it is not efficient – or even humane.

A key issue is the researchers' stance with regard to 'intake'. As Angus (1993) comments:

> Family background, social class, any notion of context, are typically
> regarded as 'noise' – as 'outside' background factors which must be
> controlled for and then stripped away so that the researcher can
> concentrate on the important domain of school factors.

Such research dehumanizes pupils – and their teachers – by reducing them to 'intake variables'. There is a stereotypical approach which appears to sympathize with the underachieving school for the 'poor quality' of its intake. The possibility that the definitions of 'achievement' or of 'the good pupil' stem from the interests of the ruling class, of males or of ethnic majority groups, is ignored. As the Congress of Mendes in Brazil admitted:

> Our public schools are geared towards an ideal child. One who does not need to struggle for survival; who is well fed; who speaks the school's language; who knows how to handle a pencil and is capable of interpreting symbols and who is stimulated by parents through all sorts of means. As this is not the reality of the Brazilian families, the schools do not have the right to impose these criteria, which are valid for the middle class, upon its students' majority. Its task is to educate Brazilian children as they actually are . . .

(Quoted in Leonardos, 1993, p. 75)

Even the 'value-added' approach, which seeks to measure what schools are able to add to initial pupil attainments, still implies that dross must be converted to gold. Reducing ethnic, gender and wealth inequalities and cultures to statistical 'intake variables' (for which a school should compensate rather than acknowledge richness) only serves to consolidate the idea of cultural deficit. The state can blame the schools; but schools and teachers can, if necessary, convincingly blame 'the home'.

Ironically, then, effectiveness research can be self-defeating. While directing schools and governments to take action for improvement, it can still, through its presentation of complex and dehumanized sets of 'factors', enable all participants to shift key responsibility elsewhere in the cycle.

COMPARATIVE EFFECTIVENESS STUDIES IN DEVELOPING COUNTRIES

We now examine in more detail some of those more quantitative research studies undertaken specifically in developing countries to see how they relate to the above critiques. In 1993, Reynolds reported the empirical base to be over 60 studies, with reviews to be found in Avalos (1980), Fuller (1987), Fuller and Heyneman (1989), Lockheed and Verspoor (1991) and Walberg (1991). Jansen (1995) traces the history in three 'generations' – 1960s, 1970s, 1980s – evidencing increasing sophistication in statistical techniques, and more lately, multi-level modelling. However, if we look at these studies, we find that they are primarily based on student achievement as the key outcome measure, either across the curriculum or in specific subject areas such as science or maths. They often go wider than Western studies in that they compare countries and seek to find common factors across them. The flavour can be found from a list such as Fuller's (1987; Table 2.1), which provides the 'quality indicator' addressed and the proportion of studies which confirm its importance in student achievement.

The significant feature of this table is that there is by no means agreement on all the factors. 'Specific material inputs' appears to show the highest consensus, with, for example, 16 out of 24 studies confirming the importance of texts and reading materials, and 15 out of 18 confirming the importance of library size and

Table 2.1

School quality indicator	Expected direction of relationship	Total number of analyses	Number of analyses confirming effect
School expenditures			
1. Expenditures per pupil	+	11	6
2. Total school expenditures	+	5	2
Specific material inputs			
3. Class size	−	21	5
4. School size	+	9	4
5. Instructional materials			
Texts and reading materials	+	24	16
Desks	+	3	3
6. Instructional media (radio)	+	3	3
7. School building quality	+	3	2
8. Library size and activity	+	18	15
9. Science laboratories	+	11	4
10. Nutrition and feeding programmes	+	6	5
Teacher quality			
11. Teacher's length of schooling			
Total years of teacher's schooling	+	26	12
Years of tertiary and teacher training	+	31	22
12. In-service teacher training	+	6	5
13. Teacher's length of experience	+	23	10
14. Teacher's verbal proficiency	+	2	2
15. Teacher's salary level	+	14	5
16. Teacher's social class background	+	10	7
17. School's percentage of full-time teachers	+	2	1
18. Teacher's punctuality and (low) absenteeism	+	2	0
Teaching practices/classroom organization			
19. Length of instructional programme	+	14	12
20. Homework frequency	+	8	6
21. Active learning by students	+	3	1
22. Teacher's expectations of pupil performance	+	3	3
23. Teacher's time spent on class preparation	+	5	4
School management			
24. Quality of principal	+	7	4
25. Multiple shifts of classes each day	−	3	1
26. Student boarding	+	4	4
27. Student repetition of grade	+	5	1

activity. The overall expenditures on a school, however, are not always highlighted as significant, and the 'School management' findings are not dramatic. The area of 'Teacher quality' is even more mixed: 'Years of tertiary and teacher training' seems relatively uncontroversial in terms of their effects on pupil performance, yet other aspects of length of teacher experience and teacher's background are less often supported.

A clue to this puzzle can be found in Harbison and Hanushek's (1992) huge study of the *Education Performance of the Poor* in Brazil. This compared rural schools over a seven-year period. Their evidence was unequivocal that having good teachers was extremely important for student achievement, but that it was impossible to measure inputs from specific teachers. Simple proxies for teacher quality such as the level of teacher education, or the amount of teacher experience, were not consistent indicators. Teachers who knew their subject matter unsurprisingly performed better, but types of activities in the classroom and range of materials used did not match with any systematic differences in student performance. A significant comment from the authors was:

> Unfortunately, overall findings such as these are frequently misunderstood. They should not be interpreted as implying that differences in teachers are not important. To the contrary, we have strong evidence that teachers vary widely in their teaching abilities. Rather, the findings about specific teacher characteristics simply indicate that conventional measures of good teachers are not very accurate. Also apparent is the fact that there are many other aspects of good teaching that were not measured. Others may not even be known. Teaching may simply be more art than science. Skill in the classroom has been only crudely captured by subject matter tests and other measures of the teacher's background and preparation. The conclusion is that it is foolish to choose among prospective teachers solely on the basis of credentials and experience.
>
> (Harbison and Hanushek, 1992, p. 199)

This is an amazing admission from such a large-scale and lengthy study. The implication is that the taken-for-granted ways we have of comparing teachers and their schools may be largely irrelevant. We return to the problem of focusing only on that which can be measured and counted up. Just as the choice of student achievement measured through tests ignores other more subtle and deeper aspects of educational outcomes, the choice of quantitative differences between teachers such as their years of formal education ignores other far more important aspects of their 'art'.

Using words such as 'impossibility', Harbison and Hanushek imply that we will never be able to get at what makes a good teacher (and implicitly a good school). This is true if we insist on continuing with the obsession with the statistically measurable and comparable. What is also significant about their study is that throughout the book there is little mention of organization, management or climate issues. Words such as 'principal' or 'head' or 'leadership' do not appear in the index. Yet there are tantalizing clues to the potential of such frameworks. In reviewing 187 studies of 'production function' from the United States, for example, they conclude that 'the research reveals no strong or systematic relationship between school expenditure and student performance'. Their note of caution about this startling finding, and about how results can be distorted, includes the example that

> the actions of school administrators could mask any relationship . . . If the most difficult students to teach were consistently put in smaller classes,

any independent effect of class size could be difficult to disentangle from mismeasurement of the characteristics of the students.

(ibid., p 20)

It is our premise, however, that administrative actions are a critical key to what schools are able or want to achieve, and they should not just be explored because they may 'distort' or otherwise 'mask' apparently more significant statistical findings. We look at 'class size' in more detail in Chapter 8; our point here would be that *on its own* it has no meaning as a factor. It depends on whether class sizes are arranged in order to provide equity, or compensatory provision for those requiring more help, or child-to-child teaching; that is, how class size relates to the overall mission and political aims of the school.

What then can we salvage from the often inconclusive and misinterpretation-prone effectiveness studies? Four potentially important areas within quantitative studies in developing countries are as follows:

(a) The effects of educational processes on student achievement are larger than in developed countries

A variance of up to 28 per cent has been found in some studies. That is, the school a pupil attends makes more of a difference to their eventual academic attainment compared to their home background than it does in industrialized nations. (Yet it must be remembered that even in developing countries, nearly three-quarters of the variance in achievement between pupils stems from their social origins.) But the reasons for this North–South difference are worth exploring. One argument is that homes are more alike and schools are more dissimilar in developing countries, so that greater differences between individual schools are found (for example, as between rural and urban areas, or between elite and community-financed schools). Another reason put forward is that there is a greater disjuncture between the local culture of the home and Western-style education, so that few parents are able to provide 'cultural capital' to their children in coping with the demands of school. This contrasts with a larger proportion of educated middle-class parents in industrialized nations who are able to get their children successfully through their educational career *whatever school they are in.*

An interesting variant on this theme comes from a fascinating study of schooling in rural west Mexico (Martin, 1994), which found low achievers in school strongly associated with tough 'old-fashioned' discipline in the home, such as physical punishment. Also, the more patriarchal the family, and the greater degree of sexual differentiation in the home, the lower the performance in the school – *for both boys and girls.* Martin argues in fact that the values of the home are not a rejection of demands from the school for some middle-class or elitist 'cultural capital' – quite the reverse. 'In Acatlan, the school is a paragon of equality, not inequality and selectivity, as Bourdieu would have it. It is the school's levelling, egalitarian tendencies which are a stumbling block for the community. More than half the population do not operate according to notions of equality, and may even not believe in them' (ibid., p. 271). Traditional family solidarity and moral codes necessary for family reputation and survival sat uneasily with the 'disconcertingly open-ended quality' of schooling, its material costs and its tendency to project people into the uncertainties of wage labour.

Whatever the nature of the disjuncture between home and school, this potential antithesis becomes a key explanation for variations in achievement. It appears important at this stage to acknowledge the more influential role of the school in deciding people's life chances in developing countries. If schools also have more impact than in developed societies on other outcomes (such as political orientation), this has profound implications for policy.

(b) The factors associated with school effectiveness may be different from those so associated in industrialized societies

Walberg (1991) concluded from his review of studies in developing countries that factors promoting science achievement were:

- length of instructional programmes
- pupil feeding
- school library activity
- years of teacher training
- textbooks and instructional materials

Factors which were not particularly associated with achievement were, contrary to expectations:

- science laboratories
- teacher salaries
- reduced class sizes
- pupil grade repetition

We can see that these lists are not the same as those found in Western studies, and could speculate why. 'Pupil feeding', for example, would not be so critical in a society where most pupils received sufficient nutrition, but could be a key discriminator where food was scarce or unequally distributed. In South Africa, pupil feeding programmes have had remarkable results; a further concern is now the high percentage of pupils who have worm infestation, and for whom the nutrients are not being absorbed. 'Poor concentration, a slowness to catch on in lessons, the inability to absorb information, are all the effects of severe worm infestation' (*Sunday Tribune*, 23 June 1996, p. 11). Such factors have not appeared in societies where both piped water and the wearing of shoes are taken for granted. Similarly, 'instructional materials' also assume far more importance in contexts where some schools may have only one textbook per class than they would in systems where the factor refers to the difference between 30 and 32 textbooks, or to whether the textbooks were written in 1986 or 1996. Class size, on the other hand may be important in the West when it refers to the difference between 15 and 30 children, but has far less impact on teaching style and pupil achievement when it is the difference between 60 and 75 in a class.

Again, it is interesting that management or leadership are not directly mentioned, but we could assume that such features would have important input into areas such as the time spent studying or whether pupils have enough food. Vulliamy (1987), in his study of school effectiveness in Papua New Guinea, pointed to the centrality of the principal in determining school outcomes, but also to key material inputs such as the presence or absence of a spirit duplicator (which expands dramatically the scope of teaching and learning methods). Often a head is central *because of* his or her ability or inability to obtain resources in conditions of stringency. This was a feature confirmed by Ngegba's study of effective primary schools in Sierra Leone (1993). Here, the most 'effective' principal was the one who had thought laterally, setting up a savings scheme for teachers so that irregularities of salary payment did not hit them so hard, and building a small fish farm which both generated income and provided science experience for the students.

(c) The factors differ within countries labelled 'developing'

Lockheed and Komenar (1989), for example, compared Swaziland and Nigeria and found incongruent effects. In Nigeria, those students who spent more time listening to the teacher introducing and reviewing a topic performed better than those who were less exposed to such direct instruction, but such effects were not found in Swaziland. Conversely, the amount of time a teacher spent monitoring was positively associated with achievement in Swaziland but had no effect in Nigeria. This can be explained only by reference to local culture, concepts of learning, interpretations of 'monitoring' and so on.

(d) The factors generate significant findings for goals of economic growth

In a review of the relationship between schooling and the state, Avalos-Bevan (1996) looked at the studies on the relationship between curriculum subjects and economic growth. Benavot had investigated the variations in annual instructional time in eight subject areas at primary level in 60 (of which 43 were 'less developed') nations, and linked these to changes in GDP over a 25-year period. There was a positive economic impact of total yearly hours of instruction across all subjects, with two subjects having significant impact: science with a positive effect, and pre-vocational or practical education a negative effect. Contrary to popular wisdom, no effect on economic growth was noted of instructional time allocated to maths and language. In the case of the less developed nations, the finding was, however, of a positive impact of instructional hours devoted to the arts and music. While cautioning about taking these at face value for immediate policy, nonetheless, it is implied they constitute dramatic warnings about simply pouring resources into 'basic skills' or vocational courses. It is suggested from Fuller and Holsinger's (1992) research, on the other hand, that

> science curricula serve important functions which are at the heart of
> those who search for relevant education: provision of an empirical
> approach to the solution of problems, acquaintance with innovations
> associated with agricultural and rural development, sensitizing to

problems in the natural environment and introduction to innovations related to health, nutrition and family planning.

(Avalos-Bevan, 1996, p. 64)

These large-scale longitudinal research designs can enable queries to be raised about seeing effective schools as those who achieve highly in maths and language, and who devote many hours to these topics: such emphases may in fact be counter-productive to national goals of growth. Dzvimbo argues from his interpretation of effectiveness research that teachers in South Africa need to spend more instructional time in school: 'This will definitely enhance the learning process in schools' (1995, p. 15). Yet the studies reviewed above will ask for the crucial refinement: 'Instructional time in *what*?' Important choices must be made, and old assumptions tested.

The four areas which we have now outlined focus mainly on measured achievement in traditional curriculum subjects; nonetheless, the interesting variances in them begin to address some of the critiques raised in the early part of this chapter. The inferences of the studies, and the salvageable benefits of such styles of effectiveness research, are twofold. One inference is the need to focus on goals; the other is the perhaps belated recognition of the importance of culture – whether national, community or internal school culture. Fuller and Clarke (1994, p. 119) attack the 'policy mechanics' who

seek universal remedies that can be manipulated by central agencies and assume that the same instructional materials and pedagogical practices hold constant meaning in the eyes of teachers and children from diverse cultural settings.

The heritage of school effectiveness research is that we cannot tell what an effective school is unless we identify clearly a set of outcomes which it is trying to achieve. The linked warning is that these outcomes may vary significantly between countries, communities and individuals, not just in their wanting different outcomes, but also in the way that similar-looking goals can be interpreted and aimed at in the light of different cultural imperatives. It is always instructive to highlight how different schools and their members subvert any 'tidy' findings from the studies. (One effectiveness researcher we know admitted that he initially left out the girls from his study because they 'messed up' the findings.) Our interest, particularly from developing countries, might be to focus directly on the discrepancies, not in fact on the areas of agreement.

CASE STUDIES OF EFFECTIVE SCHOOLS

In looking at how far schools are actually meeting their expressed and diverse goals, we can get more information from single country studies than from those that attempt to aggregate data from different settings. The most interesting departure from conventional effectiveness writing to date is Levin and Lockheed's 1993 collection, *Effective Schools in Developing Countries*. This contains a number of case studies of different countries and their independent projects for improvement, albeit using these to extract some common themes. The difference from quantitative effectiveness theorizing is that each country or programme is assessed *in its own terms* rather than simply providing a comparative benchmark.

The Colombia New School Programme, for example, represents a significant shift from conventional views of the formal school – and its evaluation. The programme is designed to provide a complete primary education, using active instruction, a stronger relationship between the school and the community, and a flexible promotion system adapted to the lifestyle of the rural child. More will be said about this programme in the final section of this book, but the point to stress here is the match between the expressed goals of the schools and the way in which they have been evaluated. The curriculum is to promote 'active and reflective learning, the ability to think, analyse, investigate, create, apply knowledge and improve children's self-esteem ... [It] seeks to develop children's co-operation, comradeship, solidarity and civic, participatory and democratic attitudes' (Colbert *et al.*, 1993, p. 55). That this is not empty rhetoric is demonstrated by the tenor of the evaluations:

> ... the level of creativity among students of New Schools where a teacher
> is responsible for several grade levels does not differ significantly from
> rural schools where there is a teacher assigned to each grade ... children
> in the New School Programme are found to have a much higher level of
> self-esteem ... the fact that the self-esteem of girls equalled that of boys
> is particularly important; more participatory classrooms appear to help
> girls' self-esteem ... in tests of socio-civic behaviour, self-esteem and
> selected subjects (mathematics, Spanish), New School children scored
> considerably higher than those in traditional rural schools.
>
> (ibid., pp. 63 and 64)

It is indicative that subject competence appears *last* on this list, with creativity and self-esteem featuring strongly beforehand. Gender equity is also seen as important. If one wants to know the real goals of a school or system, one looks at what is assessed and disaggregated, not what appears in policy documents or mission statements.

The Brazilian study compared newly formed 'democratic' schools, called CIEP schools (Integrated Centres of Public Education), with 'conventional' state schools. The CIEP teachers held firm beliefs that their actions would bring about change. Students' cultures were not only respected but enhanced. Teachers taught higher-order thinking skills throughout the curriculum, whereas the conventional schools did not think low-income students should be exposed to what they saw as 'middle-class' values. Thus CIEP schools were not reducing students to a 'poor intake', as was discussed earlier in this chapter, but were working creatively with them. CIEP schools appeared to have a higher promotion rate, but 'since the CIEP schools are based on a totally different philosophy and educational strategy from the conventional public schools, it seems reasonable that the criteria for promoting or retaining students also differ in some respects' (Leonardos, 1993, p. 85). Leonardos continues:

> It is important to assess the types of skills actually being acquired by
> students. The findings of the case study reported here suggest that CIEP

students may be acquiring different skills from students of conventional public schools . . . CIEP students are being trained to undertake more creative tasks while students in conventional schools are being trained for more routinized activities.

The implication is that establishing common comparative measures of 'effectiveness' will be problematic, since the learning goals differ. Nonetheless, the 'working climate' for both staff and students was able to be assessed as being better and more constructive – a definite management concern.

Also in the Levin and Lockheed collection, Tsang and Wheeler's account of school improvement in Thailand looked at cluster schools as a means of improving primary school quality. They raise, for our purposes, interesting questions of accountability. School effectiveness and improvement policy is all about being accountable, providing value for money, and using human and material resources to maximum effect. Yet, as was argued earlier, this may lead to an undue focus on the 'measurable'. In the Thailand study, the cluster influence led to a dilemma:

> . . . increased school receptivity to cluster influence would mean increased pressure on principals to focus on accountability, which typically would mean teacher-centred classrooms emphasizing rote memorization of facts rather than the more student-centred instruction that principals might otherwise seek to promote . . . in our studies the principals of improving schools viewed tests and test results as one of many tools, and not the most important one at that, for improving performance . . . The real tools for improvement were their own efforts . . . to promote greater collaboration among teachers . . . to promote shared decision-making . . . to promote good school–community relations.
>
> (Tsang and Wheeler, 1993, p. 126)

The message from these three studies is how the identification of ways to measure goals in the end drives the work of the school and the style of the organization. This warning had been given earlier in Vulliamy's study of Papua New Guinea. He pointed out that the ideology around effectiveness presupposes a consensus on the desired outcomes of schooling, which tends to disembody schools from their wider social, political and economic context. He found that senior staff in schools were, however, acutely aware of a conflict in aims as reflected in government policy and rhetoric, a conflict between the attempt to raise academic standards and the attempt to provide relevance to those going back to the village without further schooling:

> An interview with the National Superintendent of High School Inspections suggested that he was almost as worried by schools that obtained very high rating indices as he was by those obtaining very low ones. This is because some schools may be artificially improving their results by over-coaching and by increasing core subject teaching at the expense of other subjects . . . In the Papua New Guinea context it may be that a school with relatively poor examination results is providing a relatively better preparation than other schools for those of its students who are likely to return to their villages.
>
> (Vulliamy, 1987, p. 220)

Our first task in school effectiveness research and thinking is the obvious one: that we should identify the most desired outcomes of a schooling programme and devise precisely matching evaluative measures. There is no point in stating that the aim of a school is to produce concerned citizens, but then measuring the school only on academic achievement, hoping somehow that significant clues about organization policy will emerge which might be relevant to democracy or citizenship. Conversely, there is little point in thinking up an outcome measure and then engaging in statistical international research to compare schools and countries on its achievement. If schools are not geared into this measure, then the way they organize will have different meanings. One might identify, for example, 'education of parents' as an important measure, but a school educating parents about the importance of academic achievement for their children will be different from a school educating parents for their own literacy, and different again from a school educating parents about HIV/AIDS.

The World Bank recognizes the need for school and classroom-level processes and interpretation in its shift towards 'quality'. The new approach is to recognize

- that operations within school and classroom . . . are to a large extent independent of national policy;
- that the educational process in individual schools contributes significantly to the effectiveness of education; and
- that (school-level) factors are not independent but come together within the school to form a social system that conditions the learning that can take place there. (Heneveld, 1993, p. 6)

Jansen (1995, p. 195) comments: 'it remains to be seen whether the Heneveld proposal on *quality* translates into large-scale funding of school research and investments comparable to the *effectiveness* agenda which dominated from the decade of the 1980s.' Jansen himself is of the view that studies of effectiveness and studies of quality, because of their fundamentally different histories, represent 'competing and incompatible agendas for school and class-room based research' (p. 194). We would agree the historical discrepancy, but would see a future for some sort of match between the traditions as long as the problems identified earlier in the chapter could be addressed.

This chapter – and this book – will try not to fall into the trap of seeking generalized 'principles' of management which lead to school effectiveness. The aim has been to show that 'effective management' evolves from two key interlocking variables: goals and cultures. With regard to goals, it will have become apparent that we are interested in the democratic society as one important goal for education. By a happy coincidence, so is the World Bank. Our emphasis is not idiosyncratic, but develops a key shift in international thinking about what schools are for. Our argument to be developed in the final section is that effective management for flexible, co-operative democracy which benefits the community is not the same as effective management for competitive academic achievement which benefits the individual. Only when the goals are agreed can we start looking for underlying principles.

Even then, secondly, such principles will be mediated through local cultural understandings. Vulliamy found teachers believing in the headteacher as the most important single factor in school quality, stating that only if he (*sic*) were very firm about them carrying out their duties would they do so. In Thailand, the importance of the principal derived in part from cultural traditions that emphasized hierarchical decision-making and deference towards leaders. The Colombian and Brazilian examples, on the other hand, might be working through their democratic pro-grammes with very different traditions or expectations of 'leadership' – or indeed its absence. Transposition of 'the effective school' from West to East, from North to South, cannot be done, even if the goals were held constant; nor can one developing country's success be directly transposed to another, just because they are both working in contexts of stringency.

CONCLUSION

This chapter has argued that improvement programmes in developing countries which are linked to that style of effectiveness research which compares schools on examination success are doomed to failure, in that not all schools in a selective system with winners and losers can be 'good'. Effectiveness research which relies solely on standardized test results ignores and marginalizes all the other possible goals of the schools and of student learning. We have shown concern that effectiveness research which reduces the diversity in students and staff to crude notions of 'intake variables' may act to stereotype and confirm inequalities. Those apparently common factors across countries and institutions may be subject to opposing cultural interpretations, or to subversion if they do not meet vested interests. It has been stressed that 'good management' is not an end in itself, but can be interpreted only in the light of its possible involvement in the end goals of all the school's participants.

Effectiveness research can be most usefully valid when it uses outcome measures consistent with expressed goals, or uses a *range* of such measures when those goals appear inconsistent or contested. The research is best turned into improvement programmes if:

- it is confined to one country or region
- the identified goals are acceptable to government, teachers, students and parents
- the goals are potentially achievable by *all* participants
- the goals are turned into relevant recognizable indicators, even if these are not tidy, or short-term, or statistical.

As we turn now to the messy realities of school management in developing countries, the need for equally messy but more revealing evaluations of school effectiveness should become clearer.

PART TWO

Contextual Realities for School Management

Chapter 3

School as an Organization: Bureaucratic Façades

INTRODUCTION

> There is nothing on earth intended for innocent people so horrible as a
> school. To begin with, it is a prison. But in some respects more cruel than
> a prison.
>
> (George Bernard Shaw quoted in Meighan, 1995, p. 18)

Though some studies of school management have indeed compared schools to
prisons in their organizational style (Handy, 1984), the organizational model most
commonly used to describe the school is a bureaucracy or rule by officials. The
most influential writer on bureaucracy was the German sociologist Max Weber who
argued that bureaucracies exhibited the following characteristics (quoted in
Albrow, 1970, pp. 44–5):

(a) Staff members are personally free, observing only the impersonal
    duties of office.
(b) There is a clear hierarchy of offices.
(c) The functions of the offices are clearly specified.
(d) Officials are appointed on the basis of a contract.
(e) They are selected on the basis of a professional qualification, ideally
    substantiated by a diploma gained through examination.
(f) They have a money salary and usually pension rights. The salary is
    graded according to position in the hierarchy. The official can always
    leave the post and under certain circumstances it may also be
    terminated.
(g) The official's post is his or her sole major occupation.
(h) There is a career structure and promotion is possible either by
    seniority or merit and according to the judgement of superiors.
(i) The official may appropriate neither the post nor the resources that
    go with it.
(j) The official is subject to a unified control and disciplinary system.

Schools share many of these characteristics. Hughes (1987, p. 8), for example,
argues that:

> Schools and colleges, particularly large ones, conform to a considerable
> degree to Weber's specification of bureaucracy as judged by their division
> of work, their hierarchical structures, their rules and regulations, their
> impersonal procedures and their employment practices based on
> technical criteria.

While there are debates about how well the bureaucratic model fits different types of school (see, for example, Burgess, 1986, pp. 156–9) these are in terms of schools as more or less bureaucratic rather than not being bureaucracies at all.

Historically, mass schooling in industrialized nations developed from the end of the nineteenth century to meet the demands from churches and businesses for increased basic literacy and adopted the dominant mode of organization of the period: bureaucracy. A key purpose of the spread of formal education was therefore to socialize young people into the norms and behaviours required of workers in large-scale bureaucratic organizations, such as factories and offices. This model of school organization was exported to those countries now referred to as 'developing' either directly, through colonialism, or indirectly, through having been the first to provide an authoritative definition of what a modern school for the masses looked like.

The development of a bureaucratic mode of organization in schools has been criticized in terms of diminishing the dignity of the individual, being associated with low levels of satisfaction and power and as a source of alienation. However, the defence of bureaucracy has been rested on the grounds that it has promoted rationality, orderliness and consistency and therefore efficiency (Musgrove, 1971). One Nigerian writer, for example, argues that:

> Weber is often criticized for ignoring the human aspects of administration
> and attempting to reduce workers to machines by advocating strict
> adherence to impersonal organizational rules and regulations. A close
> look at this model, however, reveals that it is used in education and that
> in our schools, which are very human institutions, Weber's bureaucracy
> promotes efficiency.
>
> (Edem, 1982, p. 27)

It is, however, the contention of this chapter that bureaucratic school organization does not necessarily promote 'efficiency' and, moreover, that in developing countries schools do not actually operate as bureaucracies according to the Weberian model. Alternative ways of managing schools more effectively will be discussed in Chapters 8 and 9.

BUREAUCRACY AS INEFFICIENT AUTHORITARIANISM

Weber himself was clear that bureaucracy with its emphasis on hierarchy, technical expertise, appointment rather than election, and secrecy, is a form of domination, and that, in terms of the way that power is used in policy and decision-making, it is quite distinct from democracy. In Chapter 4 the autocratic role of the headteacher at the top of the bureaucratic pyramid and its implications for school management and school effectiveness will be discussed. Here it is important to note that the policy deliberations of the head with the senior management team are not usually made public and the staff who are not part of the senior management team feel excluded from important aspects of decision-making because this is seen as a specialist function carried out by 'management' (Ball, 1987, pp. 101–3). As Jeffs (1988, p. 48) documents, the price paid for this can be widespread servility amongst staff and a reluctance to act in autonomous manner or show initiative, while in the main accepting as given the existing concentration of authority. It also often results in permanent staff oppositional groups, organizational guerrilla warfare and the quiet resistance to any management initiative, good or bad.

For pupils, the experience of bureaucratic hierarchy is even more that of subordinate cogs in the machine. Shipman (1971, ch. 2) suggests that schools have been organized bureaucratically to teach the impersonal, contractual values and relationships that typify the transition from agricultural to industrial society. Thus the values which are enforced in the school are those which are needed for the functioning of bureaucratic organization and the maintenance of social order – obedience, abiding by the rules, loyalty, respect for authority, punctuality, regular attendance, quietness, orderly work in large groups, working to a strict timetable, tolerance of monotony, the ability to change readily from one situation to the next and the ignoring of personal needs when these are irrelevant to the task in hand.

In developing countries the existence of what Fuller terms 'fragile states', lacking deeply rooted legitimacy, especially in rural areas where the majority of people tend to live, means that governments must attempt to enhance their shallow authority by appearing 'modern'. One important way of doing this is to persistently signal to the population the existence and constant extension of meritocracy and mass opportunity. Schools as government institutions signal and symbolize modernity and must therefore be organized in a 'modern' way:

> The younger, more fragile state, common across the Third World, plays a much stronger role in importing and legitimating the bureaucratic structure and moral order of the Western school. Bureaucratic administration signals 'modern practice', particularly in societies where rationalized organizations or firms are still a novel form. Here the visible contours and symbols of 'modern organization' take on enormous power. The Third World school may fail to hold deep effects on children's acquired literacy or secular values. But the fact that the school is tightly administered – with tidy accounts, a sharp schedule of classes and attractive gardens – signals the attributes of a modern organization. The institution is recognized by local parents as a concrete instrument of modernity, even if the school's technical objective of raising literacy is rarely accomplished.
>
> (Fuller, 1991, pp. 43–4)

We shall return to the discussion of modernization and 'fragile states' in Chapter 5. Here, it is important to note that this organizational concern with modern form and appearance has unfortunate outcomes for education in developing countries, as the attempt to organize schools along bureaucratic lines has meant that the hierarchical and authoritarian power relationships of the bureaucratic model have shaped the nature of classrooms. In some instances, moreover, the authoritarian features of modern bureaucratic forms have coexisted easily with the authoritarian features of the bureaucracies of traditional cultures (Harber, 1989, ch. 5). Even though schools and classrooms in reality may not actually operate as classic Weberian bureaucracies in terms of such principles as merit, the fair and equal application of rules, consistency and honesty and integrity, their attempt to appear to do so means that in terms of the way power is distributed in the organization they inevitably adopt or reinforce authoritarian values and behaviours. However, because these values and behaviours are not transmitted in a consistent, reliable or predictable manner, pupils are subjected not only to authoritarianism, which is inefficient in its own terms as an organizational model for schools, but also to the inefficient practice of authoritarianism. The bureaucratic façade thus results in messy and incoherent authoritarianism.

Yet any authoritarianism, messy or not, is at odds with what should now be required as key goals for an effective education. Internationally there is now an emerging consensus on the need for democracy. Indeed, multi-party democracy is now one of the major conditions attached to World Bank structural adjustment programmes. The United Nations Development Reports for 1992 and 1993 also stress the need for democratization as an integral part of development, but recognizes that this will require a long process involving the creation of a democratic political culture and civil society – a democratic 'way of life' – and that this can only be achieved on a long-term and sustainable basis through education (UNDP, 1992, 1993). This means the creation of independent, confident, analytical, articulate, flexible and critical democratic citizens through education. Moreover, even before this pressure from international organizations, many developing countries had already framed educational policies aimed at encouraging more independent and enquiring work in schools. Education for *kagisano* (social harmony) in Botswana would be one example, and education for self-reliance in Tanzania would be another.

However, we would argue that both primary and secondary schools in developing countries as presently structured do not provide suitable classrooms for the development of a democratic citizenry possessing the qualities outlined above. The following examples illustrate the general nature of classroom relationships in developing countries, and, although their actual operation may be subject to the inconsistencies of school organization signalled above and described in more detail in the final section of the chapter, authoritarianism is clearly predominant.

Classrooms in Africa are well described by Datta (1984, p. 40):

> In most African schools the classroom is highly structured in terms of the formal distribution of space. The teacher in the classroom exercises unquestioned authority in such matters as seating arrangements and movement. He not only initiates the activities to be pursued by pupils, but also controls communication channels and all types of interaction within the group. We do not know the extent to which this kind of classroom environment determines the political orientation of pupils, but forced conformity to an authority system throughout childhood and early adolescence, if supplemented by other factors, is likely to encourage passive acceptance of authority in later years. A democratic and participatory classroom environment, on the other hand, is supposed to contribute to the development of a critical and reflective attitude among pupils.

This type of authoritarian classroom environment has frustrated policies theoretically aimed at greater participation and pupil involvement. In Botswana, even in 'Education for *kagisano*' a rigid rote learning approach is dominant, so that children sit passively while teachers talk (Prophet, 1987). In Chinese countries the situation appears little different:

> The teacher as high authority figure seems pan-Chinese, a fact verified by the dominance of the lecture method and teacher-centred classroom not only in Taiwan but also in the People's Republic and Hong Kong. In regard to instructional methods used in the People's Republic of China, Unger says that 'Chinese teachers have utilized an approach over the past 30 years that remains surprisingly traditional – the teacher-centred classroom . . . Chinese students have been cast as passive recipients of whatever form of instruction has prevailed.'
>
> (Meyer, 1988)

Similar teacher-centred, lecturing methods stressing the recall of factual knowledge are also predominant in Thailand and Nigeria (Anderson *et al.*, 1987). The situation in South and Central America does not seem very different. One survey of 16 countries in the region found that whereas teachers claimed to use a variety of teaching methods, the pupils were unanimous in claiming that teachers rarely used anything except traditional, didactic methods (Villegas-Reimers, 1993). In Brazil,

> There was little oral interaction between teacher and students over instructional issues. The dominant type of schoolwork was solitary in textbooks, workbooks, notebooks and worksheets. Children were required to do filling in exercises that called for short answers to factual questions . . . Verbal interaction between teachers and students was limited to procedural issues, control and to economical question-and-answer sequences . . . The extensive use of solitary drills and exercises excluded the use of other modes of teaching and other activities.
>
> (Da Silva, 1984, p. 274)

Even in socialist countries little seems to have changed. In Tanzania, despite the aims of education for self-reliance, one very common teaching method is 'copy-copy' where the teacher copies notes or words from a textbook or notebook onto the blackboard. The pupils then copy these into their own notebooks and in the examinations 'copy' their notes onto the paper from their memories (Mbilinyi, 1979). In Cuba,

> The structure of the classroom itself seems to have resisted the winds of revolution. In the classrooms which I visited, the method of instruction could best be described as catechistic, an authoritarian teacher-centred approach characterized by a single teacher talking at a class of passive students. Little genuine motivation or interest was evinced by the students.
>
> (Bowles, 1976)

In a survey of teaching practices in developing countries Lockheed notes that in Nepal, 78 per cent of fifth grade science instruction was lecturing and less than 7 per cent was student participation. In Thailand, 54 per cent of fifth grade mathematics instruction employed teacher lectures, explanation or demonstrations; another 30 per cent of the time was spent on written seatwork and only 4 per cent of the time spent was used for oral work of any kind, including discussion. In Jamaica, observers noted that 59 per cent of classroom time was taken up by teacher talk, with teachers dominating the lessons and posing few open-ended questions. Lockheed concludes that 'Group work, which encourages discussion, is rarely encountered' (1993, p. 31).

The classrooms of 'bureaucratized' schools in developing countries are there-fore largely aimed at the three 'r's – rote, retention and regurgitation. Investigation, problem-solving and independent thought are highly unlikely to result from these processes of teaching and learning. As Fuller notes (1991, p. 127), the state may preach the virtues of self-reliance, higher productivity and entrepreneurial initiative but the authority structure previously found in colonial schools continues to be reproduced. This may often, of course, be entirely deliberate as the last thing authoritarian governments in developing countries want is a questioning and critical citizenry. In this sense schools, from the government's point of view, are highly effective in that they help to subordinate and control the population. In terms of their genuine contribution to social, economic and political development, however, they are presently highly ineffective. As Handy and Aitken (1986, p. 95) say:

> Interestingly, however, modern businesses are moving away from hierarchies towards networks in response to the need for more flexibility and in order to give more room to the individual. It may be that in aping the bureaucracy of large businesses the secondary school has been adopting a theory of management that is already out of date.

SCHOOLS AS INEFFECTIVE BUREAUCRACIES

Ironically, while the role of schools in many developing countries may be to symbolize or signal 'modern' bureaucratic institutions, their actual operation is regularly markedly different from the characteristics of an ideal type bureaucracy described by Weber and outlined above. They also display none of the behavioural norms listed by Gunnar Myrdal (1968, pp. 61–2) as being associated with the efficient functioning of bureaucratic organizations: efficiency; diligence; orderliness; punctuality; frugality; honesty; rationality in decisions on action (liberation from reliance on static customs, from group allegiances and favouritism, from super-stitious beliefs and prejudices); preparedness for change; alertness to opportunities; energetic enterprise; co-operativeness and willingness to take the long-term view and forgo short-term profiteering.

There is also the question of how far even an 'ideal bureaucracy' contains within it unexplicated cultural values. Some interesting discussions have emerged in the context of developing countries on whether, for example, bureaucracy is inherently gendered (Mannathoko, 1995). This refers not so much to the numerical proportions of males and females occupying various positions in the hierarchy, but to the acceptance of hierarchy and the way that this can be used for dominance and power, often along gendered lines. Critiques of bureaucracy centre on the problems of hierarchy and so-called impersonality and advocate the possibility of 'decisions without hierarchy' (Ianello, 1992). As feminists argue, objectivity can be seen as just another name for male subjectivity. The apparently objective features of a bureaucracy are, ironically, one way to mask a number of cultural and gendered assumptions.

The following discussion, however, concerns how schools can actually operate as 'pseudo-bureaucracies' or bureaucratic façades in developing countries. This will inevitably seem negative in that it will focus on what are commonly seen as 'problems' in putting Western organizations into operation in non-Western cultural economic and cultural settings. Nevertheless, two important points should be borne in mind. First, while contradictions and conflicts do occur, schools can also function 'normally', smoothly and predictably according to Western models in some ways, while at the same time exhibiting inconsistencies in others. Second, when staff, parents or pupils behave in what might, for example, seem an irresponsible, lazy or venal manner this is not necessarily or only because this is the nature of the individuals concerned. Social pressures and organizational structures may leave them little choice. Possible reasons for the behaviours described below are discussed in other chapters: Chapter 1 provided a discussion of contextual factors affecting the operation of schools as organizations in developing countries, while explanatory theories of school management in developing countries are discussed in Chapters 5, 6 and 7.

ABSENTEEISM AND LATENESS

These are problems often referred to in relation to schools in developing countries. Research in Nigeria, for example, found that it affected both teachers and pupils. Surprise visits made by government officers to schools revealed that teachers were late or absent without good reason (Harber, 1989, pp. 116–17). Similar problems exist in Tanzania (Saunders, 1984, p. 134). One obvious reason for staff absenteeism is that they may well have a second job in order to survive. Surveys in Indonesia, Liberia and Somalia, for example, all showed that substantial proportions of primary teachers had second and sometimes third wage-earning jobs (World Bank, 1990, p. 25). This directly contravenes Weber's seventh characteristic that the official's post is his or her sole occupation.

The second job may not always be outside teaching, however. In Colombia in 1975, when state and national systems were fused, it was found that large numbers of teachers had been holding full-time teaching positions in both state and national schools, and sometimes in municipal schools as well. Although this was strictly illegal, the lack of co-ordination between the national and state systems had permitted it and the low salary scales encouraged it (Hanson, 1986, p. 99).

The need for money can also cause periods of absenteeism among pupils as is illustrated in Nigel Barley's description of an encounter in Indonesia in his book *Not a Dangerous Sport* (1988, p. 109):

> As I passed later that evening, a lone figure in the flimsy shirt of a high school student detached itself from a group and hailed me.
> 'Hallo, boss. Where you go?'
> 'Johannis! Why are you in school uniform?' It was hard to place the age of Indonesians. Surely he was too old to be still at school?
> He waved a book at me. *Introduction to Biology*. 'There's no electricity at my house and they complain if I burn paraffin just to read,

so we have to come here and study under the street lamps.' A wave of post imperial guilt struck me. I thought of my own world of bedside lamps, scholarships and libraries. 'You are still at school?'

He sighed. 'I should be married but, yes, I am still at school. I have to keep stopping my studies to go back and work in the rice fields. Or I work in the hotels to get money for school fees. It takes so long.'

However, absenteeism must be set in a broader context of the large amount of teaching time lost in developing countries:

> Time loss for unscheduled school closings, teacher absences, disruptions and inclement weather is much greater in developing countries. For example, in Haiti the school year in 1984 had 162 days – 18 short of the international standard – but it was made significantly shorter by unofficial closings and delayed openings. The school day often began late. Teachers were frequently absent on Tuesday and Friday (market days) and forty-eight public holidays were celebrated instead of the twenty-eight holidays built into the school year. Teacher absences due to administrative procedures are also common in developing countries. For example, many teachers must travel considerable distances to be paid, while others are assigned to schools far from their homes; both situations contribute to teacher absences and reduced instructional time.
>
> (World Bank, 1990, p. 19)

DEVIANCE: TEACHER INDISCIPLINE, EXAMINATION FRAUD AND STUDENT VIOLENCE

As bureaucracies, schools depend on suitably qualified and motivated staff. Indeed, one of the Weberian tenets of bureaucratic organization cited above was that staff are recruited on the basis of a professional qualification, ideally substantiated by a diploma gained through examination. One immediate problem, as was pointed out in Chapter 1, is that the drive for mass schooling has meant that schools in developing countries, especially in rural areas, are often staffed by untrained teachers. With the expansion of the number of teachers the status of teaching has also declined and has become far less popular as a career, many educated young people preferring, if they can, to work in private or other government employment. Moreover, the poor remuneration and working conditions described in Chapter 1 also hamper staff recruitment, lower staff morale and contribute to staff deviance.

Discussion of 'deviance' in schools is usually confined to pupils. However, it is an issue that also applies to staff. Authors of textbooks on educational adminis-tration from developing countries seem aware that these issues exist, as they provide occasional hints, glimpses and clues as to the sort of problems that might be encountered. Under 'Discipline of Staff', for example, Ozigi (1984, p. 28) notes that

> All human beings have shortcomings and it is inevitable that you will meet cases of indiscipline among members of your staff. Such cases may include, for instance, laziness, frequent absence from school, refusal to participate in extra-curricular activities, incitement of pupils against

authority, drunkenness, financial embarrassment, fighting in the staff room or in class, misuse of school property or funds, threatening behaviour or acts of discourtesy.

Musaazi (1982) provides this list in a section on staff management:

Teachers can be disciplined for disobedience in carrying out orders from their superiors, engaging in strikes, drunkenness during working hours, constant absenteeism from duty, or serious professional misconduct e.g. a male teacher having an affair with a female student . . .

However, perhaps the most interesting clues in such books come from the examples given in sections other than those specifically on staff control. Olembo and Cameron's section on 'School accounts' (1986, p. 31) warns that

Receipts of all expenditure must be collected and filed carefully immediately the money is spent. If the person who gives the money cannot give a receipt, the head must provide one for him to sign. It is a good idea to have a third person present to sign the receipt as a witness . . . It is dangerous for the head to delegate financial responsibility to another member of staff. If this is absolutely necessary, the head should keep a close eye on him . . .

For management training, the problem with such generalized examples is that they are removed from their socio-economic and cultural context and no explanation for the behaviour is provided. The rest of this chapter will examine real examples, while Chapters 5, 6 and 7 discuss explanatory factors in more depth. Davies (1993) studied the national press in Zimbabwe for a six-month period and found 53 items that posed serious problems for an effective school organization. The largest category was financial – the embezzlement by heads or senior management of school funds or examination fees. The second largest category was sexual – the rape of pupils or teachers, or schoolgirl pregnancy where the father was a teacher. Favouritism and nepotism came a close third, with claims about preferential treatment with regard to salaries. Alcoholism, running illegal dormitories, examination fraud, absenteeism and excessive corporal punishment also featured. Davies started to build up a typology of such forms of deviance from 'victimless crimes' through to 'abuses of power'. The importance of theorizing such deviance will be returned to in Chapter 6 when we look at prismatic society. This section will at this stage provide illustrative detail of some of the categories concerned.

Financial pressures are obviously one factor in the existence of corruption and cheating in schools. At a less serious level, financial problems can lead to a teacher selling iced water to her pupils in Ghana (Oppong and Abu, 1987); to teachers selling sweets and snacks to pupils in Nigerian classrooms (Omokhodian, 1989); and to the headteacher using the school playing field to graze his cattle (Davies, 1988). Yet more serious forms of corruption contradict such classic features of bureaucratic organization as the observation of impersonal duties by staff, no appropriation of resources, selection by qualification and promotion by merit or seniority. In Sierra Leone:

Part of the reason for the large number of unqualified and untrained teachers at the primary level is the corrupt way high school students are employed as teachers. The various inspectors of primary schools are authorized to appoint teachers, who are ultimately approved by the Ministry of Education in Freetown. It is in the exercise of this authority that corruption occurs, especially for high school leavers who need employment. It is not unknown for supervisors to demand two months pay as bribes in order to employ an untrained teacher. Part of the bribe is shared with the official at the Ministry of Education in Freetown. With virtually no prospect of employment, the school leaver is forced to acquiesce.

(Banya, 1991, pp. 132–3)

The following (Barley, 1986) describes Cameroon:

It was the same in the schools. They are all weighed down with an incredible bureaucratic apparatus for strictly determining which pupils shall be expelled, which promoted and which obliged to take a year again. The amount of time spent in the abstruse calculation of 'averages' with arcane formulae is at least equal to that spent in the classroom. And at the end of this, the headmaster arbitrarily decides that the marks look too low and adds twenty across the board, or he accepts bribes from a parent and simply changes marks, or the government decides that it has no need of so many students and invalidates its own examinations. At times it becomes bad farce. It is impossible not to smile at the sight of question papers being guarded by gendarmes with sub-machine guns when the envelope they are in has been opened by a man who sold the contents to the highest bidder several days before.

In Tanzania 'it is frequently alleged that teachers switch examinations around, taking a "bright" child's number and giving it to a relative' (Ishumi and Cooksey, 1985, p. 35). In Ghana teachers have charged to teach extra classes while they neglect their normal ones (Dadey and Harber, 1991, p. 7). In Kenya, where private tuition by teachers is not officially encouraged, unofficially teachers may be persuaded to give extra lessons to the children of higher government officers (Kinyanjui, 1990). An exercise on teacher deviance during a class held by the authors involved international students anonymously giving examples of corruption in education from their own countries. In Pakistan, as in Ghana, teachers have charged for private classes and neglected their own classes in order to encourage their private business; in Brunei a headteacher was jailed after falsifying bills for food to be paid by the Ministry; in Uganda a headteacher was sacked after embezzling funds from a community school.

In Nigeria, in one state the Teaching Service Commission announced that eight headmasters would have an embargo placed on their salaries until they turned up and showed their certificates at promotion interviews. The Commission commented that most teachers in the state did not have the certificates they claimed to possess and preferred to remain in their grades without promotion. It also noted that 159 disciplinary actions ranging from warnings to dismissal had been taken against its staff. It thought that the absence of a code of conduct for teachers in the state had given rise to embezzlement, certificate forgery and immoral relations with female pupils. In another state a commission of enquiry was set up after 5340 teachers withdrew their services in protest at alleged corrupt practices and nepotism in the teaching service. The commission found that teachers received salaries unrelated to qualifications and experience and that there were fictitious names on the payrolls (Harber, 1989, p. 117).

Cheating is not necessarily confined to staff, however, as the following examples illustrate:

- *Bangladesh*: Students enraged at attempts to stop them cheating attacked police and teachers with homemade bombs, knives and rocks at the start of month-long secondary school examinations in Bangladesh, police said yesterday . . . Police opened fire to disperse crowds at Baidyerbazar, 40 miles from Dhaka, after students and their friends and relatives rampaged through examination halls . . . During certificate examinations last year students chanted 'We seek the right to copy' and 'Expel unsympathetic invigilators'. Cheating is a regular feature of secondary school and university examinations, despite regular attempts to stamp it out.
  (London, *Guardian*, 18 March 1989)

- *Egypt*: Teachers are beaten up, examination papers are stolen, outside loudspeakers broadcast answers to students sitting exams – all part of cheating scandals that have been exposed in some Egyptian schools. So serious is the problem that police are forming temporary anti-cheating squads in parts of the country as high school students prepare for year-end examinations next month.
  (Swaziland, *Weekend Observer*, 30 May 1987)

- *India*: A small crowd gathered outside (the school). Several people carried books. Shortly after 2pm, a piece of paper was passed out through a window. Those with the books hurriedly consulted them and soon notes were being scribbled and passed inside . . . Behind the window 100 or more pupils were sitting the exam. Outside, in a breath-takingly brazen attempt to secure satisfactory grades, parents, friends and private tutors were helping the pupils to cheat. The invigilator did not intervene.
  (London, *Independent*, 15 April 1989)

- *Thailand*: In rural Thailand, four steps were taken to ensure that pupils passed examinations:
  1. Giving more weight to pupils' pre-examination performance.
  2. Giving extra marks when marking final papers.
  3. Providing pupils with answers during the examination session.
  4. Raising the final examination score.
  (Chantavanich *et al.*, 1990, p. 145)

- *Nigeria*: The West African Examinations Council announced that it was withholding 33,000 Nigerian results because of malpractice such as cheating, having fore-knowledge of the questions and collusion.

(*New Nigerian*, 3 November 1977)

Finally, bureaucratic systems assume that decision-making and rule application will take place in a predictable and peaceful context. This is not always the case in African schools, however, where there are regular accounts of violent riots and demonstrations by pupils in the press. Examples from Nigeria and Tanzania are provided in Harber (1989, ch. 7) and it is also a problem in Ghana (Dadey and Harber, 1991). The following examples are all from Kenya.

- At Baricho secondary school 450 students were sent home indefinitely after a riot. A contingent of armed police were called into school by the headteacher after which a fierce battle erupted between the students and the police. The trouble started when the students demanded a refund of 350,000 shillings which their parents had paid for the purchase of a school bus which had not been bought.

(Nairobi, *The Standard,* 11 July 1990)

- About 500 students at Kerugoya Boys High School were sent home following a riot. Trouble started at night when a few students started inciting others by disconnecting electricity lines from the main switch and throwing stones at the roofs of the dormitories. The headteacher informed the police when the students started shouting and waking the teachers and neighbouring residents. The students then went on the rampage smashing windows, doors, offices, dormitories and staff quarters. The students were demanding the repair of the school's television set and a record player.

(Nairobi, *Daily Nation*, 26 July 1990)

- Nineteen girls died and many were raped during a riot by boys at St Kizio school near Meru. The boys had planned to stage a strike against the headteacher over being barred from a sports competition and the girls refused to join the strike so the boys attacked them.

(London, *Independent*, 16 July 1991)

Such violent disturbances are not necessarily the result of a few malcontents or simply the reflection of a 'violent society'. Rather, as is discussed later in this book, they stem from the dysfunctional nature of school organization, and the role of the headteacher in particular.

CONCLUSION

During the period of colonialism developing countries inherited a model of mass schooling that originated in the industrialized colonial powers at the end of the nineteenth century. Originally this was just for the few but, following independence, social demand and the needs of the state have meant the steady spread of schools with dramatic increases in enrolment. That such schools, especially in rural areas, are of poor quality is to miss the point that their role has been as much to do with signalling and symbolizing development and 'modernity' by mimicry of Western schools and elite schools in the capital as with providing a genuinely useful education. Hence the majority of schools have styled themselves on the 'modern' organizational model *par excellence* – bureaucracy.

Unfortunately, as this chapter has argued, in terms of decision-making, bureaucracy is a rigid, closed and non-participatory form of organization which has severe shortcomings in a contemporary world of rapid change and uncertainty, which is why many businesses have already abandoned many aspects of it. In schools its effects are particularly harmful on pupils, who suffer the routinized and authoritarian modes of teaching and learning it inevitably promotes. This is as true in industrialized societies, where schools face many problems, as it is in developing ones.

Moreover, as this chapter has also argued, contextual factors mean that many schools in developing countries do not actually operate as efficient bureaucracies anyway. Any proposed improvements to school organization must therefore recognize this and not simply or solely recommend the fine tuning or tightening up of bureaucratic mechanisms. Rather the post-bureaucratic school needs to begin again with the basic questions 'What sort of people do we want?' and 'What sort of society do we want?' and design school organization accordingly. This will not be an easy or quickly accomplished task but, if we are really serious about education as opposed to just putting pupils in buildings called schools, there seems to be little alternative to beginning as soon as possible.

Chapter 4

'Leadership': Headteacher as Taxi Driver

INTRODUCTION

'Leadership' is often seen as a key variable in school effectiveness studies. In day-to-day management terms at school level the headteacher or principal is identified as a crucial factor in school improvement and school effectiveness. A list of the main factors in school effectiveness from a book that provides a summary of research in the field, starts with: 'The leadership role of the principal and senior management team is vital.' However, it also notes that 'there is little scientific evidence to support this frequently reported assertion' (Reid, Hopkins and Holly, 1987, p. 29). If headteachers are so important, and if they are all doing the job they were supposed to, then there would be little need for the enormous amount of expensive school effectiveness research and the resulting school effectiveness literature, as most schools would already be effective and be led by effective headteachers. If this is not the case then something is clearly getting in the way of headteachers leading effective schools. This chapter examines the roles played by headteachers or principals, in particular in developing countries, in the light of the evidence that we have and argues that the contextual realities of schools in developing countries mean that there is a serious mismatch between the prescribed roles for headteachers and the actual job of headteacher. The chapter begins by describing how heads fit into the authoritarian nature of schooling discussed in Chapter 3, then reviews what we know about the actual work of headteachers as opposed to what they are supposed to do, before concluding with an account of the work of headteachers in three developing countries in Africa – Ghana, Botswana and Tanzania.

HEADTEACHER AS DESPOT

In Chapter 3 we argued that power relations in schools in developing countries are largely authoritarian and bureaucratic, and that this is both an ineffective way of educating for peace and democracy and also means that schools operate in an ineffective manner. If school organization is like this then headteachers must play a role in maintaining it as such. In this section we examine the political role played by most headteachers in schools, while in the remainder of the chapter we explore the day-to-day work of headteachers in developing countries.

In their book on effective schools, Holmes and Wynne (1989, p. 58) describe the most frequently found type of headteacher as the 'benevolent despot'. In Ball's UK study of the micro-politics of schools he emphasizes the role of the headteacher as being significantly concerned with domination in order to achieve and maintain particular definitions of the school over and above alternative definitions. The political model presented in Ball's case studies is authoritarian, with the headteacher at the top of a hierarchical chain of command. The role of teachers in this authoritarian model is that, while they are 'consulted' about policy, this is not regarded as binding by headteachers and teachers have no real access to decision-making. Rather these 'rights of participation' are a political ritual which lends support to what is in reality a system of autocracy (Ball, 1987, pp. 125–6). What is true of most headteachers' relationships with teachers is also true of their relationships with students.

In Chapters 5 and 6 we examine how both international influences and local cultural influences have shaped the authoritarian nature of schools and classrooms in developing countries. Here it needs to be noted that in developing countries headteachers emerge from the teaching population and have had little or no training for the job (Giorgiades and Jones, 1989). Classroom teaching experience is the key factor in the selection of heads. In Chapter 3 we saw that evidence from a wide range of developing areas strongly suggests that classroom teaching is overwhelmingly authoritarian in style. Given the nature of school organization, their own identities as teachers and the top-down, highly centralized systems of education in most developing countries, it would be unlikely for the majority of headteachers to be anything other than despots, benevolent or otherwise. This is undoubtedly reinforced by gendered notions of 'leadership' with masculinist notions of strength, hierarchy and dominance being traditionally the paramount managerial model and with both men and women subscribing to this model. In Nigeria, for example,

> In theory, it is expected that most heads of Nigerian schools will fall into
> categories like autocratic, democratic or laissez-faire, but most heads
> tend to be authoritarian, if not altogether autocratic. To a certain extent,
> this tendency can be attributed to the traditional ways of life, in which
> the elder or the man in authority . . . has the final say in all matters and
> must be obeyed.
>
> (DuBey, Edem and Thakur, 1979, p. 37)

Giorgiades and Jones (1989, p. 2) begin their study of headship in developing countries with the following letter to a newspaper in Malaysia:

> A headmaster in my old school never misses an opportunity to lecture
> students but never takes the trouble to know them personally. What
> resulted is this: I have not yet encountered a student who remotely likes
> or respects the headmaster. Frustration is the cause for the graffiti and
> broken chairs and tables in the school. Ninety percent of the writings on
> the wall are often directed at the headmaster.

In Thailand the same authors asked a sample of headteachers about how their school was organized: the most commonly used term was 'hierarchically' (ibid., p. 41). This is supported by Tsang and Wheeler who, in discussing the role of headteachers in Thailand note that 'This role derives in part from cultural traditions that emphasise hierarchical decision making and deference towards leaders' (1993, p. 124). In Indonesia the attempt to introduce more student-active forms of learning has been hampered by the fact that little training has been provided to the headteacher as to how the learning should be implemented or operated in his/her school. The Cianjur Project was an attempt to use in-service education to introduce more active forms of classroom learning in one area of Java. It found that in order to change classroom relationships between staff and students it had to begin by changing the usual and predominant pattern of authoritarian and hierarchical relationships between inspectors and headteachers and headteachers and staff (Giorgiades and Jones, 1989, p. 45; Departemen Pendidikan Dan Kebudayaan, 1987).

In South Africa until very recently headteachers have had to carry out instructions from the centre and to manage their institutions along 'autocratic and bureaucratic lines' (Tsukudu and Taylor, 1995, p. 110). One ethnographic study of a school in rural South Africa described the head as follows:

> She told the other teachers what to do and to teach and when and how to do so. She set the timetable and decided on pupil admissions . . . She spent most of her day wandering from class to class, now and then issuing curt instructions to teachers or pupils. The principal was the only person who appeared to make any decisions with regard to education matters and her style was, in regard to the formal activities of the school, extremely authoritarian.
>
> (Moll, 1995, p. 14)

The following three newspaper reports all come from Kenya:

> Parents of the Kamiru Boys' High School on Thursday went to the school and took away their children, leaving the institution deserted. Several parents told the *Sunday Nation* that they took the drastic step after disagreeing with the headmaster over a number of issues. They accused the headmaster of being arrogant. They claimed that he had refused to tell them about their children's academic progress. They said that when a parent goes to the school to ask about what his or her child's progress or mistakes are, they are told to go home with the child.
>
> (*Sunday Nation*, 5 April 1992)

> Parents at Malava Secondary School yesterday criticized the management for failing to diffuse student unrest and urged the authorities to order the immediate reopening of the institution. The parents accused the headmaster of allegedly misleading the board of governors into approving the school's indefinite closure without proper investigations. They contended that if the headmaster had accepted to talk with the students, the tension would have been diffused.
>
> (*Kenya Times*, 26 March 1992)

> A primary school pupil was taken to hospital in a critical condition after he was beaten by his headmaster in Lamu District. The pupil had absented himself from school for three weeks. When he reported back his class teacher caned him before sending him to the headmaster who also caned him several times, inflicting serious injuries.
>
> (*Daily Nation*, 21 July 1990)

A survey of 16 Latin American countries (Villegas-Reimers, 1993) found that the majority school principals did not involve students in school management and, with the exception of Colombia, which is discussed in Chapter 9, in those that did, participation was tokenistic and shallow.

THE JOB OF HEADTEACHER

Despite the importance attached to the headteacher as being central to the success or failure of a school, we still know relatively little about what a headteacher actually does. Books on the subject usually provide a list of functions. The following, for example, is one from the Commonwealth Secretariat's headteacher training programme for Anglophone Africa, which began in the early 1990s:

- implementers of the policies and procedures of government
- administrators of educational institutions
- head teachers and lead providers of interesting, challenging and relevant learning experiences
- facilitators for creating school communities in which co-operation, creativity and achievement are prized
- leader, *primus inter pares,* of teams of professional educators
- managers of the supply and effective use of resources (human, financial and material)
- enablers of parental and community involvement in teaching/learning processes and in school management and development
- co-ordinators of quality assurance mechanisms, including monitoring and evaluation, which lead to useful and continuing changes and innovations (McNie, White and Wight, 1991, p. 7).

Leaving aside the inaccuracy of *'primus inter pares'* in the light of the foregoing analysis, such lists are usually both generalized and prescriptive and often become a set of exhortations. This is from a textbook on educational administration (Musaazi, 1982, pp. 167–8):

> The school head must know that he [sic] is an employee and that his employer, the Ministry of Education, expects from him good quality work, loyalty and integrity.
> The school head as the leader of the teaching staff has the responsibility of promoting effective teaching in the school. It is also his duty to ensure that his employer appoints qualified and competent teachers to his school.
> If the school head is to achieve his goal of improving the curriculum programmes he must have an understanding of the teacher and the teacher's role, and he must always be prepared to work effectively with the teacher.

Ball (1987, p. 1) argues that the reason for this tendency to ignore what head-teachers actually do is that theoretical writing on school organization has been overwhelmingly influenced by systems theory and has not been sufficiently grounded in empirical reality:

> It is my contention that organizational analyses – I include both work in organizational theory and the sociology of organization – have had little of any significance to tell us about the way in which schools are actually run on a day to day basis. Indeed, a great deal of the writing in this field has actually tended to bypass and obscure the realities of organizational life in schools. To a great extent organizational theorists have remained locked, explicitly or implicitly, within the stultifying parameters of systems theory and have tended to neglect description in favour of prescription or to move uncertainly between the two. They prefer the abstract tidiness of conceptual debate to the concrete messiness of empirical research inside schools.

This emerges clearly when we ask the question: what is an effective headteacher? An effective headteacher or principal, presumably, is one who comes close to the sort of lists given above. In fact, large-scale empirical research on effective headteachers in the West has come up with not dissimilar findings. Smith and Andrews (1989), for example, studied over 2500 teachers and 1200 principals and found that effective principals were engaged in four areas of strategic interactions with teachers: (1) as 'resource provider', (2) as 'instructional resource', (3) as 'communicator' and (4) as 'visible presence'. Of these the 'instructional leader' role was found to be particularly important in identifying the effective head. While all these characteristics of the effective head are hardly surprising and border on the obvious, what is more interesting is that only 21 of the 1200 were actually effective instructional leaders. Two other studies found that only 10 per cent of headteachers functioned effectively according to their criteria (Fullan, 1991, p. 151). Fullan, in writing about headteachers in the industrialized nations of the West, nevertheless makes a telling point about the need to look at what headteachers actually do (p. 145):

> Nearly all school district role descriptions (and courses in educational administration theory, which nearly all school principals take) stress the instructional leadership responsibilities of the principal – facilitating change, helping teachers work together, assessing and furthering school improvement and so on. However, how principals actually spend their time is obviously a better indicator of their impact on the school.

Indeed, it may well help to explain why most headteachers seem to be ineffective and unable to live up to the models of perfection of their role descriptions. Fullan's review (ibid., p. 146) of the studies that have been done of what headteachers actually do in Western schools found a series of consistent trends:

- Virtually all the time of headteachers is taken up with one-to-one personal encounters, meetings and telephone calls.
- Headteachers' workdays were sporadic and characterized simultaneously by brevity, variety and fragmentation.
- Headteachers perform on average 149 tasks a day with constant

interruptions – in one study 59 per cent of their observed activities were interrupted.

- Most of their activities (84 per cent) were brief (one to four minutes).
- Headteachers demonstrated a tendency to engage themselves in the most current and pressing situation. They invested little time in reflective planning.
- Most of their time is spent on administrative housekeeping matters, maintaining order and crisis management.

One study concluded that:

> The global response to any and all concerns means he never has the time, energy or inclination to develop or carry out a set of premeditated plans of his own. Containment of all problems is his theme. The principal cannot be a change agent or leader under these conditions.
>
> (House and Lapan, 1978, p. 145)

In developing countries we know even less about what headteachers actually do. One study of headteachers in developing countries, published by the World Bank (Giorgiades and Jones, 1989), provides the familiar list of headteacher tasks, this time from a study in Thailand: staff personnel services; curriculum and instruction development; school business and management; school law; pupil personnel services; school community relationships; school plant planning; facilities and human relations (Pinkoompee, 1979). However, Giorgiades and Jones (1989, pp. 19–20) make the following important comment:

> This list could have come from any beginning text on educational administration used in any university in the UK, Canada, Australia or the United States. But what is missing is a description of what these phrases mean in the day-to-day operations of a school. There is virtually nothing available in Pinkoompee's study or any other that described the 'average' day, week or year in the life of a headmaster within a developing country. Only one partially ethnographic study of the work of the principal was found in our literature search. Woodard (1985) worked with elementary principals in South Thailand and concluded that most of her sample principals had little influence over decisions that affected the quality of efforts in the schools. Based on her structured interviews she furthermore found that most of her sample principals were quite unclear about their roles in improving the teaching–learning process in their schools. She also noted that principals were especially reluctant to deal directly with pupil misconduct and resistance, perhaps because of the societal importance of the avoidance of conflict. Based on the reported studies there appears to be more interest in determining what a headmaster or principal *should* do.

Yet it is likely, given the contexts of developing countries outlined in Chapter 1 and the nature of school organization as discussed in Chapter 3, that, even if the job of headteacher is just as messy, fragmented, untidy and event-driven as in schools in developed countries, the actual events, tasks and problems faced by headteachers will be substantially different. This has become clearer since the appearance of data not available at the time of Giorgiades and Jones' literature review. Sealy (1992) shadowed four primary heads in Barbados and found that in one week the total number of different activities performed ranged from 113 to 194, with a daily average of 30 activities – almost 50 per cent more than Minzberg's 22 activities for the business executive. The activity with the largest amount of time was in fact 'personal' – having lunch or reading, for example. This was followed by unscheduled meetings (9.7 per cent), paperwork (9.2 per cent) and correspondence (8.7 per cent). As none of the schools had a secretary, and only one had a typewriter, the combined paperwork and correspondence took up a large proportion of their time: 60 per cent of activities were performed in their offices. However, there was constant change and interruption. One-third of all activities took less than five minutes. Less than 5 per cent lasted more than an hour. There appeared to be few occasions for any concentrated periods of time for development planning. Yet, in the light of our discussion of structure and agency in Chapter 7, it is important to note that heads were able to carve out some differences in daily use of time. Only one out of the four engaged (from choice) in timetabled teaching. Another head delegated significantly more time than the other three (including things like assembly as well as clerical work) and was able to spend more time visiting classrooms and consulting with staff. One head, on the other hand, spent ten times more time than the others on counting money.

The next section of this chapter reports data on the actual job done by headteachers in developing countries in Africa.

REALITIES OF HEADSHIP IN AFRICA

> Uncertainties and exigencies at the school level are enormous: pupil attendance is irregular and drop-out rates are high; instructional materials don't show up due to fuel shortages; pay cheques come late, usually requiring the headmaster to take the bus or hitch-hike to the District Education Officer's office; a political figure may be visiting the region, requiring teachers to organize youthful well-wishers and dancers.
>
> (Fuller, 1991, p. 90, writing on Malawi)

This account of the work of headteachers is primarily based on two sources. First, a detailed ethnographic study of the work of three headteachers in Ghana. The researcher shadowed each head for three weeks of intensive observation and interviewing (Dadey, 1990). The second source is work done by Harber in Botswana. This second piece of work is best described in Walker's (1974) phrase as 'condensed field work'. It is a concentrated qualitative study of shorter duration (in this case three weeks) than an ethnography, relying principally on interviews, the collection of documents and short periods of observation. These two sources will be supplemented by some research done in Tanzania, thereby including schools and headteachers in east as well as southern and west Africa. A number of sub-headings are used to organize the material in order to make it readable, but it must be borne in mind that this is a logical framework imposed on an untidy reality, where events could be classified in a number of ways and where there are few clear-cut categories.

Management of staff

In Botswana and Ghana headteachers have little say about who teaches in their schools. The Unified Teaching Service in Botswana allocates staff, including heads, to schools. The argument for this is that it contributes to national unity: teachers would tend otherwise to stay in their own area or go to the capital. The head of one secondary school, however, felt that her school had been used as a dumping ground for poor teachers. Of three she had recently had, two had a drinking problem and the other came from the royal family and she felt that he was beyond her control. Moreover, schools in Ghana and Botswana, as elsewhere in Africa, regularly face shortages of trained staff, and headteachers may have a third to a half of their staff untrained, with the situation worse in primary schools than in secondary schools. There has also often been little ministry provision for their training. Heads therefore have to attempt to organize 'on the job' training for these staff as best they can.

Some countries in Africa, and Botswana is one of them, also have large numbers of expatriate staff to help overcome the teacher shortage. One secondary head commented on the problems associated with this:

> Expatriate teachers vary greatly in respect of cultural and other differences and this is bound to have an effect on our schools and our children. We must be vigilant in this matter and strive to make sure that the effects are not pernicious. In addition, I think that we should not in future cast our net too wide. If we recruit from a wide area, the cultural differences may prove too many to contain. Not all speakers of English present a sufficient grasp of the language, as Zambia discovered to its cost. Then there is the problem of continuity, or rather the lack of it. Teachers from abroad often come to us at the most awkward of times and, perhaps more seriously, leave us at awkward times. I realize that other countries operate a different academic year. The National Commission on Education recommended that teachers should be recruited to start work in January at the start of the academic year but this has not been followed and makes for problems in teacher allotment in particular areas. A teacher is given an examination class and leaves before the course is completed; another arrives after the start of the course and cannot be given a class that needs his experience and expertise.
>
> (Ramatabele, 1984, p. 266)

Another problem faced by heads in Africa is frequent and compulsory transfer of staff, including headteachers themselves (Harber, 1989, pp. 122–3). This was brought home dramatically when gathering data on headteachers in Botswana. The researcher was discussing the problem with a secondary head who described how he himself had been moved to his present school on this basis and how the transfer of teachers could happen at very awkward times, thereby creating extra workloads for those left behind. His phone rang: it was a friend, another headteacher, who had just been informed that he was to be moved against his will and was seriously considering resigning from the profession.

Lutanjuka and Mutembei (1993) note that in Tanzania teachers who have completed teacher training courses are posted to schools with instructions to 'report to your head and you will be paid your travelling and subsistence allowances'. However, the head is not allocated sufficient funds to cater for these expenses. This immediately causes ill feeling between the headteacher and the new staff, who can be in the school for five months before being paid. They report an incident in a secondary school in the Kagera region in 1992. An angry teacher who had not received his salary for three months rushed into the head's office and confronted him demanding to be given a loan of five thousand shillings. The teacher refused to leave the office and threatened to beat the headteacher if his demand was not fulfilled. The head eventually called the police for help but these cases are not that unusual. 'This is the unpleasant and unsecure environment that heads of school have to live in.'

Headteachers face other problems in regard to staff discipline, as we saw in the previous chapter. Sometimes a Ministry of Education might actually encourage deviance by introducing rules that are difficult to comply with. In Botswana, for example, the Ministry has a rule that all male teachers have to wear a shirt, jacket and tie to school. In a country which is regularly very hot this rule is much observed in the breach. Heads get round it by suggesting that teachers come to school in the morning so attired but that the jacket is hung up somewhere on arrival.

Other forms of teacher misbehaviour such as lateness, absenteeism, alcoholism and sexual harassment of female students stem from a weak code of professional ethics and cultures of power and gender. Many teachers are untrained or poorly trained; many did not want to go into teaching in the first place and only remain there until they find a better job. Morale and motivation are often low because of poor pay, lack of promotion and inadequate resources. While headteachers cannot solve the larger problems responsible for teacher deviance, they can attempt to ameliorate some forms of undesirable practice at the school level. This issue is important for headteacher training and the following two examples illustrate the type of contextually relevant material that might be used for case study/problem-solving exercises in the countries concerned.

In one Community Junior Secondary School in Botswana the head was aware that the staff were not punctual in arriving at lessons. A spot check one day revealed that five out of ten staff were not in their classrooms at the beginning of the lesson. Four of the five who were on time subsequently had to go and fetch material they had forgotten. (Only one student was late for lessons that day.) The head put a paper on the staff-room noticeboard asking 'Who has the lateness problem?', 'Who has the organizational problem?' His strategy was to play on consciences. This demonstration that he was aware of the issue and was keeping an eye on it helped improve punctuality greatly.

In Ghana one headteacher faced an issue over remedial classes. Originally these had been organized in the afternoons for students of the school who were academically weak, and no fees were charged. Gradually this changed so that teachers ran them in the vacation for all students regardless of achievement and for students outside the school who wanted to attend. By the time the headteacher was appointed to the school, however, teachers were organizing extra classes during term-time for additional fees and had begun to take their remedial classes more seriously than their ordinary classes. The head decided that the only way to make regular classes meaningful was to put an end to all remedial classes. 'This hit the teachers involved at the most vulnerable point – their pockets. My unpopularity started from then' (Dadey, 1990, pp. 216–17).

Finally, headteachers in Africa have to deal with a diverse range of auxiliary staff: kitchen staff, generator maintenance staff, bursars, groundsmen, cleaners, messengers, nightwatchmen, typists, librarians and administrative assistants. One primary school visited in Botswana employed 22 'stampers' – women who stamp sorghum in wooden pots with long poles in order to make flour for the students. Dadey (1990, pp. 331–2) provides some examples from Ghana of how this can take up the head's time. The day watchman in one school reported to the head that he had caught a sixth former smoking at the weekend. The head told him that the school's disciplinary committee would soon discuss it. The watchman then told the head that delays in disciplining students demoralized his fellow watchmen: he wanted instant justice. The head therefore spent some time explaining to him why it was proper for a committee to look into the matter again and keep records of final decisions before students were punished, including being suspended or withdrawn from school. With some difficulty (because technical words in English had to be explained in the local language) he tried to explain how the 'rule of law' operated even in a small society like a school. He subsequently arranged a meeting with all the watchmen (day and night) so that the management could explain these matters to them. The head said he saw the watchmen 'not as a group of semi-illiterate guards' but 'partners in school administration'.

A second example from Ghana concerns the manager of the school farm who felt that he was not getting enough attention from management. Dadey (1990, p. 183) observed that 'every day between 9.15 and 10.00 a.m. Mr Mensah (the head) went round as much of the school as possible. Now he had to go to the farm as well. He decided to go to the poultry, sheep and goats and only do the rest tomorrow.'

In Tanzania many heads complain of a shortage of support staff such as accountants, typists, clerks, labourers, technicians, cooks and watchmen. The problem has been aggravated by a government directive (in the light of the structural adjustment programme) to reduce the number of employees and stop further employment. Heads are not clear about how they should fill vacancies created by members of supporting staff who leave their jobs. Lutanjuka and Mutembi (1993) argue that lack of support staff causes many administrative problems, which have bad consequences for the head as he or she is later blamed for the things that go wrong. They cite the example of a school that they visited which had neither an accountant nor a financial clerk. However, this school was annually allocated a sum of Tsh30 million from the government and collected fees worth Tsh4.8 million. 'Unfortunately, the head of school has no idea about the government accounting system. How does head of school escape from the audit queries raised by the Controller and Auditor General?'

External relations

One key group that heads have regular contact with is parents. This can happen in a number of ways. In Botswana many children who pass the primary school leaving examination fail to find a secondary school place. The Senior Education Officer in the Department of Secondary Education said parents should start looking for vacancies for their children two weeks before schools opened as by then head-teachers would know who hadn't turned up (*Daily News*, 15 January 1989). Thus for the period preceding the first term of the school year, and for two to four weeks after, many secondary heads face a procession of parents who come to persuade, beg and cajole to get their children into school. In one of Dadey's case study schools in Ghana the head was stopped while walking across the school compound by a parent who had come all the way from another town to arrange his boy's admission into the school. The head commented 'People in this part of the world think they can get the best out of you face to face. They do not like the use of telephones for this reason and, of course, for the other reason that the telephone lines are often faulty' (Dadey, 1990, p. 250).

Parents are also responsible for paying fees to help cover educational costs in both Botswana and Ghana, and again it is the head who must ultimately ensure that these are paid. Dadey's study records headteachers in Ghana regularly dealing with problems created by the non-payment of fees. On one occasion, for example, a parent came to see a head because his son's boarding fees were in arrears, and to ask if he could withdraw the boy from the boarding house to stay with his mother-in-law in town. However, day status is not normally accorded to students whose parents do not reside in the school's catchment area and the head was concerned that, as the student was in Form 4, he needed adequate conditions to prepare for his school certificate. The head therefore promised to take up the matter with the Scholarships Secretariat to see if a hardship bursary could be arranged.

On another occasion the bursar told the head that he was unhappy about the large arrears in boarding fees which the auditors were likely to comment on. So the head instructed housemasters to tell all students who still owed boarding fees to go home at once and collect the fees. It subsequently transpired that some of the students had retained the cheques given to them by their parents. A decision was taken to write to all parents telling them not to send fees with students, but to pay direct to the bursar. However, parents now began to call in to see him regularly to plead to be given until the end of the month to pay their ward's fees in full. A housemaster then brought two students who owed fees and who had been found hiding in the dormitories. One was the son of the Senior Education Officer in the Director's Office.

The collection of school fees can cause tensions in other ways. The Parent–Teacher Association (PTA) of one rural primary school in Botswana wanted to know why the money from fees was not banked in the post office but kept in the headteacher's house without accounts or receipts. Perhaps not surprisingly, he was suspected of being corrupt. In Ghana, on the other hand, school grants from the government are not usually received at the time most urgently needed and this sometimes results in heads taking emergency steps, like taking bank loans, to save the situation. After the December 1981 coup in Ghana and the setting up of probes into the activities of government establishments, it was revealed that heads had borrowed from banks to balance their inadequate grants but that the loans could not be repaid in full because income fell below expectations (Abbey, 1989).

Parents in Africa are also often expected to contribute towards the buildings and basic facilities of schools through the PTA. In one rural Community Junior Secondary School in Botswana, for example, in order for water to be connected, and reflecting the cattle-based nature of the society, each household was expected to contribute the equivalent of one beast. Dadey (1990, p. 172) records one headteacher in Ghana noting that the PTA had recently provided the school with 80 dining-hall tables and 160 forms to sit on, though he still needed more. Getting donations not only means regular and good relations with the PTA but also that the local community can expect favours in return. In the Community Junior Secondary School in Botswana, for example, during the annual agricultural show the head opened the classrooms for people to sleep in. The local Kgotla (council), clinic staff and Land Board were all allowed to use the school's photocopier. The school also had a large tarpaulin which the head loaned out for funerals and weddings; quite often he had to transport it (and school chairs) to functions himself. Relationships, however, are not always harmonious. One head in Botswana, for example, caused considerable conflict because he held back leaving certificates because parents had failed to contribute to the school's building fund (*Daily News*, 31 January 1989).

Parental expectations can go beyond a resource *quid pro quo*. The head of a Community Junior Secondary School in Botswana noted that parents came to see him about out-of-school matters: 'My son didn't come home on Saturday night, what can you do about it?' Yet the problem is that the traditional way of life is not necessarily congruent with a geographically fixed 'modern' institution such as the school. Parents often have a home in the village, one at the 'lands' where crops are grown, and one at the cattle post: students often live with aunts and uncles, grandparents or neighbours, who do not have the same control over their charges as parents. Conversely, the same situation can arise if parents get jobs in the modern sector in Gaborone or Francistown. Complaints about extra-school discipline come to the head not only from individual parents but also through the Board of Governors. One such complaint concerns the 'rudeness' of students; often this means that the students have simply not acquiesced to the parents' viewpoint. 'Education for *kagisano*' in Botswana is supposed to encourage a critical and enquiring mind. Yet when schools manage to achieve some success in this direction, the danger is that parents will see the resulting behaviour as rudeness.

One particular group with which a headteacher has to maintain good relations is local dignitaries. However, this has its dangers as well as its benefits. As one head in Ghana put it (Dadey, 1990, p. 119):

> The problem with keeping local dignitaries interested in the school is that they tend to regard the school as their personal property. Very soon the school becomes a local school and not a national institution. The next step is that the local dignitaries will want a local person to be headmaster and the troubles begin.

The most significant dignitary that heads in Ghana have regular contact with is the local chief. One head put it: 'The chiefs are our kings. Anytime they call on you, you must put aside everything and receive them first.' On one occasion the message from the paramount chief was simple. There was going to be a meeting of the chiefs in that region and he wanted the school truck to carry his drums and royal paraphernalia to the meeting. On another occasion, the aide-de-camp of one of the most influential chiefs in the area arrived to tell the head that the chief was coming to see him in half an hour. The head dropped what he was doing and told the rest of the school administration to gather to receive the chief in the traditional way. He noted that 'Chiefs are the custodians of traditional authority and they must be received in accordance with their dignity. They gave us this land and they feel the school is for them.'

On arrival the chief reminded them that he had given them the land in the hope that their children would be able to get places in the school. Now the majority of places had been offered to students from outside their area whilst their children roamed about in the streets without secondary education. His people were angry and he warned that if things did not change one day there would be an outburst. He himself had a son whom he expected to be admitted the following year. Politely the head replied that he had taken note of the point but that the school was a public institution run on directives issued by government; he was just an agent of the government. He would therefore place the views of the chief before his Board and the education service officials. On the question of the admission of the chief's son, he advised the chief on admission procedures and expressed the hope that the boy would make the grade and come to the school the following year. The head then engaged the chief in conversation, arguing that the school was a government institution and must not be run on a parochial basis. In the end he seemed to have won over an opponent who would be able to explain school policies to the local people – so much so that the head received an invitation to the chief's palace at the weekend (Dadey, 1990, pp. 259–61).

Another problem for heads is that of maintaining external relations at all in the light of poor communications and transport difficulties. Schools, particularly those in rural areas, are not on the telephone. The waiting list for a phone line in Ghana is 30 years (London, *Observer*, 17 March 1991). As a result one headteacher at a rural school in Botswana described himself as a 'glorified messenger'. Not having a telephone, when the school needed to contact the local branch of the Ministry of Education in the nearest town or to collect supplies he had to use his own car. The nearest town is a two-hour drive away, so this role can take up one day each week. Sometimes a visit to a larger town such as Francistown or Gaborone to collect something needed by the school takes a couple of days. Moreover, although the Zonal Central Transport Organization is supposed to provide trucks to transport students, for example to sporting events, this arrangement is unreliable, and those few staff with transport, including the head, often have to do the transporting themselves.

In this role of transport officer, which took up a significant part of his time, one head in Botswana was often asked by parents and teachers to get something for them as he was going into town anyway. The head of a nearby primary school made the journey to the local town on an even more regular basis, publicized the fact and then charged for lifts. On pay day he took half of the staff into the town to shop and on the next day the other half. Headteacher as taxi driver. His possession of a vehicle also enabled him to visit another small town locally to get medicines and then sell them back in the village. In this way he supplemented his income, not by having a second job as many teachers in developing countries do, but by creating a second job out of his first one.

Problems of communication between the schools and the ministry in Tanzania has caused problems concerning registration of students. At one school the head was unable to inform the students or to explain what was happening as regards their exam registration: 'Ultimately, the desperate students went on riot and caused damage to school property. Today the damage is beyond repair. Suppose the school had a telephone or telex to communicate with the ministry in time, such an incident couldn't have occurred.' Moreover, lack of transport results in other serious problems. At one school visited by the researchers a teacher had died the day before and his body was lying in the mortuary because there was no transport to take the body to its place of burial. Luckily, the school was near enough to a town for the headteacher to be able to use his influence to get transport but, as the authors comment, what if this happens in a school without transport 40 miles from a town? In the Kagera region only 14 out of 34 schools have any transport (Lutanjuka and Mutembei, 1993).

Boarding schools

Only a minority of schools in the West have students in residence. In Africa post-primary institutions are often boarding. In Ghana, for example, 80 per cent of such institutions take boarders. The boarding tradition in Africa dates back to the colonial period when Christian missionaries thought that the most effective way of educating African children was away from 'pagan' home influences. This may still be a factor in Christian-based secondary institutions. An important factor in explaining the persistence of boarding schools is the widespread geographical location of secondary schools, often far away from the homes of students attending them. This is the result of a socio-economic context in which only a minority go on from primary to secondary education, so that secondary institutions are not available in all locations. Even where distances are not large, transport can still be a problem. Boarding schools may also be favoured because many homes (over-crowded and without electricity) do not have adequate facilities for study. Another factor in many countries is that student meals are subsidized by the government, so it may cost less for parents to have their children fed in boarding schools than at home. As Dadey (1990, p. 19) notes:

> The boarding school system contributes a great deal in making the
> secondary head a busy person. In effect, boarding school heads are on
> call twenty-four hours a day. At weekends they have to ensure that
> recreational and religious activities are organized to meet the varied
> needs of students. The situation is worsened by their responsibility for
> providing catering facilities for their pupils in a period of economic
> recession.

An example of the problems that boarding schools can present to a headteacher is provided by an incident at a secondary school just outside Gaborone. The head of this school recounted how one boarding master had been rather too lax and easy-going with the students, to the point where indiscipline in the hostels had begun to

73

spill over into the classrooms. As a result the boarding master resigned and a new one was appointed who was more firm. But the students had become used to a more laissez-faire regime: one boy assaulted the new boarding master and was sent home. The other boys therefore boycotted meals in protest and subsequently persuaded the girls to join in and also to boycott classes. The school came to a standstill and when the head tried to persuade the students to return to class all but a few refused. The head threatened to send the students home but they in return issued an ultimatum – they wanted the boy reinstated and the master reprimanded in their presence. The head refused and felt that she had to report the matter to the Chief Education Officer. By this time about 450 students were marching to the ministry until they were stopped by the police. The CEO talked to the students and only convinced them to return to classes because they misunderstood him and thought he wasn't reprimanding them. The atmosphere at the school was tense for some time afterwards. This is not an isolated incident in Botswana, as other reports indicate (for example, *Daily News*, 10 April 1989) and student disturbances are a problem faced by heads elsewhere in Africa, as will be discussed below.

The head of the school referred to above felt that the boys wanted to put the new master in his place and resented being treated as children. The oldest students in this school were in their early twenties. The head is managing a school that ranges from children to adults. Indeed, there has been some discussion in Botswana about whether married students should or should not be allowed in schools.

One problem facing heads of boarding schools is keeping students amused, especially at weekends. Schools organize clubs, debates, discos, bands, newspapers and games, but heads admit it is difficult keeping students occupied all of the time.

Heads also have to take final responsibility for feeding students. While this was seen as adding yet a further complication to the job of the secondary head in Botswana, in Ghana it can take on more serious proportions. At 7.20 am in one of Dadey's case study schools (1990, pp. 178–82, 247–9) the school bursar, domestic bursar and matron rushed into the head's office to complain that the food contractor had not delivered the yams and there would be nothing for the students to eat at lunchtime. The headteacher dealt with this by changing the lunch menu and organizing the school truck to buy yams from the local market for supper. The head asked the bursar to arrange an imprest as the local market women wouldn't accept cheques. The head remarked:

> 'You see now why the headmasters' conference has been pressing
> government to take the responsibility for feeding students off our
> shoulders. We are not caterers but teachers. We should have enough time
> to attend to curricular matters than to solve food problems.'

Luckily, on this occasion the food contractor eventually arrived and the head was relieved of responsibility for a change in the menu. His sense of relief was due to the fact that food supply problems are often a source of student unrest. Indeed, later that same morning the Assistant Director of Education called in on the head and told him that there had been trouble over a change in the menu at a neighbouring school the day before. Moreover, in another of the Ghanaian case study schools the head had problems with food supply and claimed that 'more than 50 per cent of our time is spent on this aspect of school life'.

It is not therefore surprising that part of the World Bank's structural adjustment programme in Ghana is to encourage 'deboardization' in secondary schools to save on the cost of housing and feeding students. However, this is being resisted by parents because of poor local transport, loss of food subsidy and a general belief that school can do a better job of bringing up children than they can.

Student control and discipline

Perhaps the first problem that primary headteachers can face in a rural context is getting students to come to school and stay there. While distance to the nearest school is one reason for non-attendance mentioned in a survey on school enrolment in Botswana,

> The single most important reason for non-enrolment, according to this survey, was the opportunity cost of having a child at school; for example, boys are needed for herding cattle and smallstock. This is especially true for poor, rural, female-headed households. The opportunity cost of keeping girls in school is lower partly because the need for girls in agriculture is seasonal. Another important reason for non-enrolment . . . was the direct cost – fees, school uniforms, etc.
>
> (Kann, 1984, p. 90)

During the school year there are periods when the traditional economy can cause widespread student absenteeism. In Ghana, Abbey (1989) notes that,

> The times of serious absenteeism and lateness due to pupils' engagement in farming varies from region to region. In the Kade area of the Eastern region, for example, this occurs in the main rice harvesting season (i.e. July to October). In Ashanti, Brong Ahafo and some parts of the Eastern Region, this problem is encountered during the main corn harvesting seasons of June to July. In the Asante-Akim area of the Ashanti region, this problem is at its peak during the snail season. During these times some schools are compelled to reschedule their start and finish time to accommodate the situation since the problem is understood by all.

In Botswana there have been discussions at ministerial level about whether it was possible to align school holidays with agricultural operations so that students could help parents at the lands. The education minister told parliament that he had sought expert advice from agriculturalists who said it could not work because the school calendar would have to be based on the predicted times and natural rainfall but this was not precise (*Daily News*, 16 March 1989).

Another problem facing headteachers in Africa is that of violent riots and demonstrations by students. We have already made mention of this in regard to both Botswana and Ghana and further examples from the press in Nigeria, Kenya and Tanzania are provided in Harber (1989, ch. 7). The root of the problem is that schools in Africa (as elsewhere) are authoritarian institutions in which students are socialized to depend on the authority structure of the school. However, at the same time students are very anxious about their success, as families have spent considerable amounts of money on their education and will have high expectations of them. Yet because of resource problems, poor communications and untrained staff things frequently go wrong. These problems ignite deeper feelings of malaise and frustration. The essence of the problem often seems to be communication: poor communication and a high-handed approach by the head generates misunder-standing and suspicion. When the system the students depend on fails them in some way and no explanation is forthcoming, resentment grows until a small incident sets off serious disturbances. One headteacher in Dadey's study in Ghana, for example, listed what he thought were the major causes of student disturbances in Ghana. The first four in importance were all about communications (Dadey, 1990, p. 80):

- absence of information flow and slow flow of information
- breakdown in communications
- headmaster keeping students at arm's length
- lack of interest in students' welfare matters

Any other business

'Instructional leadership' is one of the key characteristics that is supposed to define an effective headteacher. However, in countries with a centrally defined curriculum, and in the light of everything else a head has to do, the scope for curricular initiatives is likely to be small and come under 'AOB'. Some curriculum initiatives can be forced on a head through resource stringency, however. In one secondary school in Botswana, for example, the science curriculum had to be altered because the head had been forced to take higher numbers of students than she wanted in a context of limited laboratory provision. As a result, out of an intake of 240, 60 did three pure sciences, 60 did one pure science with some combined science, and 120 did combined science. Another example comes from Ghana, where supplies of textbooks and stationery often arrived after the middle of the term rather than at the beginning. 'In such circumstances the heads have the problem of deciding what learning ought to take place in the interim. Old and outdated textbooks were used, some with missing pages' (Abbey, 1989).

Other curriculum changes might be in response to social pressures. One head in Dadey's study, for example, had introduced a drugs education programme, while in Botswana the introduction of sex education (in the light of schoolgirl pregnancies and AIDS) is much discussed in the media and schools.

Finally, there are the hundreds of minor tasks, rarely noted or recorded, that go to make up the 'general dogsbody' aspects of the job of headteacher. One junior secondary head in Botswana cheerfully recounted cooking fifteen chickens for the prize-giving and end-of-year party on one occasion and unblocking drains on another. In a rural school if the roof blows off or the water pipe breaks then the head must see that they get mended, and this often means being physically involved in doing the mending. The writer can vouch for this particular head's painstaking efforts in planning a treasure trail for that year's school-leavers' party, as he helped in touring the locality with the head searching for possible clues. Such is ethnography.

CONCLUSION

A major concern of school management debates in recent years has been the need to train headteachers. Headteachers, so the argument goes, are chosen because they are good at one thing (teaching) and then put into a managerial role which can demand quite different skills. However, if more headteacher training is to be provided in developing countries, where it has tended to be neglected, then it must be grounded in the reality of the nature of the work in that particular country or area. This means that some form of research will be necessary to establish what the needs stemming from that work are. As one study of the training needs of educational managers in developing countries put it:

> Research is a greatly neglected area. Very little systematic study of the training needs of the clients is carried out. When there is some effort it is usually done by the trainers who frequently have little or no research background.
>
> (Rodwell and Hurst, 1985, p. 123)

Moreover, such training cannot ignore the question of goals: what is the education that headteachers manage supposed to achieve? Hence it will need to be guided by clearer (and often different) notions of effectiveness in terms of goal priorities for a particular context. Are, for example, democratic values and practices, gender equality and safe sexual practice more or less important than knowing how to do equations, mix chemicals in a test tube and recite poetry? The second important question to explore is to what extent the goals can be realistically attained in their given context.

PART THREE

Explaining School Management: Levels of Understanding

Chapter 5

The Macro Level: Transformational and Development Theories

This chapter is the first of three in this section which explore explanations for the realities of schools described in the previous section. We use 'macro' for those theories looking at global relationships and their impact on development or underdevelopment; 'meso' for explanations related to national or local cultures; and 'micro' for insights at the institutional or individual level. Clearly these levels and explanations intersect; but their theoretical bases have different histories, and our intention is to distinguish them initially, before assessing their combined implications in the final section.

Here we examine those contemporary explanations for school conditions which are to be found in 'macro' or global theories of the relationship between education and national development. In fact, such theories do not often focus directly on school effectiveness as such, being more concerned to depict and explain the history of broad educational systems, or the overall functions of schooling. Yet it is important that such theories be interrogated, for a number of reasons. Firstly, education planners have been influenced by, and often trained within particular 'paradigms' of development theory, for example, modernization or Marxism. Secondly, all those working within the management of education, whether head-teachers, classroom teachers or inspectors, carry round with them explicated or unexplicated theories of what schools are for, and these theories should be surfaced in order to assess their impact on practice. Thirdly, it is crucial to redress the political void in much First World effectiveness literature (already mentioned in Chapter 2). While it might conceivably be possible to analyse school effectiveness in developed countries without mention of the place and history of those countries in world relationships and markets, it is impossible to do this for countries which are locked into varieties of interdependent relationships with 'richer' countries or with neighbouring 'peripheral' states and regions.

This chapter cannot cover all the complexity of development theorizing. Instead, it selects four examples of theory, in order to begin the analysis: modernization; dependency; transition states; and fragile states. Each theory examines why a country has or has not transformed itself into a 'developed' one, and the role of education in this process. Our aim is to assess their usefulness in three ways:

(a) identify a definition of 'effectiveness';
(b) explain school effectiveness or ineffectiveness in developing countries; and
(c) indicate areas for possible school improvement.

This, it will be seen, involves distinguishing two types of theorizing: explanatory and prescriptive. Explanatory theories may stop at the 'cause and effect' stage, leaving the implications for change implicit or unformulated. Prescriptive theories, those that say what ought to be done, may on the other hand begin with the changes and leave the explanations for the current situation implicit. Most development theories are, at least initially, explanatory ones. For our purposes, it is important to assess their usefulness in providing pointers for future action, and to see how they mesh with meso and micro theories to be discussed in the following two chapters. It is not the intention to enter what has been called the 'paradigm wars', that is, to embark on detailed dissection of the relative merits of different theories as they pertain to particular countries or epochs. There is now the view that the whole of 'development theory' is in 'deep trouble', or has reached an impasse (Leys, 1996). We would share the concerns about wanting to avoid 'metatheory' or grand designs. In contrast, our concern is the particular relation of education and development, and our task to see whether a simple overview can be helpful in understanding the specific question of for whom and for what schools are to be effective. What is interesting is that, for our purposes, each theory appears to arrive more or less at the same place: the seeming inevitability of authoritarian, bureaucratic and hierarchical school structures.

MODERNIZATION

Modernization theory was at its most popular in the 1960s and 1970s, and has suffered a decline, both because of the critiques it received, and because of the changing nature of development itself. However, it is undergoing something of a comeback, albeit in an altered state, and hence merits exploration.

Modernization is part of a developmentalist tradition which sees societies as all moving from simple, undifferentiated, agrarian systems to complex, differentiated ones, that is, to modern industrial societies. Wealth and economic growth is linked to the degree of development along this continuum. If societies are poor or 'underdeveloped' it is because they have not evolved the social, cultural and political structures necessary for industrialization to take off. Such modern structures rely on particular values, such as entrepreneurialism, the need for achievement, the work ethic, punctuality and aspiration; also needed is investment capital as well as modern technological equipment and the skills to use this effectively.

> It is further suggested that the less developed societies can be helped
> towards 'enhanced adaptive capacity' (a functionalist euphemism for
> social change) by a process of interaction with the more advanced
> nations.

> (Harris, 1989, p. 30)

Under this model the role of formal schooling is clear: to teach the skills necessary for using modern technology and, more importantly, to imbue a future workforce and future parents with the values necessary for economic take-off. The more a schooling system and its values mirrored those of advanced nations, the more geared it would be to producing people attuned to economic success. Links with developed countries could only be beneficial: the colonial education systems established by missionaries and colonial governments began the task of modernization, which can be further enhanced by continued Western expertise, consultancy and aid.

Closely aligned with modernization approaches is human capital theory. The rapid and successful growth of developed countries is seen to derive from their investment in people. This investment in human resources or human capital, that is, the money put into mass formal schooling, is argued to have paid off in terms of a skilled and psychologically attuned workforce. The correlation between economic growth and numbers of years of formal schooling was seen to be a causal one, that is, that mass education contributed to economic expansion, rather than the other way round. Similarly, the fact that educated people earned more on an individual level was seen to demonstrate the investment potential of education, both for parents and for the nation. The claim is that educated people earn more because they are more productive. This can only be good news for families and for governments.

The holes in modernization and human capital theory are perhaps too obvious to need rehearsing at length. The problem of Western impositions of definitions of 'modern', the way that earnings often do not in fact correlate with productivity, the phenomenon that industrialization preceded mass formal schooling in many countries: all these arguments have cast serious doubt over straightforward connectedness of education and development. Yet the ideas within the moderniza-tion framework are alive and well, and would underpin educational style in many parts of the world.

The definition of an effective school in this mode would be:

- one that identified and selected the manpower necessary to be productive at a range of levels of the economy
- one that prepared for the skills necessary in a modern industrialized state
- one that socialized into the values associated with entrepreneurialism
- one that socialized into the values associated with hard work and profit

If these sound familiar, it is because contemporary schooling still resembles colonial schooling in ethos and aims. It is selective and competitive, for two reasons. First, there must be selection and competition into the next level of education and hence position in the workforce; and second, there must be daily competition in order to teach the individualism necessary for aspiration and upward social mobility. Schools must also teach the values associated with modern living: this includes adherence to a modern bureaucracy of timetables and punctuality, as well as some of the Western ways of life which are held in higher esteem than traditional modes. Kamuzu Academy in Malawi, for example, prides itself in taking poor but bright children from the bush and teaching them to use a knife and fork, to sleep on a bed, and to wear the varied but arcane sets of clothes associated with differentiated activities in boarding school life.

The investment value of education is stressed throughout developing countries. In private schools, children are exhorted to work hard to repay their parents' investment; in state schools, they are exhorted to work hard for the economic payoff that this will generate. In countries with a long tradition of mass education and a relatively long tradition also of high unemployment, the myth that hard work at school will guarantee a good job has been exploded; but that myth is harder to shift in countries which have had a shorter period of mass education and where memories of educational qualifications being the only way out of rural poverty are still fresh.

Whether or not it is analytically sound, elements of a modernization theory are likely always to be with us in conceiving of the effective school. Particularly in an age of high technology, it would seem imperative that schools enable children to be computer-literate. The 'gap' between developed and developing countries will only get wider if children do not gain the skills and the attitudes towards technology, as well as the different learning habits now associated with the use of computers (Hawkridge *et al.*, 1990).

However, we would argue that schools have not always taken on board completely the full message of modernization in terms of the entrepreneurialism. The subtle balance between obedience and initiative, between rule-keeping and innovation, has often swung towards the more authoritarian end of the spectrum. Rote learning and respect for authority are not typical of the successful tycoon; indeed, the biographies of economic, political or cultural heroes will often show them as rebels, or unappreciated in their school life. The actor Peter Ustinov's school report read 'This boy shows great initiative, which must be curbed at all costs'. Schools are uneasy about initiative. The development of the First World was not linked to a mass education system which treasured and promoted inventiveness, questioning or lateral thinking. Indeed, it is instructive that Japanese economic success has been built on other types of educational and cultural values, to the extent that there are recently some concerns about the lack of inventiveness in the school system, and whether Japan can continue to hold a top economic position in a postmodern world. Income, in Japan, has been based on loyalty to the company and length of service, not skills and training (Brown and Lauder, 1996).

Everywhere there are of course differences between elite schools and those for the masses. Yet elite schools are not necessarily transformative for the society. The prestigious private schools in all parts of the world may have promoted leadership, but that is not quite the same thing. Acceptance of the existing social patterns of stratification, and one's place within it, is not the same as seeing new ways of ordering one's own and others' existence. Perhaps the best one can say is that successful entrepreneurs have flourished *in reaction to* school life rather than because of it. Spending ten years coping with boredom and repression leads some to very creative strategies. If one had to go to school to learn walking, this would no doubt be a gross and expensive failure; similarly, if we did actually teach (and assess) innovation in school, we would be guaranteed a generation of people who classified themselves as no-hopers.

Put crudely, modernization theory would depict effective schools as those which enabled children to fit into a modern society, on Western terms. The schools would need to be efficient in terms of repaying the financial and human capital put into them. To the extent that schools contain inefficiencies such as high drop-out rates, absenteeism, superstition and corruption, they would be deemed ineffective. School improvement practices would involve a Western view of rationality, the

Weberian perfect bureaucracy mentioned in Chapter 3, whereby people worked at the level of their competence and skill, and where the values of neutrality, individualism, hard work, and high achievement were paramount. Materialist values would also be high on the agenda, but coupled with knowledge of the system, so that if people did engage in rote learning or certificate-passing, it was in full knowledge that this was but a game to be played for future prosperity. A degree of latent innovativeness would need to be encouraged – for some, at least.

It was argued earlier that these concepts of 'modern' and of the effective school are making a comeback – if they ever departed. With the current global emphasis on markets and market ideologies, what used to be called Thatcherite values of consumerism and competition are pervading all areas of social life. Structural adjustment policies and World Bank conditionalities impose neo-liberal approaches which focus very sharply on the role of the school in a modern market economy. Vocational education, the subject of much critique and doubt as being second-best, and associated with colonial reproduction of a manual class, is now reasserting itself, particularly in terms of links with industry and a closer association of school and the business world. The Zimbabwe 'School on the Shop Floor' scheme is one example of this, using work placements with the hope of continuing this into employment after school.

Interestingly, some of the recent initiatives with regard to gender equality fit firmly within a modernization framework which seeks to extract women from the tradition-bound family and village and allow them to participate in the modern business economy. The family and village are seen as the blockages to progress, and women portrayed as the bearers of traditional values; their 'emancipation' is held as crucial to a rational, market-oriented society (Scott, J., 1995). What seem like radical democratic arguments for equity may rest on nothing more than a conception of a public/private divide whereby the private is a barrier to the public; women must be 'integrated' – as if they were somehow otherwise outside the normal business of society. Effective schools under a modernization framework would therefore promote a degree of equity – not just in terms of efficiency and the identification of talent, but also to challenge 'traditional' gender roles and the importance of family which might impede the march of modernity. Yet this would not necessarily be done in the name of equal rights. Liberal theories and initiatives must be scrutinized closely to establish the underlying concepts of the place of the individual in society.

DEPENDENCY

Diametrically opposed to modernization theory in its explanations for underdevelopment is dependency theory. Again, initially an economic theory, it proposes that the underdevelopment of a country is a direct result of the development of a richer one, that the relationship between the 'metropole' or powerful Northern manufacturing countries and the 'periphery' or poorer producer states is an essentially exploitative one. Rich countries get richer by the trade relationships they have been able to establish which set low prices for primary goods sold to them; and in turn they are able to export consumer items again at favourable rates to themselves. Colonialism had established local elites who were more attuned to foreign interests than they were to their own people. Developing countries become – or remain after colonialism – dependent on developed countries for their own markets, and take on developed countries' definitions of progress. Rejecting indigenous goods in favour of imported ones (the Coca-Cola culture), they are also dependent on them for expensive consumer items, or for arms. To pay for luxury high-tech goods, workers are encouraged to seek work in large multinational organizations. In this way, economic dependency becomes cultural dependency, and in turn educational dependency. Particularly because of the power of world languages such as English, developed country publishers are able to sell textbooks and educational resources at competitive rates, undermining the establishment of indigenous publishing firms. The textbooks and the Northern examining boards drive the curriculum and local assessment, and schools become locked in a cycle of neo-colonial education which may not fit the cultures or needs of their people.

Within a similar analysis, aid from 'donor' countries has been analysed as imperialism (Hayter, 1971). Aid is often in fact a loan, with a number of conditionalities attached. These conditions to be met before loans are given relate not just to the project but to internal political arrangements, foreign and export policy, and treatment of foreign private investment. There have recently been severe critiques of World Bank structural adjustment policies (SAPs) as imposing a number of restrictions on public and welfare spending, and on wages and food prices, leading to the increased poverty of certain sections of the population (Monshipouri, 1995). The particular impact of structural adjustment on women has received much attention (Gordon, 1994).

Debates around dependency theories have led to the growth of 'world capitalism' theories which take a global analysis of capitalist production. The international accumulation of capital resides in the multinational corporations. There is global division of labour in these companies which maintains the dependency of underdeveloped nations. The question then revolves around the different models of production in a country, and whether capitalist and non-capitalist modes can co-exist, or conversely whether countries can embrace world capitalism but then develop their own independent forms. The rise of the 'economic tigers' of SE Asia has led to some revisions of the inevitability of dependency relations.

The Marxist origins of dependency theories mean a primary focus on the economy and hence on modes of consumption, production and distribution. The links to education then have to be made. 'Correspondence' theories which explained how schools in America developed in order to provide a direct match between the organization of schooling and the organization of the workforce (Bowles and Gintis, 1976) can also be applied to developing countries. The divisions created in schools to produce different tracks for the elite and for the proletariat are mirrored everywhere. A different formal and hidden curriculum ensures that the future elite become attuned not only to greater independence of thought, but to an international outlook. The future working class on the other hand learn subservience and to cope with routine and boredom at work. Yet even the elite are but 'dominated dominators' – in some versions mere pawns in the international capitalist game. In thrall to Western economic values, they would be less interested in distributing wealth or their own expertise within their own country. All pupils, elite and proletariat, would be locked into the acceptance of capitalism, with mathematics lessons teaching profit and loss rather than a calculation of the number of people who were unemployed, or suffered under apartheid. In this sense it might be argued that schools were – and are still – very effective in maintaining world capitalism and its relationships.

An interesting version of this is Hunt's 'incorporation' analysis, which argues that interest groups within countries, and through their influence the country's education systems, are being incorporated into global productive systems of activity and into competitiveness. Case studies of countries like Malaysia, Singapore and Australia as well as regions of Western Europe and America showed how the difficult economic circumstances of the 1970s and 1980s were associated with attempts to use education increasingly as a sorting and sifting mechanism. Key people in government and industry have used strategies to increase, or at least maintain, personal and group achievements in status, wealth, influence and other areas of interest. Monetarism and privatization go together with diagnoses of a lack of economic competitiveness and are used 'to justify the marshalling of resources, including the educational process, to enable societies to compete more effectively, and increase or restore the flow of benefits to members' (Hunt, 1987, p. 128).

Dependency and incorporation theories therefore explain the marked similarity in school *process* between developed and developing societies. The former may, as we saw in Chapter 1, look very different in terms of poverty, overcrowding and so on; but the actual function of schooling to stratify and indoctrinate into capitalist values remains identical. This requires the same emphasis on discipline, on competitive assessment, on routine and on respect for authority roles.

An effectively *dependent* school in a developing country therefore is

- one that divides students into elites and workers
- one that attunes elites to a place within an international elite, looking outwards rather than inwards
- one that produces a mass exploitable workforce for multinational corporations and bureaucracies
- one that teaches the economic and consumer values of world capitalism and market competitiveness
- one that teaches acceptance of the superiority of Western culture

However, the message of dependency theory is that such dependent and exploitative relationships are wrong and unjust, and that even if capitalism is to be embraced, there must be independent capitalism. Countries that have asserted not just political but economic independence from neo-colonial powers have attempted to build in self-reliance in all sectors. An effective education would be one that enabled pupils to have a political awareness of global trends and pressures, and to contribute towards an independent nation. This would involve either being personally self-reliant, or learning skills useful in indigenous enterprise. The classic formulation of this is Tanzania's Education for Self-Reliance (ESR), where emphasis was to be moved from competitive academic achievement towards a philosophy of self-help and education with production.

Yet unlike modernization theory (which is both explanatory and prescriptive) and where the role of the school to 'modernize' is relatively clear, dependency theory is primarily an explanatory one, and the role of education in breaking free from dependency is not so straightforwardly depicted. Some versions would see no way out via mass formal schooling; others promote a form of liberation education. The work of Paulo Freire has been pivotal here, in its notion of 'conscientization' of the oppressed, and the need for awareness of patterns of national and international oppression (Freire, 1970). Arguments for how to break the chain of dependency vary with whether the model is for a country or region to be virtually self-reliant, or whether the model is for them to take their place in world markets, *but on their own terms*. Either way, implicitly, an effective *emancipatory* educational enterprise would

- create and support nationalism
- enable understanding of the country's past and current place in the world economy
- teach science and technology skills useful in the creation and maintenance of local industry and enterprise
- revive traditional cultures and language
- teach advocacy and communication skills necessary for global competitiveness
- teach responsibility to fellow citizens and compassion for the disadvantaged

The stance towards equity is a contradictory one. Clearly, local leaders and local revolutionary cadres will be necessary, albeit geared to indigenous values rather than foreign ones. Scott again points to the masculinist notions within much dependency theory, which, like modernization theory, posits women as vulnerable and 'backward' within a definite public/private split. This is because of:

> chiefly, the way in which male dominance in the household is accepted as 'natural' and the causes of women's subordination are shifted to predatory colonial capitalism. At the same time, women are invited to enjoy the gains of the revolution to the extent they are able, through class positions and family ties, to take advantage of civil and political rights conferred in the public sphere.
>
> (Scott, J., 1995, p. 103)

The problem of global patriarchy is not high on the agenda in Marxist or dependency frameworks, and their emphasis is on local *class* formations. Anti-dependency effective schools would challenge those class forms which merely reproduced the relations of world capital, and instead promote control by workers. Freirian political literacy sits well with such endeavours; the debates then are often over which language(s) to be literate in, in order simultaneously to feel a self-sufficient nationhood and to participate powerfully in world trade.

TRANSITIONAL STATES

An interesting development from dependency theory is Carnoy and Samoff's (1990) notion of the 'transitional state'. They prefer the term 'conditioned' capitalism rather than dependent capitalism, arguing that 'dependency' implies some degree of correspondence between economic or social change in the centre and a change in the periphery. For them this proposed correspondence fails to account for social structures and social changes which are shaped by a local dynamic.

> The Third World state . . . is conditioned by the nature of the peripheral role its economy plays in the world system and the corresponding enormous influence that the dynamic of world capitalism has on its development process. The Third World state is also conditioned by the significant noncapitalist (postfeudal) elements in its own political system.
>
> (Carnoy and Samoff, 1990, p. 20)

This prefigures the discussion of 'prismatic society' in the next chapter. 'Postfeudal' is an interesting term here. In advanced industrial societies, the state has expanded greatly in the context of increased economic demands by the working class, or the 'employee society'. These 'politically democratic capitalist states' are characterized by a significant degree of political participation or accountability. Yet in peripheral states such a compromise with the working class is not possible. The armed overthrow of the capitalist state is viewed as the most logical path in societies where political action by subordinate groups for increased political and economic power cannot be diffused by existing institutions. The personnel in conditioned Third World state bureaucracies, although allied with important sectors of industrial and financial capital, still operate largely as if they were independent of the long-term needs of those groups. 'The bureaucracy promotes capital accumulation, but does so within the context of enriching state bureaucrats, and state funds are used primarily to enhance the political networks of those in power' (ibid., p. 21). The conditioned state does not have a mandate for action derived from mass partici-pation in the selection of state personnel. It never therefore develops institutional legitimacy. Instead, it seeks its mandate through populist policies and charismatic leaders.

Carnoy and Samoff argue that they cannot observe a democratic transition to a postcapitalist society in the Third World (or anywhere else?). The long history of particularistic, authoritarian, corrupt or colonial structures, which the revolutionary movement seeks to overthrow, has resulted in a highly underdeveloped political culture and, historically, low levels of political participation. The citizenry may therefore support the *ideals* of the revolutionary movement, but the institutions do not exist through which that support can be translated into direct political action or influence. Carnoy and Samoff's case studies are of five societies that have attempted to create alternatives to capitalism, in four cases – China, Cuba, Mozambique and Nicaragua – by armed revolution. The exception is Tanzania. They argue that four factors condition the nature of these transition states: the state bureaucracy; the legacy of the predecessor conditioned capitalist state; the counter-revolutionary foreign military intervention, and the capitalist world economy.

Education in transition states is seen as the key to economic and social development. After the take-over of the conditioned state (whether by revolution or independence), there was a rapid expansion of both formal schooling and nonformal adult education – particularly those segments of the population least empowered in the conditioned political economy. Expansion is there both to increase skills and to reduce inequalities in access. It is also to transform social relations, to make educated labour the 'keystone' of a more productive, modernized, participative economy, based on a collectivist or socialist ideology. Wealth has to be disconnected from political power; the basis for political power is labour rather than the ownership of capital. There is also the ideal of creating a feeling of national history. In this sense, the effective school is indeed similar to that described in the previous section. However, the case studies showed the reality to be somewhat different – because of the compromises required in a world dominated by capitalist financial institutions. There is a demand for traditional skills in order to meet short-term production and organizational needs – needs accentuated by economic sanctions, political subversion or destabilization and military intervention.

> Education in transition states . . . continues to be characterized by formality and hierarchy. In part, this reflects the emphasis on the development of basic skills and the importance of maintaining centralized control in a situation of persisting external threat. In part it stems from the uncritical adoption of external models. And in part, it is due to the tendency by revolutionary leaders to increase bureaucratization and control . . . there seems to be a clear relationship between increased bureaucratization in the transition state and increased reliance on traditional hierarchical formal schooling as the principal means of defining and transferring knowledge.
>
> (Carnoy and Samoff, 1990, p. 363)

Education, then, has failed to create social and political consensus. A highly significant statement is that political parties 'have to face the unpleasant reality that either education has to be made devoid of all critical analysis (and that critical analysis has to be suppressed in general) – severely limiting further social transformation – or political organizations have to be made participative and accountable, and thus potentially threatening to those in power' (ibid., p. 364). Literacy ended up being about functional requirements for economic growth rather than for a political foundation for social transformation. In Tanzania, literacy class participants were more often required to memorize the names for agricultural implements than asked to label their social environment. There is a constant tension in transition states between political forces that want to tighten controls and promote technocratic reforms to increase economic growth and groups that want to promote increased equality and socialist ideals.

The successes of revolutionary education nonetheless have been in the expansion to rural areas and to the urban poor, and the increases in literacy. The literacy programmes showed up the powerful relationship between political mobil-ization and educational outcomes. There has been some equalization of access to knowledge among social classes and between the sexes. There has been an increased capacity for self-government. Through the literacy campaigns and the development of popular adult education and rural primary education, the transition states developed the mass organizations and new local leaders to replace the old alliances, family ties and material wealth which were determining factors in local power in the conditioned states. Yet they have not achieved a totally different consciousness, collectively oriented and putting social goals ahead of personal ambition. Individual academic excellence is still the key to higher education, and contradictory to a collective and egalitarian consciousness. Ascending the ladder to political power requires individual ambition and fierce competition – as in capitalist states. Party hierarchies are male dominated, and family relations – except in Cuba and early phases of the Chinese revolution, and in some family planning movements – untransformed.

The truly effective school in a transition state has a highly difficult balancing act to achieve. It must

- create a new consciousness of collective responsibility within a new nation-state
- provide functional and political literacy
- promote gender equity and new concepts of family roles
- combine academic with practical, mental with manual
- give skills to increase material production
- give technical and managerial capabilities together with inclusive definitions of and popular production of knowledge
- promote critical awareness and participation without threatening the new state order

The tensions are between the power of the state to direct economic growth and the need to democratize and decentralize both politics and decision-making in economic units and in civil society. Emphasis on material growth means less educational spending on those areas not immediately linked to productive investment, and after the initial expansion of primary and literacy education, there have been indeed been cutbacks. Spending on university education increases, under the argument that highly trained cadres are essential to economic efficiency and independence. Are social consciousness and participation in decision-making to be attained only after high levels of traditional education and material consumption have been achieved? Political commitment without competent planning, organization and management has not worked. Yet a return to hierarchy and limited expertise did not, from the evidence, help economic growth. The task is to combine participative democratic institutions with technically specialized (and essentially hierarchical) knowledge.

THE FRAGILE STATE

Carnoy and Samoff's analysis was of those Third World states overtly attempting to make the transition to socialism. Not all developing countries have that commitment, and many might be characterized more by a need for political survival, under any system. Fuller (1991) develops the concept of the 'fragile state' to explain the relentless spread of Western schooling worldwide. The Western state has for two centuries turned to the 'medicinal magic' of the school to address a variety of social maladies, whether economic competition or moral decline. Unsteady or brittle states of the Third World, with shaky economic or political foundations, similarly 'reach out to the school institution to advance their own legitimacy' (Fuller, 1991, p. 3). To look modern, and to signal mass opportunity, the fragile state has to express faith in, and materially expand schooling. It has to maintain its interdependencies with other powerful institutions, elite groups or local communities. It often draws legitimacy from the (earlier established) school institution, using it as a stage on which the ideals and symbols of the liberal polity are enacted.

Yet the state in such economies has a 'rocky romance' with the school. The proportion of children attending primary school in Africa has doubled in the past three decades, and the state's economic resources cannot keep pace with the growth in child populations and enrolments. Although being ill able to afford it, fragile states must redouble their efforts to maintain quality and deepen the effects of mass schooling, even reverting to rekindling popular demand for it. Its legitimacy is reinforced through the adoption of a Western-style schooling with bureaucratic rules and a rationalized moral order (as we saw in Chapter 3). This is particularly true of plural states, with competing minority groups, where a common moral order is essential for social harmony. The way that the school, for example, socializes all children into a common understanding of 'work' (as that directed by authority) and 'play' (as that directed by students) is a prime instance of the imposition of a taken-for-granted common reality. Following national independence, and anxious to lessen the effects of race, caste or ascriptive merit, Third World states promptly took over colonial systems and pushed standardization of curricula, of teacher preparation and of school management.

The problem for the fragile state is that the school's *actual* effects in entering the modern economy – boosting literacy, encouraging innovative farming practices, changing health or sexual practices – are often disappointing. Traditional forms of socialization and immediate labour demands placed on children swamp the state's earnest attempt to have children grow up modern.

> Ever since the modern state successfully wrestled child socialization into the civic sphere, political leaders have worried about educational quality. Technical remedies are commonly mounted by the state: pupil exams are standardized and given with greater frequency; teachers are evaluated more tightly; the curriculum is simplified to focus on easily-tested bits of knowledge. Yet administrative remedies often run aground, due to their high cost or inability to touch the uncertain technical process of teaching and learning. Political elites, frustrated by the limited capacity of the state apparatuses to control teachers' local behaviour, engage in symbolic action to at least encourage certain moral commitments and behavioural choices.
>
> (Fuller, 1991, p. 7)

Within this already Westernized version of mass schooling comes the international aid money and projects which seek to extend school effectiveness through modern technology and/or greater rational use of existing resources. Yet, as discussed in Chapter 2, the fragile state may not actually want greater school effectiveness in terms of high numbers of academically successful graduates. The legitimacy of mass schooling can be maintained only if it simultaneously signals mass opportunity: once the link between school qualifications and employment is repeatedly shown as tenuous, then the faith in education declines. With this declining faith goes faith in other institutions of the state, and ultimately in the state itself. Like transition states, the fragile state therefore has to maintain a balancing act. It has to perpetuate the myth that *if only* schools and teachers were more effective or efficient, then both family economies and state economies would improve. Locked into Western symbols of achievement and Western bureaucratic modes of rational organization, it nonetheless cannot afford to let too many succeed in these terms. This goes back to Hopper's (1971) distinction between 'warming up' and 'cooling out'. The state, through the school, must 'warm up' sufficient numbers of children to 'work' and try to achieve, in order to maintain the ideal of mass effort and opportunity; it must then find some mechanism of 'cooling out' large numbers of these again in ways that do not reveal the impotence of the government to provide jobs. It could be argued then that there is also a 'rocky romance' with vocational education. While this should be the answer to relevance and efficiency in schooling, the links are too obvious when they fail. It is better for a fragile state to focus on academic achievement as the marker for attainment and future success. This way, when the success is not forthcoming, students and their teachers can be blamed for inability to reach the hurdles, not the state of the job market or the local infrastructure into which graduates are to be ejected.

We would claim then that the truly effective school for a fragile state at first sight needs to:

- socialize all children into a common moral order and sense of nationhood
- expose all children to a centralized academic curriculum
- indoctrinate students and teachers into acceptance of bureaucratic organizational routines
- have a relatively high level of internal inefficiency, so that not all complete
- have an individualized, competitive assessment whereby failure is internalized
- minimize the autonomy of teachers to subvert the legitimation of the system or the state
- encourage community financing and support

The delicate balances involved between community involvement or interests and the need for central control and legitimation are evident. The state cannot afford to fund mass schooling in the way it did; its position in the world economy, together with the pressures towards marketization and privatization, lead to a return to the imperative of community financing. Local economies and elites must indeed be incorporated into support for the state and its institutions. Yet this localization fragments the national order and threatens any supposed consensus over the learning objectives of the school. Ironically, the fragile state cannot depend on such equally fragile balances in the organization of schooling.

A SYNTHESIS?

Alternatives to the effective school in such states are the subject of the final section of this book. Meanwhile, a summary of the definitions or desired outcomes of school effectiveness under the four models described in this chapter (see Table 5.1) show some of the choices which are being made.

Table 5.1 *School goals under four development theories*

Outcome goals	Modernization	Anti-dependency	Transition	Fragile state
Nationhood		X	X	X
International attitudes and communication skills	X		X	
Technical skills	X	X	X	X
Political awareness		X	X	
Docility	X			X
Equal rights		X	X	
Self-reliance		X	X	
Mass literacy	X	X	X	X

This is a crude representation, and more accurately might have indicated degrees of importance among the various outcome goals. But the aim is to demonstrate that different models of the relationship between education and development will generate different prescriptions for the effective school. While all countries might claim that they want politically aware students, and that they are educating for equity, the reality is that the drives towards modernization or towards the stability of the state will mean a down-playing of these goals in favour of an emphasis on a docile workforce or on acceptance of differential achievement. Similarly, while internationalism is essential to the survival of many developing country economies, they will at the school level often focus more on nationalism and national solidarity. All societies will however emphasize literacy, because this fulfils a number of goals: political mobilization, technical competence, gender equity, and social incorporation. Technical and scientific skills are also likely to be high on the agenda, whether to enter the global competition, or to enable the society to remain relatively independent of international technical markets.

What is particularly fascinating is that all the theories analysed can be used to support our claim that most schools in developing countries are currently authoritarian bureaucracies. Modernization theory actually supports this, in both its explanatory and prescriptive, 'is' and 'ought' modes. Dependency theory agrees and deplores the reality, but, apart from Freire, does not really develop alternatives, so that until recently there were few 'anti-dependency' examples. Transitional states theory shows us how socialist countries have by and large tried but failed to change basic school organization because of their internal and external political positioning. Fragile state theory explains how such schooling is not good for development, but is necessary to maintain a precarious stability and legitimacy. Whatever the diverse imperatives, the net outcome looks like a consensus.

The extra fascination of these desired, albeit contradictory, outcomes for effective schooling is of course that they also remain at the 'ideal type' level, to be further eroded or subverted by local or cultural pressures. Decisions must be made, for example, as to whether nationalism includes a national religion, or whether a secular education best avoids potential religious tension. What sort of literacy, and in what language or languages, is another locally resolved issue. Thus the next chapter turns to the 'meso' level to establish how the broad economic functions for education become interpreted in particular contexts.

Chapter 6

The Meso Level: School Management in Prismatic Society[1]

INTRODUCTION

> My friend Chimtali, age 14, moved 10 kilometers from her small village nestled against the Zomba plateau to just outside the trading post of the same name. She had recently entered a government boarding school to pursue her secondary studies. She liked her teachers and her subjects. It was the foreign-seeming customs that she found amusing. Chimtali now was required to wear pyjamas at night. And she was relearning how to eat. Growing up in the village she simply used her hands, but now she was required to use utensils imported from London. Nor was she allowed to eat fried ngumbi, those plentiful and tasty African bugs resembling winged roaches. While Chimtali obviously enjoyed becoming modern, she had not suspected that the secondary school would require such deep changes in daily habits.
>
> (Fuller, 1991, p. 96, writing on Malawi)

In the introduction to this book we argued that theories and principles of educational management and administration are not necessarily universal and that there is a need to explore and explain the nature and operation of educational organizations in developing countries. In the previous chapter we explored theories of how global, macro patterns of development and underdevelopment affect the general nature of education in developing countries. This chapter examines the 'meso' level and uses the theory of 'prismatic society' to discuss ways in which the actual functioning of educational institutions, and hence their 'effectiveness', is affected not just by global patterns but by both continuities and contradictions stemming from their cultural and socio-economic location within particular societies. The purpose of this chapter, therefore, is not to list the problems experienced in school management and organization in developing countries but to put them into an explanatory and analytical framework in order to understand better why they occur and then later to explore alternative ways of organizing and managing schools that could be more effective.

PRISMATIC SOCIETY

The theory of prismatic society was developed some thirty years ago by Fred Riggs in his book *Administration in Developing Countries* (1964) in order to

---

[1] An earlier version of this chapter was published in 1993 as 'Prismatic society revisited', *Oxford Review of Education*, **19**, 485–97, and is reprinted here with kind permission of the publishers: Carfax Publishing Company, PO Box 25, Abingdon, Oxfordshire OX14 3UE.

understand the conflict between the highly differentiated and relatively autonomous Western modes of organization imposed at the time of colonialism and the less differentiated indigenous modes of organization. However, it has retained its relevance during the post-colonial period of 'fragile states'. During this thirty-year period the newly independent, fragile states based on Western models have striven to look 'modern' to enhance their own legitimacy and be seen as 'real' states but they have been only partially successful. Their limited economic and organizational resources have meant that the drive for modernity has been consistently stalled by the resistance and persistence of pre-modern economic interests, culture and social organization.

The theory of prismatic society is based on an analogy of a fused white light passing through a prism and emerging diffracted as a series of different colours. Within the prism there is a point where the diffraction process starts but remains incomplete. Riggs is suggesting that developing societies are prismatic in that they contain both elements of the traditional, fused type of social organization and elements of the structurally differentiated or 'modern' societies. In prismatic societies therefore 'traditional' and 'modern' values and behaviour coexist in the same organization.

Although in some ways Riggs can be classified as a modernization theorist, he is wary of the notion implicit in some modernization theory that 'developing' or 'transitional' countries are inevitably and inexorably developing towards replicas of established Western industrialized nations,

> Moreover, the word 'transition' suggests a temporary stage between a particular past and a predictable future state. May not some 'transitional' conditions turn out to be relatively permanent? Can we be certain, for example, that the present stage of public administration in Haiti or Bolivia or Afghanistan is temporary and transitional rather than permanent and final? Or if these societies are undergoing change, cannot the same be said of England, France and Canada?
>
> (Riggs, 1964, p. 4)

So developing societies, and the organizations that exist within them, are a synthesis – though not always a harmonious one – of long-lasting indigenous values and practices and relatively new imported ones. This is well captured in novels by two Senegalese writers. The main character in Miriama Ba's *So Long a Letter* (1987, pp. 18–19) is clearly aware of the tensions that exist:

> We all agreed that much dismantling was needed to introduce modernity within our traditions. Torn between the past and the present, we deplored the hard sweat that would be inevitable. We counted the possible losses. But we knew that nothing would be as before. We were full of nostalgia but were resolutely progressive.

Such tensions and contradictions inevitably affect individuals, as Sembene Ousmane illustrates in describing one of the characters in his novel *Xala* (pp. 3–4):

> El Hadji Abdou Kader Beye was what one might call a synthesis of two cultures: business had drawn him into the European middle class after a

feudal African education. Like his peers, he made skilful use of his dual background, for their fusion was not complete.

So in this sense such individuals and societies are neither 'traditional' nor 'modern'. Moreover, this synthesis of continuity and change itself may well be slowly developing in its own way, but not necessarily along established Western industrialized lines.

Riggs (1964) was also very critical of existing administrative theory and its tendency to rely on prescription rather than description. In discussing this point he makes parallel arguments to those made in the introduction to this book. Unfortunately, little has changed in thirty years:

> Indeed, the emphasis in much administrative literature is rather more on the prescriptive side than on the descriptive side. The so-called 'principles' of public administration take the following form: 'Authority should be commensurate with responsibility'; 'Staff functions should be clearly separated from line functions'; 'The span of control should be . . .'; 'Communications should flow upwards as well as downwards'; 'Equal pay for equal work'. We need not question the usefulness of such maxims. I only wish to point out that prescriptions which are valid in one context may be harmful in another . . . In other words we need a pretty complete descriptive and analytical understanding of what now exists before we can make useful judgements about what we ought to do, about what changes should be made. The model of administrative behaviour, as of economic, was inspired by the experience of Western societies in which markets and bureaus existed and corresponded, at least approximately, to the image conveyed by the model. We are not to assume, however, that the situation in 'transitional' societies can be properly described in these terms, although we may be tempted to do so.
>
> (Riggs, 1964, p. 11)

So organizations in developing societies, including schools, do not necessarily operate as a Western observer might assume because they retain aspects of the traditional form of organization:

> Hence many formally administrative structures in transitional societies turn out to be mere facades, while the effective administrative work remains a latent function of older, more diffuse institutions.
>
> (ibid., p. 34)

He termed social structures in such societies 'polyfunctional' because the fused or relatively undifferentiated nature of traditional organization will mean both that its range of concerns and roles will be much wider than might be expected from its more specialized equivalent in developed countries, and the existence of older values will mean that the new concerns and roles will be dealt with in different and unexpected ways.

Riggs in his book was primarily concerned with an analysis of the workings of the institutions of central government and public administration in developing countries. This chapter, however, argues that Riggs's theory of prismatic society is also a useful explanatory tool for understanding how schools operate as organizations within developing societies. However, before we examine some of the themes raised by Riggs in relation to the actual operation of schooling, it is again necessary to ask, this time within the context of cultural influences, why the overall structure of schools is authoritarian.

TRADITIONAL CULTURE AND AUTHORITARIAN SCHOOLING

In Chapter 3 we argued that schools in developing countries were predominantly authoritarian, even if their actual mode of operation did not necessarily conform to the tenets of models of bureaucracy. Part of the reason for this lies in inherited colonial forms of education and the post-colonial perpetuation through international influences of what is understood by 'school' and 'knowledge', and this was discussed in the previous chapter. A contributing factor to the continuation of authoritarian relationships, however, is the nature of traditional political cultures and patterns of childrearing. Such traditional cultures have often reinforced the educational values imported with colonialism. As Nagel (1992, p. xvii) says in relation to Shona culture in Zimbabwe,

> the underlying values of both tradition and modernity probably support each other. An example is the military, authoritarian English education, with its strong emphasis on obedience and discipline, which coincides with the authoritarian gerontocratic and patriarchic social systems of traditional society.

Similarly, in northern Nigeria the Hausa child's experience of authority in the patriarchal family and in the traditional Koranic school is hierarchical and authoritarian with an emphasis on strict obedience based on fear and physical punishment (Harber, 1989, ch. 5). Rather than clashing with imported, Western schooling, the authority relationships of the home and the school have been mutually supportive. In Pakistan the interplay between traditional systems of patronage and intricate networks of power creates a 'culture of fear' where teachers (and students even more so) are afraid to express their views before higher authorities (Davies and Iqbal, 1996). One study of an innovation that used teaching kits in Pakistan, for example, found that teachers were wary of using them, needing to be reassured that 'breaking an item is all right' and that they would not be penalized for using it. Some teachers found the kits did not fit their teaching style, which emphasized lecturing and rote memory rather than experimentation (Warwick et al., 1992). In Tswana culture in Botswana,

> Much of the child training consists in imparting the etiquette that an older individual (doing the instructing) feels should govern how a junior person acts towards a senior person. Basically this is training in deference . . . The Tswana are rigid and authoritarian disciplinarians who enjoy the legalistic dos and don'ts in matters of public decorum, etiquette and role obligations . . . Child training is directed towards producing a mannerly, conforming and industrious person.
>
> (Alverson, 1978, p. 68)

Moreover, Alverson sees formal education as a perfect reflection of Tswana patterns of child-rearing involving rote learning and punishment for mistakes and errors. As in the surrounding culture, creativity, self-reliance and autonomy are discouraged and docility, obedience and submissiveness encouraged.

'SALA', AUTHORITY AND CONTROL

In his book Riggs describes work by Morroe Berger (1957) in which he attempted to apply the Weberian concepts of bureaucracy to a transitional society: Egypt. Berger, however, ended up by rejecting the Weberian model because he found only internal contradictions in the concepts and hypotheses placed at his disposal by Weberian literature. He concluded that the available theory of bureaucracy could not cope with the problems raised by the facts of the Egyptian bureaucracy (Riggs, 1964, p. 72). Instead Riggs prefers the term 'sala' to bureaucracy. This term, according to Riggs, is often used for a government office in Latin America and has a similar meaning in Arabic-speaking countries as well as in South-East Asia.

The sala, because of the coexistence of the values and behaviours of two different cultures, is characterized by Riggs as exhibiting 'polynormativism':

> The sala official, while formally adhering to one set of specific norms may
> secretly reject them as meaningless or not binding. Hence the
> overlapping bifocal nature of power in the sala becomes comprehensible
> in terms of the values systems of the incumbent. For example, an official
> can adhere publicly to the norm of objective recruitment (equality of
> status and universalistic norms), but privately subscribe to more
> subjective, ascription-oriented standards (a rigid hierarchy of status and
> particularistic norms). He can publicly castigate bribery and corruption
> but secretly encourage them. He can insist, one moment, on a strict and
> literal enforcement of regulations but the next moment wink at their
> open violation.
>
> (Riggs, 1964, p. 277)

Chapter 3 contrasted the key features of the Weberian model of bureaucracy with the actual operation of schools as 'bureaucratic' organizations in developing countries. Riggs's theory of prismatic society is used to further examine and explain some aspects of this such as bribery, corruption, cheating and nepotism below. Here the concern is with the centralization of bureaucracy and the exercise of authority and responsibility. As Riggs states: 'One of the most widely noted characteristics of public administration in transitional societies is a high degree of "overcentralization"' (ibid., p. 280). Indeed, Rideout (1987, pp. 27–8) argues in relation to educational mismanagement in Africa that:

> Here children's rights are being very effectively thwarted by incompetent
> overcentralization in which no one is 'to blame' and no one is held
> 'accountable'. The sense of commitment has been dulled and the sense of
> urgency lost by bureaucracies insulated from local pressures, needs and
> demands.

Riggs points out, however, that the term 'overcentralization' is misleading because high officials are unable to exercise substantial control over their subordinates.

Despite formal centralization of authority, effective bureaucratic power permeates to lower levels of the sala; it is not concentrated at its apex. A distinction has to be made in the sala between formal and effective power – between authority and control. In developing societies authority and control often become disengaged, resulting in a situation which might just as well be described as 'under-centralized' in that there are few substantial curbs to the expediency interests of subordinate officials. In fact, power in the sala is neither centralized nor localized but highly equivocal:

> If the highest officials in a bureaucracy had effective control they would not permit bribery and nepotism since these practices undermine the effectiveness of their own control . . . If subordinates persist in referring matters to their superiors in the sala, this may not be because of their inability to make decisions so much as their unwillingness to take responsibility. If superiors refuse to delegate authority to subordinates, it is not so much because of their unwillingness to surrender power as it is their inability to impose constraints on the conduct of their staff, thus to assure rule implementation by others. They cannot delegate who cannot impose accountability.

> (ibid., p. 282)

This phenomenon also affects the operation of schools. Harber, for example, quotes a participant observer teaching in a school in Kano State, northern Nigeria, as saying,

> There seemed to be no mechanism of accountability: in many instances individuals failed to take responsibility for doing things but did not seem to have been taken to task for their omission.

> (Harber, 1989, pp. 123–4)

Although headteachers are formally head of the school hierarchy and often attempt to exercise their authority in an authoritarian manner, they also often lack effective control. They have little control, for example, over the hiring and disciplining of staff because teachers are often appointed, assigned and evaluated centrally. Davies (1993, p. 167) quotes the headteacher of a rural boarding school in Zimbabwe recounting the tale of a teacher who had made a girl in Form 3 pregnant, was sleeping with other girls in the school and was found sitting on a pile of exercise books totally drunk first thing in the morning. The head concludes: 'The ministry does bend backward to help wayward teachers, it has tied our hands . . . it is very difficult to remove someone who is inefficient.'

Disciplinary action would have to come from the Ministry but there are often serious problems there as well. A report by Chew (1990) on Uganda documented the responses of civil servants to falling levels of both salary and cash allowances. Abuses of allowance claims for travel, number of children and housing became more numerous, more blatant and more acceptable. The most visible adaptation to low pay was a massive withdrawal of working hours, with many civil servants working less than half a normal day. Administrators complained about their missing support staff and school principals about their missing teachers. Not only did everyone seem to have another business, but these required more time because of lack of spare parts or the need for personal intervention in transactions. Much of this other work had to be done in 'office hours'. Those in authority were reluctant to reprimand moonlighting staff who need to make financial ends meet. Their moral authority to insist that regulation hours be respected evaporates when they themselves are guilty of the same fault.

In one school in Harber's study of Nigeria there was a general feeling disciplinary action from the Ministry of Education was ineffectual. The teacher responsible for examinations at the school complained at a staff meeting that many teachers did not turn up for invigilation when they were supposed to. When it was suggested that he should report this to the Ministry, the teacher in question laughed and said that he had never known of 'disciplinary action' as regards teachers in Kano State and that he would believe it when he saw it.

The Ministry of Education's lack of effective authority and control over schools stemmed from a number of factors such as a shortage of inspectors and poor communications and large distances between schools but,

> Possibly most important, however, is that the Ministry of Education itself
> suffers from the same sort of problems of 'indiscipline' – delay,
> inefficiency, lack of diligence, corruption – that are a key feature of the
> rest of the 'modern' organizational sector of Nigerian society. On one
> occasion, for example, four education officers were dismissed in Kano
> State for 'drunkenness, absenteeism and gross inefficiency'. Hence,
> school Principals cannot rely on the Ministry too much for support in any
> attempt to improve the efficiency of school organization.
>
> (Harber, 1989, p. 124)

CORRUPTION, NEPOTISM AND OBLIGATION

While corruption is a feature of all countries, including Western industrialized nations,

> corrupt practices in contemporary developing societies are much more
> pervasive, much more an everyday pattern of life, and they disrupt
> economic life to a far greater degree than is the case in the advanced
> countries . . . Corruption sweeps across every sphere of life and affects
> everyone: with patients offering bribes to nurses in hospital to persuade
> them to pass on a bed-pan; traffic offenders bribing police officers to
> waive the fine; tax collectors adding their personal increment to the
> inland-revenue exactions; councillors awarding contracts to firms in
> which they (or their kin) have a financial stake; educational officers
> giving government scholarships to their cousins . . .
>
> (Hoogvelt, 1976, pp. 127, 128–9)

Such corruption inevitably affects schools, as the following two extracts from a novel set in Nkrumah's Ghana illustrate:

> It is well known that the supervisor was once, before coming to the
> Railway Administration, a bursar at one of the Ghana national secondary
> schools. As is the custom in this country, he had regarded the job as an
> opportunity he had won for making as much money as he could as

quickly as he could, and his handling of the school's finances had soon made his intentions clear. The students complained to the Ministry of Education. The Ministry, as is usual in this country, had searched for the students most responsible for the drafting of the letter of complaint and dismissed them for gross insubordination. The remaining students had rioted. The Ministry, looking for more students to dismiss, had closed the school down. There had been no financial probe, of course, but none would have been possible, anyway, since a fire had gutted the bursar's entire office during the rioting. Very shortly after that the Railway Administration was advised from above to appoint the bursar to this new job. He had brought the allocations clerk with him, and there was a likelihood that it was he who let it be known that the fire in the bursar's office was not the work of students.

The woman put her hand to her throat in a swift movement of disgust, then smiled. 'No', she said, 'I don't like made-in-Ghana spirits. But there are good drinks in the country still.'
    'Only in the homes of big shots and Party socialists.'
    'They must get them from somewhere . . . You must know people who could get you these things. After all, people don't go to school for nothing.'

(Armah, 1969)

Other examples of corruption in schools were detailed in Chapter 3. However, corruption may not be caused simply or only by greed but may arise out of the very nature of prismatic society. The following explanation of corruption, for example, is provided by Riggs. In traditional systems officials would not be paid from a central treasury fund but would get a prebendary income by taking a portion of the tributes, rents, etc. collected before passing the remainder on up the chain of command. As Riggs notes (1964, p. 44),

> The general public, long accustomed to paying officials directly for services rendered, cannot be expected to abandon this practice suddenly. Thus the opportunities and temptations for officials to augment their incomes on a prebendary basis remain overwhelming, unless very sharply curtailed by the ruler or by new political and judicial control systems.

Furthermore the customary exchange of gifts was often a normal and integrated part of social behaviour but with the change to a modern bureaucracy 'legitimate gifts' become 'disguised bribes' and expected by officials before a service will be performed (Hoogvelt, 1976, p. 135). Moreover, the need for extra money on the official's behalf is equally understandable in terms of the demands of a developing society. Often a post in the modern sector brings with it obligations to, and demands from, a large extended family network more typical of a traditional, agrarian society. The income is not commensurate with the expectations, and the result can be corruption.
    Similarly, in Thailand rural teachers are expected to pay 'social taxes', which are high in comparison with their income. One study found that every month teachers were asked to make donations to educational, official and social organiza-

tions to which they belonged. In addition, there were numerous official occasions throughout the year for which they were expected to make donations and, because teachers were considered among the most respectable people in the community, donations were expected from them for social functions such as weddings, ordination ceremonies and funerals. As a result teachers were often in debt (Chantavanich *et al.*, 1990, p. 133).

As was described in Chapter 1, teachers in developing countries often have more than one job. The cause of teachers having a second occupation is not always financial, however. Davies (1990, p. 26) quotes an example from China, where there is a widespread attitude that if peasants pay the salaries of teachers then teachers must work, and this means work in the fields. Brigades and villages have withheld salaries from teachers until they perform assigned fieldwork.

On the other hand, the persistence of traditional obligations can sometimes benefit a school. In Kenya the official policy of 'Harambee' (literally 'pull together') means that Kenyans should help one another and possess a sense of service. This particularly applies to those who have done well out of Kenyan economic development. An important aspect of Harambee therefore are the regular fund drives where rich and powerful Kenyans publicly donate large sums of money to community development, often in the form of a local school. In this way the rich are seen openly to share their wealth in a poor society, a benevolent image is maintained and the relatively new wealth and power of the Kenyan elite is legitimated. A rich businessman in Ngugi Wa Thiongo's *Petals of Blood* (p. 153) says to a teacher from the mythical Kenyan town of Ilmorog that, had his friend, the MP for the town, known of its problems,

> 'I am sure he would have organized a Harambee there – you know, self-
> help – he has many friends and they all would have contributed
> something. Charity begins at home, ha!ha!ha!'

For Riggs the persistence of the strong ties and pressures of extended family in prismatic society and the need for sala officials to reinforce their power position by recruiting staff on whom they can rely, are factors which can also result in nepotism in public appointments and the behaviour of public officials. One character, a university student, in the Senegalese writer Miriama Ba's novel *Scarlet Song* (1981, p. 48), says:

> 'The available accommodation in this university is ludicrous, compared to
> the number of students. I fought like mad to get digs here, it didn't help.
> But one telephone call from my cousin, who is principal private secretary
> to the Ministry for Education and Culture, and I immediately got what I
> wanted.'

In Papua New Guinea one attribute of the 'ideal' headteacher is that he or she should be free of 'wantokism', i.e. favouring members of his/her own language group or region, thereby suggesting that many are not (Vulliamy, 1987, p. 216).

Social pressures also exist to get school places and for pupils to succeed educationally in order to gain the paper qualifications necessary to provide a white-collar job in the urban bureaucracy. In *So Long a Letter* (p. 18), Miriama Ba asks:

'What will the unsuccessful do? Apprenticeship to traditional crafts seems degrading to whoever has the slightest book learning. The dream is to become a clerk. The trowel is spurned.'

Once in the white-collar job there are expectations that the incumbent will provide for the wider family, who will often have contributed money for his or her education. These expectations often greatly exceed the income that goes with the new post and hence the temptation to take bribes begins, as is well portrayed in the Nigerian novelist Chinua Achebe's classic novel *No Longer At Ease*.

But perhaps this desire for white-collar work is not altogether surprising. Van Rensburg (1978) commented, in regard to the people of Serowe in Botswana, that the general atmosphere and traditional experience were not conducive to a great deal of hard work. Historically, wealth is not, in any obvious way, the function of harder work and effort, but of social origin, of how many cattle a man inherited. There was little in the colonial experience to suggest that hard, manual work was the key to wealth, and those who went to the mines discovered that the hardest manual work was the least rewarded.

Officially eligibility for well-paid, white-collar work is usually determined by levels of paper qualifications, though in practice this might be the bottom line after which influence and nepotism come into play. Nevertheless, the need to attain minimum paper qualifications (what Riggs terms 'strategic learning') not only causes qualification inflation and a pool of 'overqualified' labour, as described by Dore in *The Diploma Disease* (1976), it also puts pressure on pupils and students to succeed at all costs. The cheating in examinations described in Chapter 3 can be the result.

The pressure on pupils to succeed is also a factor in explaining the violence in African schools referred to in Chapters 1 and 4. Schools in Africa are authoritarian institutions in which pupils are socialized to depend on the authority structure of the school. Yet because of the problems faced by schools in developing societies, such as poor resources, untrained staff and double employment of staff, things often go wrong. Allowances do not turn up, classes are left untaught, food is short, examination papers fail to appear. The system the pupils depend on, and which is so important to their future, fails them. No explanation is given because there is no regular system of communication and no expectation that the headteacher and staff should explain what has happened. Complaints are met with high-handed authoritarianism, so that frustration and resentment grow until in the end a small incident can spark off violence.

TRADITIONAL ECONOMY, CULTURE AND COMMUNITY

As we saw in Chapter 3, absenteeism, lateness and delay are problems often referred to in relation to schools in developing countries. One obvious reason for staff absenteeism already referred to is their parallel or alternative economic activities. During the school year there are also periods when the traditional economy can cause widespread absenteeism among pupils. In Nepal economic and family responsibilities mean that although the official school year is 220 days, few are open more than 140 days. As we saw in Chapter 4, in Ghana schools close in certain regions to accommodate agricultural needs during the snail and corn harvesting seasons. Furthermore, in the Huni Valley area of Ghana school attendance is normally poor on market days because the children have to carry bags of gari, maize or cassava to sell. Some of the children drop out of school to engage in the galamsey (illegal mining) business. Others are used by their parents as labour on their farms (Ferguson, 1993).

Chapter 4 also referred to the proposal to change the school calendar in Botswana to align school holidays with agricultural operations so that pupils could help parents on the land. Teachers in Botswana are well aware of this conflict between the purposes of schooling and the influences of the traditional way of life. In Prophet's study of junior secondary school classrooms (1995), teachers gave the following reasons for pupils' poor attitudes to school:

> 'They only want to become cattle herders.'
> 'The students have a village mentality.'
> 'Some people [parents] have never been to school and sometimes . . . they don't bother to see how their children are performing.'
> 'They are people who are used to ordinary bush life.'
> 'Some of the parents do not even know where the school is. Even when you call them they don't come. Unfortunately, they are drinking this traditional brew.'

Cultural expectations and gender relations can also influence absenteeism or lateness amongst both female members of staff and pupils. Research in rural Thailand noted a situation where two single women teachers were staying in the only teachers' house available and had asked one of the female pupils to stay and keep them company in the house. This was frowned upon by the people in the village, who accused the two teachers of discrimination for leaving the student to sleep on the verandah, asking her to do their laundry and using the rainwater from the tanks for baths instead of bathing in the canal in front of the school. Thus they were being criticized for not conforming to the people's way of life. Then, a man in the village with a criminal record of using violence started to court one of the teachers. Upon being told by the villagers that the normal practice there was for a man attracted to a woman to abduct her, both teachers felt unsafe and decided to take up residence in town and spend roughly two to two and a half hours each journey travelling to and from school (Chantavanich et al., 1990, p. 134).

In Botswana, between 300 and 500 female students a year have to absent themselves from school on account of pregnancy (Simon, 1984, p. 107). Botswana has a population of one and a half million. Not surprisingly, schoolgirl pregnancy is a widely discussed issue. The President's wife pointed out that whereas teenage pregnancy was not an issue when early marriage was widespread and females did not go to secondary school, it became a problem because females now delayed marriage but sexual practices had not changed (Daily News, 13 February 1989). Another cultural factor that has been suggested to help explain this is the need for a woman in southern Africa to get pregnant to prove that she can have babies before she can get married.

Sometimes the explanation provided may be as much to do with material conditions as with culture. Davies (1993, p. 162) reports one Education Officer in Zimbabwe explaining that male teachers having sexual relations with third- or fourth-year girls was quite understandable in the distant rural schools. In these areas, where the bulk of the adult population is illiterate, the fourth-year girls are the most articulate and interesting of the potential female companionship for the single male teachers posted by the government. Where there is no electricity or evening entertainment one way of relieving the tedium is sleeping around. However, while this may explain the motive from the male point of view, it leaves out the abuse by male teachers of their power in a position of authority. In Zimbabwe, as in many other countries, the mismatch between official, but relatively recent, policies on gender equity and traditional patriarchal views of rights, roles and relationships will mean that attempts at equal opportunities policies in school may be deeply subverted by the staff. The scripts used to justify this subversion are further explored in Chapter 7.

Motherhood can also affect teachers. In the study of rural Thailand it was found that married female teachers with children under five would often miss classes or were forced to bring their infants into the classroom because they could not afford to employ a wet nurse while they were working (Chantavanich *et al.*, 1990, p. 126).

As the above suggests, traditional, gendered cultural expectations and practices can often conflict with the needs of 'modern' schooling in prismatic or developing societies. Educational managers and administrators are therefore faced with choices over priorities about what should happen first. This account is from Malawi:

> The district education officer (DEO) faced a painful predicament when the sobbing teacher called. The teacher's uncle had just died, some 40 kilometres away, far to the south of Zomba. But the DEO's only Land Rover was in the government repair shop, having vanished into that automotive black hole from which few vehicles emerge (at least in less than six months time). The DEO, acting under a peculiar mix of state regulation and government tradition, was obliged to move the body to the preferred burial ground. (Distribution of teacher salaries and textbooks must wait under such a situation.) As the education ministry's representative, the DEO must respect this entitlement and protect the government's credibility.
>
> (Fuller, 1991, p. 89)

CONCLUSION

Judgements about 'effective' or 'ineffective' management are difficult to make on a culture-free basis. What is seen as 'poor management' by an external expert in a prismatic society may in fact be part of a skilled and well-designed strategy for managing a bureaucracy to the managers' advantage. Reilly (1987) provides the following examples:

- The lack of accurate, up-to-date staff lists, ineffective personnel record systems and few realistic manpower plans are essential for the system of patronage whereby employment can be offered to needy relatives, friends and those to whom obligation is owed.

- The ineffectiveness of financial controls and audit systems is necessary in order to permit those in charge to manipulate the allocation of funds, not necessarily for corrupt purposes, though this could be the objective, but to a favoured project.

- Authoritarian, highly personalized styles of management in which decision-making is seldom delegated are crucial if those at the top are to maintain their powerful and profitable positions.
- Procrastination and slowness in making decisions is part of a strategy to ensure that the boat is not rocked and to publicly demonstrate power and status.

The questions facing those who wish to improve school management and school effectiveness in developing countries are therefore: what aspects of the interplay between existing and 'modern' social and cultural forces can be lived with and what must be changed? Can some competing and contradictory behaviours, e.g. regular attendance at school versus agricultural need, be accepted and accommodated through open and official recognition and resulting flexibility in school organization? Are there some behaviours, such as bribery or sexual and physical abuse of power by teachers, that are always unacceptable and that need to be identified through open and democratic discussion and prevented through newly agreed school policies?

We return to issues of flexibility and democracy in the final two chapters of the book. Here it is important to reiterate that there has been a dearth of systematic empirical research into the purposes and nature of educational management in developing countries and a consequent lack of theory to explain many features of the operation of schools and other educational institutions. The concept of prismatic society is an explanatory theory of competing cultures and their values, discourses and behaviours deriving from processes of transition. From such values and discourses come the personal scripts used to describe and justify individual agency in the operation of school organization. This is discussed in the following chapter.

Chapter 7

The Micro Level: Scripts, Discourses and the Individual Agent

INTRODUCTION

The previous two chapters have looked at explanations for effective or ineffective schools at the global and national levels. Here we explore those theories which might illuminate the eternal puzzle: how is it, within the same broad frameworks of reproduction of inequality, and of heavy external constraints and conditions, one school seems to be more (or less) effective than another? This is not a return to the 'factors in effectiveness' approach, but an attempt to probe 'structure' and 'agency' in determining how an individual school or indeed individual person 'makes a difference'. As Giroux (1981, p. 107) commented on structural restraints in schools: 'They are concrete but they are not static, they can be changed.'

Much school effectiveness literature, as we saw in Chapter 2, has entered the debate about the relative importance of home and educational institution in determining student achievement, and hence about the likelihood of the school being an 'agent' of change. The concept of 'agency' is however used somewhat differently here. A 'change agent' refers to the person or institution who deliberately sets out to transform or improve some aspect of their society. 'Agency', on the other hand, as used by contemporary sociologists, refers to the role of the individual *either* changing or maintaining, *either* consciously or unconsciously, their social world. It relates to the individual biography within what Giddens (1979) calls the 'duality of structures'.

This goes back to Wright Mills' formulation in 1959:

> We have come to know that every individual lives, from one generation to the next in some society; that he lives out a biography and that he lives it out within some historical sequence. By the fact of his living he contributes, however minutely, to the shaping of this society and to the course of its history, even as he is made by society and by its historical push and shove.
>
> (Quoted in Giddens, 1979, p. 6)

The duality is that social structures condition or shape us, but that they are also dependent for their survival on the everyday reinforcement by individuals and the institutions they are in. 'Structures', in Giddens' usage, refers not so much to organizations or collectivities, nor to the reified 'needs of society', but to 'systems of generative rules and resources' (Giddens, 1976, p. 127). Members of society draw upon these rules and resources, but also change them, in a constant reciprocal process. The notion of 'agency' refers to the shaping 'however minutely' that we do of our social world, and the fact that we are all ultimately responsible (in different degrees) for the perpetuation or change in these worlds. Every time that we say

'That's typical of women' or 'There's not much we can do: it is our culture', we are contributing, however minusculely, to the reproduction of that stereotype or that culture. Conversely, every time we raise a small question mark about the inevitability of social structures, rules and allocation of resources, we cast doubts on their absolute permanence and acceptance. Not only do we as individuals use cultures and structures for our own ends (as we saw in the previous chapter); but we are implicated in their continuance and power over others.

This highlighting of agency is therefore a strong antidote to the more deterministic accounts of reproduction or 'socialization'. Early sociology was guilty in its reification of 'society' as something over and above us, that 'expected' things in its own right. The concept of agency breaks down that determinism by rightly locating society once more as a system of *interaction*, with individuals – at varying levels of consciousness – actively constituting the processes of production and reproduction of that society. Each of us is integral to the continuance of an apparent system of 'expectations'.

The notion of structuration then appears to dissolve the problem of a divide between structure and agency. There have been long debates over the relative merits of a structuralist approach, such as Marxism, and an interpretative approach, which locates major powers in the individual to make sense of their world. Yet it is possible to accommodate both, in the same way that we saw Carnoy and Samoff accommodate both global forces and a national political culture in the notion of the 'conditioned state'.

We can similarly talk of the 'conditioned individual'. This person does not operate freely; yet s/he makes choices of action which in turn condition future social phenomena. It is more of an endless loop rather than a divide. It is also a more exciting concept than that of either straight 'socialization' or straight 'resistance'. Clearly the argument is about the *relative* power of structure or agent, and this is not to deny the weight of economic conditions and the continuity of systems such as the means of production (or cultural belief systems such as organized religion). We should also not deny the differing amounts of power people have in the structuration process. As Hunt found from his studies of education systems (1987, p. 4), 'for some people [social] arrangements are instruments or mechanisms for use in the pursuit of interests, while for other, less effective people they constitute aspects of reality to which one can only accommodate'. Yet the realization that social structuring depends on all of us individually for its daily continuance and projection is a very empowering one, and one that has enormous implications for teaching and learning. It is 'thinking the unthinkable'. Just 'doing nothing' is an active contribution.

DISCOURSE AND LANGUAGE

For Giddens (1977, p. 132), 'all processes of the structuration (production and reproduction) of systems of social interaction involve three elements: the communication of meaning, the exercise of power, and the evaluation and judgement of conduct'. We can see from this the centrality of language in such processes. More lately, but closely linked to analyses of structuration, has come the exploration of 'discourse'.

In educational terms this has been defined as

a language which serves to define educational problems in a particular
way and to support an implicit political stance towards their resolution.

(Carr and Hartnett, 1995, p. 18)

The link with agency is that we 'enter into a discursive field', that we *use* language
as well as being used and abused by it. Discourse analysis is now very popular in
the field of education, although, as Maclure (1994, p. 283) points out:

> some people find some of the key propositions of contemporary work in
> discourse pretty hard to swallow: for instance, the idea that truth is the
> creature of language, rather than the other way round; that there's no
> first, last or deepest thing Out There that tethers language to reality; that
> our solid sense of self is a textual thing – the product of genres, not
> genes . . .

Without acceding to the completely relativist versions of discourse and text analysis
(because later we want to argue the merits of a democratic discourse) we can see
the benefits of discourse study. One benefit is foregrounding the definite relationship between language and 'reality', that is, that our reality cannot be explained to
ourselves and others *except* through a choice of language; a second is that language
or discourse is not just a *reflection* of 'the social', but is deeply implicated in the
constitution of the social and cultural world; and a third that meaning is ambiguous,
contested, contestable and shifting, not resolvable by recourse to an external world
of objects and certainties.

Our interest here is in the overall discourses of 'effective schooling', and the
way that individuals enter these discursive fields; plus the intersection between
such discourses and other discourses within and outside education: markets, rights,
discipline, culture, gender roles, citizenship, leadership, or career.

In writing this book we are in a way caught in the dilemmas of discourse
analysis: we are both giving credibility to the importance of the effectiveness
discourse by positioning the book within it; yet we are wanting to critique its origins
and impact, and cast grave doubts over its appropriateness as a central means of
analysing what schools do. We both work within it and attempt to stand 'outside' it.
It is like trying to push the bus you are riding in.

Discourse analysis can be used at a number of levels. One is that of
interrogating policy texts, or public discourses. By looking at key phrases, repeated
concepts, unexplicated but powerful metaphors, and sets of oppositional categories,
one can unpack the motives of the writers, and their political positions. As Leys
(1996, p. 26) comments: 'The World Bank's annual *Development Reports*, in
particular, came more and more to resemble flip charts for neo-liberal propaganda,
a sad decline for what was once, for all its faults, a formidable intellectual machine.'
In contemporary educational discourse, we can explore the insertion of various
terms which have come to be known as 'hooray words' – those that appear to evoke
a cheer and which seem incontestably Good Things. Hooray words such as
'ownership', 'choice', 'whole school', or 'progress' may mask any analysis of who
exactly owns, chooses or makes progress. If 'progressive' is set against 'regressive',
it becomes a hooray word. If, on the other hand, as in UK government literature,
'progressive' constitutes what Ball (1990) refers to as a 'discourse of derision' –

here coupled with 'trendy' and set *against* 'radical' – then we begin to understand the ways that particular teachers and teaching practices become categorized. Davies (1986) conducted a similar exploration of developing country education policies, finding common hooray words such as 'equality' and 'relevance', but many internal contradictions and unexplicated areas such as: relevance for whom? At school or college level, textual criticism can be used to explore school policy outlines, mission statements, school development plans and everything from notes sent home to graffiti in the toilets. Even school uniform is seen as a 'signifier', a symbol of the school's position with regard to membership and ideology which can be 'deconstructed' in the same way as a piece of writing.

Educational research and theorizing of itself can be subject to discourse analysis, an example being Mannathoko's (1995) account of teacher education ideology in Botswana, where she traced discourses of teacher competencies and individualized, depoliticized learning, and linked them to discourses around gender to form a powerful critique of contemporary positioning of women teachers. This links with the macro and meso analyses in Chapters 5 and 6, where it is possible to trace discourses from Western conceptualizations, and see how far they appear to condition actions and behaviour at the classroom level. Davies (1992, p. 129) noted from her research on school power cultures under economic constraint:

> . . . I interviewed a Headmaster in a rural secondary school in Zimbabwe, in his 'office', which was a small cupboard off one of the three classrooms (for 300 students). In the hour that I spent with him, I heard from the adjoining classroom not a sound except for the voice of the teacher dictating notes, and the odd scrape of a chair. When I asked him about the school philosophy, he stated quite firmly 'child-centred' – and I think he believed it.

We can see a hooray word such as 'child-centred' being used in a definition very different from those original proponents arguing for children determining their own pace and content of learning. It could be argued that child-centred here meant, quite correctly, the best way in the child's interests to get them through the examinations. Yet discourse analysis does not seek to say either this head or the researcher were 'wrong' in their interpretation. It merely examines the power of such a word to legitimize and shape action, and conversely how people's interpretation and continual use of a discourse will eventually change and shape that discursive field.

It is of course more difficult to deconstruct one's own output, and if one equally sees one's own writings as just a set of discursive positionings, borrowings, colonizations, or derisions, then one is not in a position to claim any greater legitimacy for them than for *Mein Kampf* or for *World Football Weekly*. We take the view that, in line with agency theory, you have to state your position and challenge unjust discourses, or all academic writing becomes a luxurious and leisurely sport. The ultimate accolade is of course when other academics or writers see your work as important enough to deconstruct. We await that moment with interest.

CLASSROOM DISCOURSES AND SCRIPTS

The notion of a discourse implies a whole set of shared language practices and beliefs, albeit embedded sometimes in one word, such as 'child-centredness'. However, a particular interest, if we are looking at school improvement or decline, is how a discourse becomes shared, and part of taken-for-granted reality. In examining pupil deviance in secondary schools, Davies (1984) developed the notion of 'scripts' and 'typescripts', particularly in explaining the way that pupils positioned themselves within various gender 'roles'. A typescript resembles a discourse, in that it is the broad set of expectations attached to a social position, such as man/woman, or bank manager, or criminal, or teacher. A script on the other hand is a much more individualized and possibly experimental statement, which acts to say something to oneself or others about who you are and where you stand at a particular moment. It can range from a one-liner 'I didn't mean to do it' to a more longstanding admission 'That's me all over' or 'I can't help myself, I have to hit back', right through to a career positioning statement such as 'I always wanted to be a teacher, and now I've done it'. What Davies found from the study of female pupils categorized by the school as 'difficult' was that they had a number of scripts at their disposal, and that this was a much broader repertoire than would be conveyed by the notion of 'the delinquent girl'. They could use a 'feminine' script, 'fluttering their eyelashes' at male teachers, and using tears or weakness to elicit sympathy; or they could use a 'male' or 'macho' script, often resorting to physical violence or fights, and justifying this with a script around 'seeing red' or 'I wasn't standing for that'. Sometimes they would pull a 'mother' script out of the bag, talking to the male teachers in an irritated tone as if they were small boys. School for them might be characterized by scripts for 'mucking about' and 'having a bit of fun'; outside the school, they would often appear in a very different light, with conversation, even their body language demonstrating maturity, sophistication, world-weariness.

The sheer unpredictability of their scripts was what confused teachers, and led to the admission that they preferred to teach boys, where 'you know where you are'. The link with agency is that teachers would be forced into counterscripts, having to make decisions as to the most appropriate ways of playing or not playing the roles implied by the girls' choice of register or audience. Teachers who had the most difficulty with the girls were those who themselves had a limited repertoire, particularly male teachers who had only 'soft uncle' or 'stern father' roles to play with – both of which the girls scornfully rejected. The most successful teachers were those that engaged with the girls on the level of equals, opening up about their own lives and chatting with them (if invited) about friendships, family, clothes, new babies – indeed anything except curriculum.

What Davies explored at the time, and what is of particular importance for our discussion of effective schools, is how experimental scripts, the throw-away one-liners, become repeated, and then become the preferred style within a school. Teachers may operate in isolation, and, from the research, often fall back on the teacher scripts they observed themselves as pupils. Pupils, on the other hand, are exposed on a daily basis to a whole variety of experimental and semi-permanent scripts from peers, and spend their lives watching the effects. Some are tried and instantly discarded; others are refined, polished, photocopied, and subjected to endless action replays to achieve at least a temporary sense of control over the situation or a sense of identity: 'I told her, didn't I? I said to her, "You think you can lord it over us, but you're no better than us". She didn't know what to say then.'

An effective school, at least in its own terms, would be one where scripts were shared and agreed by staff and pupils. This might be a long slow process of negotiation, or might result from an uncontested discourse entered into willingly by all participants. Successful schools, for example, are supposedly characterized by 'high expectations' of students. This would be relatively unproblematic in an already high-achieving school which was able to select its intake, and where that selection process would inevitably include something to do with existing motivation and conducive family background of the pupils. In a school attempting to move from a position of minimal achievements of pupils, if teachers one day decided to move in on the pupils with scripts for 'high achievement' and 'you can all do it', they would likely be reacted to with derision rather than mutuality. Through years of failure, low-achieving pupils are conditioned to 'discourses of legitimation', or justificatory scripts – that they are inherently idle, hopeless at mathematics, have a memory like a sieve, or that the lessons are boring. To say that after all they have it in them to achieve is to upset all those carefully nurtured rhetorics. It also acts to deny and show up as senseless all their previous years of failure. Even in the face of the encouraging teacher, it is easier to maintain the script for incompetence or hostility than it is to rewrite the biography.

The problem of tracing teachers' and students' scripts in developing countries is, as we saw in the last chapter, they may derive from a whole host of traditional and modern, North and South, international and local discourses and 'rules'. A discourse of 'quality' may derive from the World Bank, but may be interpreted (for participants' own interests) in a variety of ways within a school. Not only that, but even one individual may articulate it differently according to the current audience, as Hawes and Stephens pointed out in their book *Questions of Quality: Primary Education and Development* (1990, p. 11). Asked what she meant by quality, a teacher's response would depend on who was asking the question:

> To the *parent* she will speak of examination results
> To the *inspector*, of better general standards of reading or handwriting or mathematics
> To the *chairman* of the school board she may emphasize making good use of money
> To the *professor*, good teaching and learning practices
> To the *mayor* or *member of parliament*, effective work-orientation
> To the *clergyman*, character-building
> To the *village elder*, conservation of traditional values

We can only guess what her response would be to a pupil, or what sense the pupil would make of her reply. Still less do we know how each participant would *make use* of the notion and in doing so, shape the discursive field for others.

THE ROLE OF ETHNOGRAPHY

What is needed, then, is detailed ethnographies of different schools to uncover the range of discourses, typescripts and individual scripts at play. While these are available for some schools in Western societies, they are scant in developing countries. Identification of more successful schools, or even lists of factors apparently associated with those schools, do not tell us the *processes* by which they managed to generate conducive and agreed discourses. Nor do they tell us whether they have had to challenge existing social structures and discourses in order to position themselves as exceptional, or whether they are simply better at working through the existing norms. For example, have schools which have managed to achieve greater results for girls done so by challenging existing gender roles, and encouraging scripts for aspiration, competition, ambition? Or have they done so by playing on discourses of female conformity, hard work, neatness, obedience to authority? Or have the girls themselves brought in scripts for gender equity borrowed from the media or 'exposure' to Western feminist values and discourses? Unless we listen to the exchanges, and deconstruct the language of interaction, we cannot tell.

In tracing the fate of curriculum innovations in Botswana, Prophet (1995, p. 136) usefully engaged in intensive ethnography to account for the lack of any real change. Classrooms continued to be teacher-centred, with whole-class teaching, and continuing student involvement in listening and silent desk-work:

> On the part of the students, this appears to fit with their expectations of 'what a classroom should be like'. From extensive interviews with the students it was clear that apart from the regular use of corporal punishment in class they seemed content with the status quo. Even when offered the opportunity to take more control of the classroom situation through group work, they preferred instead the security of silent and individual desk work.

Prophet relates this to the culture of the classroom and the shared notions of how teachers should teach. He instances an event in a mathematics class, where the desks had been arranged in groups, in line with the new curriculum philosophy (ibid., p. 136):

> The teacher had set the class to work on a series of exercises . . . He encouraged them to work in groups and stressed the importance of them helping each other. The class started work and as usual most worked silently on their own. However, at one group of desks, two boys started discussing a problem and as they became engrossed in their joint work one leaned over the desk to look at the other's book and they carried on their conversation in that position. The teacher started to walk round the class and as he passed these two boys, he took hold of the shoulders of the boy leaning over, straightened out his back and sat him down firmly in his own seat.

Here we see the teacher using the official discourse of co-operative learning, yet being unable to cope with its implications. The language was not internalized. Prophet himself refers to the 'stickiness' of teaching behaviours in Botswana junior secondary schools – a nice term from Fuller and Snyder's discussion (1992) of 'Teacher productivity in sticky institutions'. Discourses are the glue of culture, and not easily dissolved.

A fascinating account by Thaman (1995) revealed the different language usage around education in Tonga. Three terms, *ako*, *ilo* and *poto*, are widely used in the context of Tongan education. *Ako* currently means to teach or to learn, and is used variously to mean: to learn; the learning process; instruction; training; to study; to practise; schooling; to receive instruction; and the formal education system. It is interesting that the same word is used for both teaching and learning. In English two words imply the notion of independent activity. *Ilo* means to find, discover, know experience; it may be obtained naturally or through active searching. *Poto* is the 'fundamental' concept of Tongan education, which is 'to be clever, skilled, to understand what to do and be able to do it'. There are various ways to be *poto*; it implies the positive application of *ilo*; the educated person (*tokotaha poto*) is one who applies *ilo* with positive and successful results. *Poto* has become reconceptualized to include formal education; yet interviews with teachers revealed that they emphasized the need for students to use their school knowledge (*ilo*) for the welfare of others, and not to be selfish with their education. Thus although modern education is valued in Tonga, it is valued not so much because it is good in itself, but because it helps people to find jobs, which in turn enables people to fulfil their social obligations to their respective groups, whether family, community, school, church or country. Hence 'all is not lost with regards to ensuring that children acquire useful Tongan cultural knowledge in school in order to survive a rapidly modernizing world' (Thaman, 1995, p. 12). Yet Thaman is concerned that Tongan teachers do not appreciate that the scientific–industrial paradigm of education, the rapidly expanding market economy and associated growth mania and consumerism, is destroying and exploiting their culture and values:

> Theories which rely on a biological model of interaction and a view of
> personhood comprising a distinct, physically bounded genetically
> determined self-actualizing individual . . . [are] opposed to the view,
> prevalent in most of our island cultures, of person being defined through
> their placement in different social settings.
>
> (ibid., p. 15)

Another important concept is *wah* – the space between you and another person, which must be kept at all times. Therefore there should be no confrontation and, similar to some Chinese cultures, you should not make another lose face. It is therefore difficult to ask questions in class, or to challenge a teacher. On the other hand, you also must share your learning, not be 'selfish' with a degree. Thaman argues for reclaiming indigenous discourses by placing greater emphasis on their cultures and their vernacular languages in curriculum planning, teacher education and research activities.

This analysis is interesting in the connection between a discourse as a means of shaping behaviour in school contexts and the actual discursive fields particular to one language, in this case a language with concepts not easily translatable to other languages. As with prismatic societies, Western concepts of individualism and self-actualization seem to sit side by side – or to jostle – with Tongan concepts of shared identities and shared learning. Discourse analysis in developing or previously colonized countries will have simultaneously to note the usage of

Western definitions of effectiveness and how they intersect with – or contest – local discourses around the functions of education.

CHANGE OR RESIGNATION?

Our key concern around school effectiveness in contexts of stringency is the interplay between the absolutes of stringency and people's interpretations of them. Do people develop discourses which posit financial hardship as conditioning everything (what we shall refer to as a 'discourse of resignation'), or do they develop a discourse of change? In order words, how far do heads, teachers and students really think of themselves as positively 'agentic'? Some research done by one of the authors in Zimbabwe illustrates the degrees of difference.

The research was a case study of Mashonaland East, as part of a larger project on Performance Management in the Education Service (Davies, 1995b). Its aim was to explore the role of the Regional Education Officers (or inspectors); to this end she shadowed the inspectors as they visited schools, as they talked with heads and as they observed lessons. In this way the different discursive fields of inspector, head and classroom teacher could be uncovered, and the relative power of each discourse analysed. Let us contrast just two schools, which were apparently very different in their degree of effectiveness.

School A was understandably labelled by the Regional Education Office as 'disadvantaged'. It was in a remote area, and built on rock, so that no water supply was possible. The teachers had to walk two kilometres at the end of each day to fetch water from the village wells for the next day's use; some days the villagers were reluctant to give them this water if they themselves had little to spare. The head was not 'substantive'. That is, he was an acting head, not confirmed into the post. The school had had some trained teachers in the past, but now the majority were untrained. Materials were short, and in the local community not even newspapers were common, so that recommendations from the inspector for English to 'use current events' in lieu of textbooks was a difficult task. There was no duplicator, no Banda, and of course no telephone. The school had very poor examination results, and even poorer attendance. 12.3 per cent had passed an O level, but this year's results were likely to be worse.

Understandably what characterized the school was a rhetoric of resignation, that they could not influence change. The head commented on a European Commission grant which had been given to some schools for resources: 'We were unlucky last year, some schools benefited from the EC, we didn't get anything. Perhaps we were forgotten.' He had tried to follow this up; but to get the only suitable bus down to the Regional Office meant leaving at 4am, and a day's task, and this was not undertaken lightly or frequently. The school was supposed to have a School Development Plan, produced or revised termly. 'This term we have not come to that yet.' The head was unable to find the plan, when asked, after searching through three different files in a cupboard. The pupils, too, dropped out, either physically or mentally. They were 'seasonal' and did not come in the winter when it was cold. They said 'We are not feeling like coming to school'.

The head claimed to visit classrooms regularly, but the positive effects of this were not apparent. The following are extracts from field notes from an English lesson with Form IV (fourth year secondary). My commentary noted at the time is on the right. The EO was sitting beside me, and gave a whispered commentary as well. Even these notes start to show different discourses and expectations at play from participants and observers.

Teacher comes in.	*No greeting, no smile.*
Writes POEM *on the board.*	*No explanation.* EO: We don't do literature here, so there's no reason to go to poetry.
Turns round: What's a poem.	*Even the question is delivered in a monotone, no rising inflection.*
No response. Then someone tries:	
P1: It's a saying.	*T ignores this response.*
T: What techniques are there.	*Difficult to hear. Classroom door*
No response.	*creaking continuously in the wind, she makes no effort to close it.*
She throws in personification, metaphor, simile.	
T: Give me an example of a simile.	*Never says please, just orders.*
T reads a poem from a book.	EO: There are no resources, but she
T: What's the difference between a poem and a story.	could at least have written a poem on the board. The lesson is straight after
P1: There is personification.	break. I expect the teachers to do their
T: The message is sort of hidden, isn't it.	bit for these kids.
All chorus: Yes!	
T asks the class to write a short poem on 'My Teacher'.	*No explanations. No connection with previous poem read.*
History teacher comes in to collect scme exercise books for the other inspector.	EO: Teachers have no order. He should have been prepared. Teachers are not disciplined.
Pupils write their poems. T walks round. Class write in silence, the odd whisper. She collects the poems.	*No suggestion that they use personification etc.*
Reads one out.	
T: What can you say about this poem.	*Why not the pupil himself?*
P2: He did not follow the instruction, he is not writing about my teacher.	*It's actually very good, written from the standpoint of the teacher.*
T: Someone else.	*Gives no feedback on this response.*
P3: The poem sounds like a story.	*Only boys ever answer.*
T: Why do you say it sounds like a story.	*She never uses their names. Does she know them?*
Silence.	
T: But he tried to use something. What.	
Reads it again.	
P4: He used some smiles *(sic).*	
T does not comment. Reads the second poem.	*Also very good.*

117

T: 'Busy during day and night'. What's wrong with this.

Only finds negative comments.

Pupil comes to the door.

T: You're late. Get out.

Boy just leaves again without protest.

T carries on reading poems.

Some are very amusing. T does not laugh when pupils laugh, though.

T: What can you say about this one. There is something wrong.

Does not laugh at all, in fact.

This time she does not want repetition.

T: Even though there is poetic language, it is a bit bad.

Little positive reinforcement.

Boy goes and rings bell.

Is this the end of the lesson or not?

T just packs up and goes.

No conclusion, no farewell, just leaves.

Here appears (to an outside observer) to be a teacher who does not know, like or understand her pupils, and does not know, like or understand English literature. The whole process is ritualized, a job to do, a stab at a teaching situation. Understandably the EO cautions her severely, and she has to bring her exercise books and lesson plans down to Marondera in six weeks' time, to assess improvement.

After that, we watch a history lesson, which is much better, and positively stimulating by comparison. Yet the dialogue with the EO, where critiques were made, reveals a mixture of defensiveness and acquiescence from the teacher.

The EO asks whether the teacher thought he had achieved his objectives.

T: Perhaps it is not for me to say I have achieved my objectives. You were observing.

The EO comments on the very varied levels of understanding of the pupils, the need for group work, and the difficulty of some of the words the teacher was using:

EO: Did they understand them?

T: They are supposed to understand. They should have come across them.

EO: Do they have English dictionaries?

T: I'm not quite sure whether the English Department has some . . .

T: For the past three years I have been teaching maths. When I was transferred to this school, I was given history and geography. I am still new to the subjects . . . I wanted to come to Marondera and consult with you, but I did not have the chance.

[*There are only seven textbooks for the two classes. One day last week the library door had been left open and pupils stole some textbooks.*]

EO: We have to improvise. They don't have to be spoon-fed. You can cyclostyle some notes.

[*The teacher agrees straight away. I point out that the school has no duplicator.*]

EO: You can get a stencil cut, bring it to Regional Office. Get newspapers, magazines, get them to analyse a passage.

T: But my pupils don't want to participate.
EO: But you are asking them to discuss something they do not know about.

In the above exchange, we see a clash of scripts. The EO has a view of learning as about understanding, group discussion and use of a range of resources, with the onus clearly on the teacher to achieve these. The teacher does not want to take responsibility. It is the pupils' duty to understand the lesson, they are 'supposed' to know the words. He did not 'have the chance' to go to Marondera. It is not his fault he is teaching the wrong subjects. He agrees without question that he could cyclostyle notes, clearly having no intention or means of doing so, but wishing to keep favour with the EO. Nowhere is there a discourse of the professional teacher, one who has autonomy or takes initiative.

We are not being judgemental here, merely pointing up the way that a disadvantaged school generates disadvantaged scripts. The head said quite categorically in interview 'Most of our pupils are academically incapable'. It is unsurprising that his teachers go through the motions without believing or wishing that what they did made any difference. In this context there would be no point in imposing academic ideas of whole-school improvement. The EOs are doing their best in this context, and given that they have power to write reports on teachers and hence have power over promotions, they are able to generate change in some teaching behaviours, in some schools. But with inspections few and far between (this visit had only been made because the researcher had transport), the few orders that inspectors make are unlikely to get beyond being adhered to at the ritualistic level.

In School B, a municipal school much nearer to the office, a different atmosphere was immediately perceptible – to start with, at least. The head's office was an amazing Technicolor display of coloured timetables, roster lists, mottoes, banners and pictures. There was a staff development programme, and the previous term they had had a workshop on 'Teacher as Leader'. They had found the Ministry handbook 'too general', so had written their own policy. Every teacher had to read and sign it. They had a tree-growing project, poultry, a maize field. The head was clearly a charismatic figure who wanted to put his school on the map. He had clear ideas about management, and had delegated considerable powers to the deputy. He knew about ownership with regard to the community:

> 'The parents have got to feel that the school is theirs . . . I have given
> them the correct position, "without you we will not survive, you give us
> the children, you give us the Durawall, rooms". I suggest the fees, but
> they choose. They decided the uniform.'

The School Development Plan was an impressive list of proposed new buildings and projects.

Here then is a script for ownership, a discourse of progress and 'modern' management. Yet the question remains: what difference does this make to children's learning? Observation of lessons revealed the underside to all this progressivism. In the first class, there is indeed a banner on the wall: 'Let us read to be tomorrow's leaders.' Yet the EO spots a length of fan belt on the teacher's desk. He is grave. 'This should not be here. We do not want to see such things.' Apparently the fan-belt is for corporal punishment, and only the head is allowed to administer corporal punishment. Every class we go in has a length of fan belt on the desk; some teachers have sticks in their hands as well.

The lesson which ensues spends the full 30 minutes on 'neither–nor', with no one being much the wiser as to why they were learning it. [I discover later that this must be where they are in the textbook: I talk to another expatriate researcher in my hotel who had gone up-country in a completely different direction that day and watched a lesson on . . . 'neither–nor'.] The inspector had visited the school before and had run workshops on Bloom's taxonomy. Apparently alone in the inspectorate, he was enormously keen on Bloom (having had some training in South Africa). His own scripts revolved around objectives, and different levels of them. He takes the teacher to task afterwards about her questioning techniques. She is adamant that she has used different levels of difficulty; yet in reality all her questions were factual ones, with none inviting any lateral thinking or creativity. It is clear that she has only partially understood or internalized Bloom's taxonomy, and in fact deep questions might be raised about the impact of such languages – more of a 'mystifying technology' (Foucault, 1977) than an emancipatory discourse.

Another teacher had assiduously prepared Remedial Record Books in line with the school's policy. Here the teacher is supposed to record the specific difficulty the child has, and the action taken to remedy it. Yet perusal of the book just has every item marked with a tick, or 'Now can do this'. Not once is there any indication that further work would be needed; it is suspiciously successful. The EO is rightly dubious, and demands to see the exercise books where this work was undertaken. These cannot be found. Record books for the other pupils have but two standard phrases 'Must work harder' and 'Must put more effort', apart for five pupils who get 'A hardworking boy'. As with School A, there is no real ownership of the teaching/ learning initiative. It is the pupil's responsibility to work harder, not the teacher's to prepare interesting material, or to think of ways to overcome specific difficulties in learning. The question-and-answer session revealed answers coming only from one half of the room; clearly the class was divided into 'fast' and 'slow', and they responded accordingly.

The impact of the development plans, the mission statements and the recording routines did not seem to have percolated down to the classroom level in terms of any difference in learning styles or relationships. The teachers were 'scheming' and preparing lessons to the extent of writing down what they were going to do; but the effect of this was rigidity rather than flexible learning. Lessons were planned up to six months ahead, according to the scheme books. It was not apparent that there would be any change if an evaluation showed that a lesson did not work.

School A was not successful on any measure of effectiveness, except for 'fragile state' effectiveness in terms of maintaining the faith in mass schooling and not producing too many successful graduates to flood the job market. It was outwardly and inwardly a failing school. School B was outwardly a successful school, but inwardly had remarkably similar teaching–learning discourses to School A. Nothing had changed the teacher's conviction that physical punishment and necessary boredom were the bedrock of learning, and that it was the student's responsibility if they failed.

WHO HAS THE MOST POWERFUL SCRIPT?

In examining who defines effectiveness, and whose script for action takes hold in any particular situation, we have then to look carefully at claims that 'leadership' is everything, and the head has the power to make or break the school. Certainly, as we see from the above, the head can create an atmosphere, and provide a surrounding discourse of either resignation or modernization. Yet the teachers' own scripts are what count in the actual classroom situation.

It must of course not be implied that Zimbabwe is alone in this. Here is an extract from a qualitative research study in Thailand:

> Being the sole authority in a school often leads headmasters, such as Khruu Somchai and Khruu Prasop . . . to be dogmatic, verging on tyrannical. Khruu Praneet, for instance, often held back information on opportunities for teachers to further their studies because he was afraid that his teachers would miss work at school. Khruu Prasop on the other hand, taking no heed of teachers' protests, suddenly ordered that the Waaj Khruu ceremony (during which students pay their respects to teachers) be held because he had seen his nephew leaving home one day with candles and joss sticks on his way to the private school in the district. Khruu Somchai insisted on putting the rubbish burner in front of the school without informing the teachers of his reasons, which were to remind teachers and students to keep the school clean. As a result the teachers resented his actions.
>
> Headmasters' relationships with pupils were no better. They usually did not know their students nor the nature of their problems. Often, headmasters tried to resolve problems when it was already too late, as illustrated by teachers helping students during examination sessions. As part of this study students were asked to write about their headmasters. The reports received showed signs of intimidation and detachment. The one exception was Rung Pithaya school, where students praised acting headmaster Khruu Rachanee:
>
> 'We like Khruu Rachanee because she is a very good teacher. She makes things easy to understand. She dresses well. She is kind and not very strict. She also speaks politely and can sing.'
>
> (Chantavanich *et al.*, 1990, p. 121)

Here the students' definition of the 'good teacher' is highly significant. The students focus of course on her teaching capabilities, not her management ones. If effective schools are, by anyone's definition, about what pupils learn, then it would seem imperative that the analysis starts there, and not with the surrounding contexts or ritualistic trappings and languages of school management, development plans, mission statements and record keeping.

Micro-level analysis of a school enables the interplay of discourses to be discovered. It also reveals which discourse in the end has an effect. Scripts for Total Quality borrowed from Western contexts may appear highly powerful; but teachers do not necessarily enter these discursive fields, and may position themselves very differently, drawing on ancient cultural scripts for power in the classroom.

This is very apparent in the clash of gender discourses. Western notions of equality of opportunity, of feminism, of what constitutes sexual harassment, sit uneasily with some traditional discourses of masculinity and sexuality. Research by one of the authors in Southern Africa had revealed an acceptance of the imperative of male teachers' sex drives, whereby female pupils were to blame if they somehow 'provoked' them. If the teacher told the girl to bring her homework to his house, and she complied and was raped, it was still her fault for presenting him with a situation where his uncontrollable urges had to be assuaged. When a particular teacher was fired for impregnating a schoolgirl, the ensuing debate was around the problem of other pupils having no teacher to help them through the examinations, and of his no longer earning money even if he wished to support her (Davies, 1993). He was cast as 'unfortunate'. She was cast as siren. The power of these very ancient patriarchal scripts is significant, and not easily overlaid by newer scripts for female assertiveness or equal rights. The language of parents is revealing here:

> The fear of girls becoming pregnant also acted as a deterrent to keeping girls at school. In the Donkwe-Donkwe group, it was said that while education was important for the daughters, 'the great problem is school pregnancy. We struggle to raise the school fees for them [daughters] but they disappoint us. This influences us to give priority to boys.'
>
> (Graham-Brown, 1991, p. 195)

The blame is firmly with the girl for 'disappointing' the parents. Parents too have agency in reproducing patterns of gender and other forms of dominance and inequality.

THE IMPLICATIONS FOR EFFECTIVE SCHOOLS

In a paper on 'Continuity and change in African value systems', Molutsi wrote:

> In my part of the world, car owners take [their cars] for doctoring before they can consider them safe to drive. It is their belief that traditional medicine is part of the road safety measures that one has to do.
>
> (Molutsi, 1991, p. 101)

It is perhaps unfortunate that such a concern for safety has not always percolated to the use of condoms against AIDS, but the point to be underscored here is the necessity to understand the prismatic societies we are undoubtedly all part of, and how scripts and discourses interweave, contradict and struggle for supremacy. If we return to structure and agency, this chapter has tried to show how teachers get their scripts from a range of discursive fields, and move in and out of them *as suits them and the occasion.* Such scripts, as we saw in the last chapter, are both Western and indigenous, traditional and modern. A script for resignation to a situation is a very powerful one, as is a script for untameable lust. In keeping the scripts for punishment and obedience, for students' incapability and teachers' (gendered) power, heads and teachers use their agency to reproduce highly traditional and bureaucratic forms of educational life. In so doing, they more widely reproduce equally ancient forms of social stratification.

As discussed in Chapter 2, the factors associated with school and teaching effectiveness appear to be a matter of using common sense. Our puzzle is always why schools and teachers appear to shoot themselves in the foot by adopting behaviours that hinder pupil learning. Why do teachers continue to shout at pupils, prevent group work, come late, not prepare lessons, and expect minimal performance from their pupils? Why do heads continue not to delegate, not to share power, not to adopt collegial practices which will help staff development, which will in turn help pupils? To understand such 'footshooters' one has to understand the cultures and logics of their position.

The implication is that there is little point in dropping in new scripts for school effectiveness unless they provide greater rewards than the old ones.

> A researcher in India, talking to villagers, found that they regarded their children's education as a lottery. You do not really expect to win, but you take a ticket just in case you, or in this case your child, draws a lucky number. The hope has not disappeared, but for many people, experience has taught scepticism.
>
> (Graham-Brown, 1991, p. 2)

Most of the discourses around school effectiveness are of course quite counter to the idea of luck and chance. They imply a rational, coherent framework which 'obviously' will improve achievement and minimize the luck element. Yet as we saw with the scripts for resignation, teachers may continue to draw on the language of 'chance' to justify lack of action or lack of success. The ineffective school is one where both life and the scripts are unpredictable.

The effective school (whatever its goals) is one where there is some coherence within the discourse. This does not deny dialogue and debate. On the contrary: it is important that scripts and discourses are surfaced, explored, shared and actively chosen from. To move from a discourse of conscious or unconscious resignation towards one of active change requires both an acknowledgement of the centrality to participants of such tried-and-tested scripts, yet finding a way to broaden the repertoire.

In the final section, we will therefore be examining ways in which discourses and scripts can become congruent, and a 'fit' can be achieved between a school's stated goals and the means to achieve them.

PART FOUR

Towards Post-Bureaucracy

Chapter 8

The Need for Flexible Schools

INTRODUCTION

> Indeed the case of Child-to-Child illuminates sharply the basic dilemma which affects all those who contemplate translating the principles of lifelong education to policy and practice.
> At the level of rhetoric everyone is in favour of it.
> At the level of policy many are frightened by the upheavals which would be implied if rhetoric became reality.
> Yet in the longer perspective those who look far enough into the future are frankly terrified at the thought of leaving education unchanged.
> Certainly the prospect of allowing primary education as it exists in many less developed countries to follow its present path towards lower standards and increased irrelevancy is profoundly disturbing.
>
> (Hawes, 1988, p. 5)

This section of the book moves on from analysis of ineffectiveness to more explicit prescription about what effective schools could look like. In the last section we stressed the need to acknowledge all aspects of the surrounding culture, whether of macro economics or micropolitics. We attempted an analysis of the prismatic intersection between traditional and modern cultures, an intersection which in turn provides a complex array of scripts and discourses for schools and individual teachers or managers to choose from. In our repeated depiction of the bureaucratic school, we cast doubt in fact on whether so-called 'modern' formal schooling is really modern, or whether it is firmly rooted in ancient organizational forms going back to colonial, military or even feudal traditions of control. Schools are based on out-of-date work patterns of the nineteenth century. Most Western schools are as anachronistic as developing country schools: the trappings of modernity such as computers and televisions do not alter the basic format of rigid timings of the day and year, learning fragmented into set blocks of time, children formally graded and categorized, school and classroom architecture predicated on identical sets of one teacher and 30-odd children. Little has changed since the nineteenth century. We can shop from home on computerized databases, but education from home is still viewed with suspicion. Even when we go out to shop, we can find a gleaming electronic supermarket strangely juxtaposed with a school in a building -- and philosophy -- which has essentially remained in a time warp since its first construction.

The interesting thing is that it is in developing countries that many of the real educational innovations have taken place. Stringency and rapid growth of school age population have forced lateral thinking about the provision of education in ways that more affluent countries have not had to contemplate. While we will in the end look back on all formal education systems as a 'hiccup in history', we are for the present locked into the need for a mass form of transfer of knowledge and a mass form of controlling the young, as argued in Chapter 5. The original INNOTECH/ IMPACT project in South-East Asia (discussed below) had derived from a neo-Marxist deschooling philosophy referred to as 'no more schools', based on the mistaken assumption of the easy mobilization of community resources. Yet this philosophy was modified in the mid-1970s, with a questioning of the idea that schools should be abandoned, particularly in a South-East Asian context where teachers were highly revered members of local communities and where governments looked to schools as essential vehicles in nation building (Cummings, 1986). Massive changes that we are witnessing in newly independent states mean that the nation-building role of schools, if nothing else, is likely to remain high on the agenda into the next century.

We need new forms of educational 'modernization' – not necessarily in terms of technology, but in tune with the world ecology and politics of the year 2000 and beyond. The keynote for a post-bureaucratic world is going to be flexibility. We have no idea what technology will bring, nor what the global environment will look like. The other keynote is going to be democracy for world peace, if we and the planet are to survive; this will be discussed in detail in the next chapter. Here, we look at the pre-conditions for a democratic effective schooling, centred on flexibility. Our argument is that flexible schooling is not just more cost-effective, but also provides the preparation for the adaptable learner which will be the only means for survival.

> Why is flexibility, which requires complex systems rather than simple ones, such a good idea? One reason is that the complexities of modern life are such that inflexible people, fitted only for a simple world, are at risk. In some situations it is necessary to be able to cope with authoritarian behaviour either by taking a lead or taking instructions. At other times we need to co-operate with others and behave democratically. Sometimes we need to be self-directing, take decisions for ourselves and act autonomously. Sometimes we need to have memorized information and at others to know how to research it. It follows that an effective education requires experience of all these approaches and an awareness of when each one in turn is appropriate.
>
> (Meighan and Toogood, 1992, p. 123)

This chapter is not however a dream-like 'forward vision', but based on those developing country innovations which signal viable pointers for the future. Many come from that strange category designated 'non-formal education' – NFE. While such innovations are often designed as add-ons, or supports for the conventional school structures, our argument is that the reverse should be true: that school systems should be built around flexibility (if that is not a contradiction in terms), with formal classroom instruction being just one component, or support, for the wider activity. It will be clear that boundaries between 'formal' and 'non-formal' education become fluid. It is a curious distinction that we have made, and probably another anachronism that we cling on to in order to justify the massive expenditure and effort that has gone into the 'formal' sector as opposed to its poorer cousin. Literature talks about 'out-of-school' children, about children attending NFE centres because they cannot have access to 'normal' schools. School is still seen as the norm, and anything else is unconventional, or abnormal. With the growth of technology and open learning systems, it is likely however that the boundary will eventually disappear. This chapter draws eclectically on a number of educational arenas in order to present its case for flexible learning. For effectiveness, we must broaden our definition of 'normal' schooling to include a vastly wider range of educational activity than has previously been the case.

Citing a number of projects as they become relevant, we extract eight themes which represent different facets of flexibility. These are: time and place; who is the teacher; what is the learning group; what is learned; pedagogy; assessment; rules; and financing. The chapter concludes by looking at the implications for management, for training and for research.

TIME AND PLACE

If firstly we explore ways of breaking down rigidities of time or location, it is indeed in the NFE sector that lateral thinking has occurred. Non-attendance or truancy is solved by recasting the problem. It would seem that children are not 'dropping out'; teachers are 'dropping in'.

In China, for example, a number of different 'teaching stations' have been set up which overcome some of the barriers that prevent girls, in particular, attending school. The list below (Chen Shao-Min, 1989) demonstrates the creativity and flexibility that has been achieved to bring education to the learner at times and places appropriate to them. There are:

morning classes
midday study classes
night study classes
every-other-day classes
pasture coaching classes
break-time coaching in planting areas (classes for the peasants' children)
mobile teaching (the teacher goes to different places to teach)
multi-grade classes
teaching stations for fishermen's children

China, of course, has seen a spectacular increase in the use of television in education, moving from the 'television universities' to a broader use of television by those students entering for examinations on flexible self-study programmes, by in-service teachers and by rural agricultural education programmes. 'Very large numbers of students can be reached quickly and at low cost through television education. There is no need, even in a vast country like China, to wait for tens of thousands of schools or colleges to be built and hundreds of thousands of teachers to be trained to teach in them' (Ma and Hawkridge, 1995, p. 35).

Distance or home-based education has an equity as well as a cost benefit. Enrolling girls in formal schools in China has been a problem, particularly where girls are caretakers of younger siblings. In rural areas, some schools provide day care for younger siblings; or preschools are established close to primary schools

(Lockheed and Verspoor, 1991). Such acknowledgement, rather than denial, of family constraints can help teachers and their attendance too.

In Colombia, similarly, a project was set up by CINEP (the Colombian Research Centre in Popular Education) to work with farmworkers' children who had to supplement the family income through work. The project was not only to provide basic education to these working children, but also to develop a pedagogic model to raise consciousness (on Freirian lines) among the learners. The features of the project were flexible schedules, where children came to school after work or during their free time to study independently or in small groups. Instructional cards were made containing contents of interest of the learners and community, designed by the teacher but based on themes selected by the learners and parents (Ranaweera, 1989).

In India, the Delhi Open School, for any student over the age of 14, has parallels with Open Universities, using correspondence instruction supplemented by periodic contact teaching, with increasing amounts of audio and audio-visual technology. Fees are charged, but they are kept low, and girls and all members of Scheduled Castes and tribes are exempted (Chaturvedi, 1989). A different style of flexibility is provided in projects for child workers in India, for example in the match and fireworks industry. Weekend classes are held, to provide informal education and raise awareness of health and working conditions issues (Lockheed and Verspoor, 1991).

A particularly interesting example is the Philippines Mobile Tent School. Here ethnographic research had indicated that the tribes in the Cagayn Valley Region transferred on a seasonal basis to temporary dwellings in remote *kaingin* sites, where children were needed to work on the farm. Tribes showed a pattern of mobility, always looking for food, and making *kaingin* on different sites each year, moving from settlement to settlement deep in the jungles. In recent years they have become victims of torture in the law and order operations between the military and the guerrillas, reinforcing their highly transitory modes of settlement. The Mobile Tent School therefore aimed to raise the quality of their life and provide greater consciousness. It consists of a single teacher, with no need for an infrastructure of classrooms and offices. The collapsible tent, collapsible chairs and tables and the blackboard are temporary facilities which are locally produced, and they are easy to store during typhoons and bad weather. A Mobile Library and multimedia instructional materials provide support to the Mobile Tent teacher. The teacher moves from one settlement to another, holding classes in tents or 'kiosks'. Such a teacher is not just concerned with education, but also assists in food production, health, civics and other concerns. Ethnic lay teachers are also employed, as the culture requires a headman, and the lay teachers can enhance pupil attendance and follow up class activities (Ranaweera, 1989).

BRAC (Bangladesh Rural Advancement Committee) has since 1985 been developing a system of 'non-formal' schools to cater for those children who do not get into the state system or drop out early. Teachers come from the local community, with the result that parents become involved in running the schools. BRACs work in providing rural credit and improving living conditions works in parallel, so that parents find it easier to send children to school. A significant description for our purposes is:

The attraction of these schools, in contrast to government schools, has been that teachers are dedicated and interested; curricula, designed by BRAC, are relevant to rural life; the schools are close to students' homes, with relatively short days, and are flexible according to the rhythms of economic life in the village. The cost to parents, apart from the 'opportunity cost' of their children's labour, is very small. This contrasts with government schools which, though theoretically free, now charge for books, materials and exams. BRAC has been particularly successful in attracting girls to enrol in its schools, and has generally low drop-out rates.

(Graham-Brown, 1991, p. 46)

Similarly, the PAMONG project in Indonesia, part of the well-known Project IMPACT, had its time flexibility in terms of matching the time and opportunities the learner had, and with the additional feature of the learner being free to stop their studies at any time and to come back without being considered a drop-out. It also had place flexibility, in that in an area one or two schools might be selected as centres for managing the project, but then 'satellite' learning posts would be set up to suit the convenience of the learners. These satellites could be community buildings, village offices 'or even ordinary houses' (Ranaweera, 1989).

The use of the phrase 'even ordinary houses' gives the implication of being extreme, but, interestingly, this should not be seen as not a last resort, for at least two opposing reasons. In Pakistan, for example, adult literacy classes for women in remote villages visited by one of the authors were all held in their houses. The women would not have been allowed to travel outside their village, and classes had to be brought to them. The spin-offs were of course that their children also became involved, and fathers were more easily persuaded that daughters could go to school. At the other end of the spectrum, secondly, the growth of information technology has meant that learning from home is not just the receiving of correspondence, but can be highly interactive. A recent conference of the Aga Khan Foundation task force (in Oxford, UK, 1996) discussed how even in a poor country such as Pakistan, home computers were becoming widely available. Networks of e-mail users on a course (such as are used by the Open University in UK) were no longer seen as a science fiction scenario. Of course the home has always been a key learning site, but confidence in it has been steadily eroded by the insistence that schools are the only places for learning.

Projects for street children again accept that children work, although some-times attempting to direct them into more valuable areas. In Kenya, the Undugu Society targets street children, mainly 'parking' boys and girls who direct motorists to parking bays, and child prostitutes, mainly girls between the ages of 12 and 16. The emphasis of the four-year informal education course is on practical skills and literacy, with children channelled either into primary schools or, more frequently, into self-employment. The Society 'has devised an alternative approach to primary education, shown that parking boys and girls can become useful members of society, promoted the informal sector, upgraded about 1000 slum dwellings, helped single mothers earn decent incomes, and organized the formation of numerous small businesses' (Lockheed and Verspoor, 1991, p. 163). As Williams pointed out from his research on the education of street children across a number of countries, formal education could learn a great deal from the initiatives with street children, for it is in the latter that focus must directly be on the practical and psychological needs of the learner to entice them into education at all. Needs for relevance, personal safety and a secure territory for their belongings are prime concerns of street children; but it might be argued that in different ways these are concerns of all children (Williams, 1992).

Finally, in discussions of time, mention is also usually made of shift systems. These have been introduced in a number of countries to tackle the problems mainly of buildings, but also of textbooks and even teachers. They have been viewed often as second-best, temporary measures, with second or third shifts of the day being unpopular with both students and teachers, particularly in hotter climates. However, the research on effectiveness finds that the effects of multiple shifts are generally positive. Academic achievement may vary between single shift and double shift, but that is often because multiple shifts serve a lower-income population. When multiple shifts do reduce class size and streamline the curriculum, achievement does not seem to suffer (Lockheed and Verspoor, 1991). Although often introduced in urban areas, shift systems can also target rural areas. If schools are segregated by sex, and institutions have not been built for girls, then shifts can give girls and female teachers access to educational facilities. 'In fact, a shorter school day might be more welcome in rural areas, where the opportunity costs associated with school attendance are generally higher than they are in urban areas' (ibid., p. 158). This returns us to the need to be flexible about children's attendance when they are in paid work, harvesting or have domestic duties.

Our first argument, then, is that breaking out of the rigid timetables and the notions of attendance associated with formal schooling is not only possible but highly cost-effective. Its success depends, of course, on the 'inputs', discussed below.

WHO IS THE TEACHER?

Teachers' salaries are always the largest proportion of an education budget. Developing countries struggle between wanting to upgrade their teaching force and knowing that this implies an increase in salary with every qualification level. Qualified teachers may be resistant to the use of unqualified staff or even 'assistants' in their schools, as this undermines the mystique or expertise of teaching by implying that anyone can teach. Yet it is imperative, in cost terms alone, that flexibility is found in terms of who – or what – is seen as able to 'teach'.

Formal schools can learn from informal projects in their use of community members and 'lay' teachers. The problem is with creating new tiers of expertise, new hierarchies, as qualified or experienced teachers would, understandably, want to be in a position to supervise less qualified or experienced teachers, and retain superior status and salary. Schools enlisting parents' help have had to work through issues of whether parents can join teachers in the staff room (if there is one), where they might be privy to confidential conversations about pupils. Yet proper job descriptions and clear boundaries around tasks, responsibilities and territories should be possible, and be part of the management capability of the school.

The most promising avenue for broadening the 'teaching force' is that of peer tutoring. Two examples are described here. The first is the Child-to-Child health education project, a well-known one which has taken root in over seventy countries. It aims at the demystification and democratization of medicine, with health care not just the preserve of doctors. Materials and storybooks generate activities for primary-age children around health issues in the community, whereby they learn and teach others about crucial aspects of health, hygiene, safety, prevention of disease, child stimulation and development, recognizing and helping the disabled, and better nutrition. They are engaged in surveys and health campaigns. There is, therefore, the 'empowerment' of the individual to take action on health issues, and active learning to create knowledge about health and apply that knowledge in and out of the classroom (Stephens, 1993). The 'empowerment' of children is both process and outcome; while the project and the materials have taken different shapes in different countries, two of the principles are that the roles of teacher and learner are interchangeable, and that learning is not confined to the schoolroom:

> . . . it makes plain that children can become teachers of their community – of parents, neighbours and siblings – and that they learn and teach in many and varied settings. That schools can admit that they are not the sole repositories of knowledge and can welcome 'outsiders' who are not primarily qualified as 'teachers', is itself a major step towards the realization of life-long education.
>
> (Hawes, 1988, p. x)

Analysts such as Hawes recognize the threatening nature of shifting from teacher-centred teaching to peer-teaching, and that rhetorics of 'student active learning' do not transform into action (ibid., p. 86):

> Often we are told that the reasons are logistical: teachers with large classes have no alternative but to stand and shout at them. Of course, this is not true, because fifty children sitting on the floor are going to learn much more by helping each other in groups of eight than they will by trying to listen to a teacher whom only half can hear (because there are five other teachers bellowing away to five other similar sized groups in the same hall!)

Different styles of questioning are required, with far more pupil–pupil questions. Children may be working outside the classroom, away from the teacher's reach. Children will have a longer topic cycle, planning enquiries in advance, conducting them out of class and discussing them and making deductions in later lessons. If all this sounds fanciful, the growth and success of Child-to-Child and its pedagogy show what can be done even in previously autocratic systems and systems with very small budgets.

Project IMPACT also used children as tutors, usually older children to younger children. Cummings quotes Woods' ethnographic assessment of 'tutors' in Jamaica (Cummings, 1986, p. 63):

> How do tutors behave towards tutees? Quite well, on the whole, would be the short answer. A cuff here and a pinch there were also seen, but these are commonplace, given the way Jamaican children treat each other.

Actually, tutoring can serve many purposes which can be lumped under the heading 'personal development'. It can build confidence and self-esteem – 'the children are nice to me' – which can be fuelled by the award of prizes, and it can provide roles and opportunities for modelling, even if this is sometimes exaggerated. In these respects tutoring can certainly help the low achiever and the student with behavioural problems; it can provide a career try-out for teacher.

Not just one-to-one tutoring, but also the power of the whole group may be important, particularly when using self-instructional materials. Cummings noted in the Philippines and Indonesian contexts, that problems emerged of boredom with the materials, and of differential pace of movement through them. The second is less of a problem than in conventional classrooms, but nonetheless students may want to get to an endpoint or graduation. The problem of boredom was tackled in Indonesia through peer-group learning, whereby three to six students would form a group to study modules together. After some experimentation, modules were revised to assign distinct roles to a peer-group leader and the other members, and a procedure was developed so that the position of group leader could rotate among the members. With regard to pacing, pre-tests and post-tests for each module were devised, and no group could move on until all members had achieved 90 per cent on the post-test. Post-tests were administered by the group leader and checked by members exchanging papers:

> Once students realized they were responsible for the progress of all their group members, fast learners manifested a more helpful attitude towards those in difficulty, and the overall co-operative spirit in the classrooms was considerably enhanced. Also, because students corrected their tests and recorded the results, teachers were relieved of considerable clerical work.
>
> (Cummings, 1986, p. 87)

In terms of peer tutoring, the programme was changed from the original one so that all students were required to take their turn at tutoring, and not just the 'bright' ones or older ones. This was introduced to quiet the complaints by bright students that they lost time when tutoring, and also to allow all children to share in the growth experience related to tutoring others.

Who 'the teacher' is, then, will be much wider than usually conceived, and include materials as teachers in their own right. A World Bank survey on *Improving Primary Education in Developing Countries* concluded from all the studies that the most promising avenues for improving the quality of teaching were to offer in-service teacher training, supply programmed materials and use interactive radio instruction (Lockheed and Verspoor, 1991). Simply trying to reduce class size was found to be a 'blind alley', a conclusion later supported by Black *et al.*'s study *School Improvement in the Developing World* (1993). Unless class size can be halved, tinkering at the margins does not improve teaching quality. It is better to support (and involve) existing teachers with the production of resources.

Programmed materials are not there to deskill teachers, but to enable larger numbers to be coped with through peer tutoring or community help. The Dominican

Republic effectively uses radio learning centres in communities without schools. Young school-age children meet every afternoon under the supervision of an adult from the community; they listen to one hour of radio lessons in mathematics and language, plus some social studies and science. 'Achievement tests demonstrate that the children in the radio groups learn as much language and more mathematics than children attending traditional schools in comparable communities. Furthermore, these radio schools cost about half what traditional schools cost' (Lockheed and Verspoor, 1991, p. 160). This is an astonishing admission, tucked away in a small section on 'nontraditional schooling'. Why do governments not then turn all primary schools over to radio-type schools? Research on *why* the children are learning better is crucial. Our hypotheses would be that it would be a mixture of the quality of the transmissions and an atmosphere where learners are taking responsibility. The adult is there to supervise, not to instruct; the relationship is not one of expert versus unschooled, but all learning together. Should not this be the model for all schools?

'Child Power' could in theory be applied to any learning situation. The argument is that the approaches to health education can 'unlock' better approaches to learning on a much wider scale:

> If children can form groups to discuss health priorities based on their own knowledge and experience, why cannot they do so in relation to other subjects? If an older child can help a younger one to practice better health habits, why cannot she help it to practice reading? If a group of children undertake a successful survey of the water sources of their community, why cannot the same skills of observation and recording be applied to the social studies and science curricula? If a health problem, say 'recognizing and preventing malnutrition' can help to integrate teaching and learning in mathematics (measurement), science (food values) and language (reading and writing about nutrition), why cannot such integration be applied to other issues that matter such as soil erosion or harmonious community relations?
>
> (Hawes, 1988, p. 4)

WHO IS THE LEARNING GROUP?

It becomes clearly not just a question of who teaches who what, but of different relationships between all those involved in the education process. In the Colombian CINEP project mentioned above, Ranaweera reports that 'the social organization of the school was set up through a process of agreement among students, teachers and parents; e.g. a group of students were commissioned for organizing the school work for each week; instructional materials were made by parents, teachers and students organized in groups; older students helped the younger ones with their assignments' (Ranaweera, 1989, p. 139).

If the boundaries between teachers and taught become increasingly blurred in flexible learning, so too do those between previous 'categories' of learners. Many education systems spend inordinate amounts of time and resources changing from 9-3-3 to 8-4-4 to 7-5-4 and back again, with such systems supposedly age-graded. In practice, one can find 'children' as old as 23 in a primary classroom.

Flexible learning is about acknowledging and building on variations of age in learning groups instead of constructing this as a problem.

In the Philippines IMPACT project the idea arose of reorganizing the schools into 'families' – seen as 'possibly the most original contribution of the Philippine experiment' (Cummings, 1986, p. 28). A single family included 10 to 15 students from each grade level, that is, about 60 to 90 children in each family. With children of all grades sharing a common area, it was easier for older children to assist their younger peers. Interestingly, this has parallels the other side of the globe with the reorganization of Madeley Court School, where the head, Philip Toogood, introduced 'minischooling'. This large comprehensive was reorganized to make a federal system of six minischools, each with its own head. The model was of a 'cluster-network' rather than line management, with children – and teachers – feeling part of a 'base' (Toogood, 1992a). Each base had its own territory, where most teaching and pastoral activities occurred. A much greater sense of ownership and belonging occurred, with children, parents and teachers feeling passionately about 'their' minischool. This is being mentioned here as it is an example of how with lateral thinking, a large impersonal institution can be transformed. Madeley Court was not a purpose-built federal school, but could be adapted 'quite easily' to the structure of territory for minischools. The main problem was maintaining 'heart units' for subject specialisms. Yet this turned out in the end to be more of a problem of constructing an adequate resource centre than constructing areas where *all* the teaching and learning had to be done.

In developing countries, parents are often enlisted to help in the construction of classroom blocks, either through fund-raising or through their own physical labour. These are often to a standard design, sometimes unremitting rectangular blocks – even in countries where other sorts of architecture is varied, curved, decorated or adjustable. With flexible learning, thought needs to be given to equally flexible accommodation for different size groups. A nice example from Vietnam was of community members supporting the project, improving the school garden and 'building simple kiosks (umbrella-like shelters) on the school grounds so that small groups could meet outside their classrooms' (Cummings, 1986, p. 27). For many impoverished schools, trees of course fulfil the same function, but are less good against rain than they are against sun. The post-bureaucratic school should have flexible but sturdy units, whose construction and arrangement do not suggest prisons or factories.

WHAT IS TO BE LEARNED?

It would be presumptuous and foolhardy to make prescriptions about the curriculum for an effective school. Each school's management should make the connections between the ultimate aims for learning and the way that learning will be organized. While the negotiated curriculum between each individual learner and teacher/school may be an ideal end state, this requires extremely high levels of resourcing. Many of the projects alluded to above have in fact quite tightly bound curricula, as they are based on predetermined instructional materials. The term 'open learning' often refers in fact to relatively closed packages, as learners work their way through sequenced steps at increasing levels of difficulty.

In other projects, materials are designed by teachers, students and parents together in terms of perceived needs.

The flexibility comes more in choices made by the learner about when and how to access such materials, and in the designers rethinking old certainties such as subject boundaries. Interestingly, the Indonesian *kejar* (catch-up) project saw a motivating factor as integration:

> The learning of language and arithmetic are integrated, not separated,
> the reason for this being that in real life situations the two are
> intermingled: nobody separates calculation from verbal explanation, but
> mixes them in conversations.
>
> (Ranaweera, 1989, p. 143)

Even greater integration might be incurred when the curriculum is focused on the 'needs now' basis. The 'Women's College' in Cape Town, started in 1992, is an NGO which reaches out to 'historically disadvantaged' women and teaches them everything from driving skills to advocacy skills for candidates in local elections. It is run on the proverbial shoestring, with five staff and two volunteers, but has had significant success in getting women elected, and generally 'empowering' grassroots women (Women's College, 1996). Lobbying and advocacy skills are undervalued areas in most formal school curricula, but would be key parts of communicative competence, possible to practise immediately in a range of contexts.

It is difficult to conceive of a National Curriculum which could fulfil the needs of the post-bureaucratic school. The time-lag between agreement of areas, constituting writing teams, design, consultation (if any!), production, dissemination, teacher induction and eventual learning by pupils is such that unless such National Curricula have a great deal of autonomy built in, they are likely to be out of date before they even reach the classroom. Arguments between 'subject specialists' and tight control of disciplines means that integration is very difficult to achieve. 'Cross-curricular themes' – even those as important as peace education – become relegated to the afternoon, to the spaces in between the 'real' learning of the differentiated areas of maths, literacy or science.

Programmed materials suffer some of these problems of time-lag, but do not carry the weight of imperative, nor force schools into rigid schedules to get through the streams of syllabuses. It is essential for effective schools that teachers and learners have choice and a degree of control over the content and application of what is learned. Coming through all the literature is always the cry for 'relevance', both to fulfil learning objectives and to motivate students. The better 'learning package' projects are those which encourage the writing of supplementary materials locally, and/or, as with Child-to-Child, have instant activities built in which force awareness of relevance to immediate community and family.

The philosophy to get across to the learner is that curriculum is just a resource, not an imperative. One of the authors recalls a research supervision with a teacher from Pakistan who was investigating teacher training courses. The teacher was using the words 'curriculum', 'syllabus' and 'textbook' completely interchangeably, and saw little difference in them. There was mutual puzzlement as we tried to arrive at a research design. By coincidence shortly afterwards, the author picked up an internal consultancy report in Pakistan on 'Supporting Factors of a Successful

System of Education' which commented in the section on 'Teachers' Training': 'Teachers should know the difference between Syllabus and Curriculum . . .' It was clearly a significant elision, symptomatic of the history of rote learning.

Flexible learning implies that any book or learning package is just there as one source of help, not to be memorized or accepted as Universal Truths, or as equivalent to all the syllabus or learning within that area. Study skills to ensure and accompany such critical reading or varied use are an essential part of effective education.

In fact, although the post-bureaucratic school projects into the future, that future is so unknown that it is better to minimize 'subjects' altogether. The effective curriculum, particularly at primary level, is one that teaches skills, not knowledge. Basic literacy is still a prime skill and source of power; perhaps a little numeracy, but not much; after that the better skills to learn are research skills and political skills. Research skills enable children to find out what is happening, and to check for evidence; political skills or political literacy enable them to survive and work together in their community. Any curriculum/knowledge packages are then there as examples of what one might do with those skills, rather than ends in their own right. As Graham-Brown concluded after her extensive review of basic education in the developing world:

> . . . post-literacy and skills training . . . will require more flexible approaches to education than those which prevail in most formal systems today. While the rhetoric of 'popular education' still runs ahead of practice in most cases, the concepts it embodies and some practical examples have at least offered new definitions of what constitutes 'education', as a concept which is not divorced from people's daily experience. It also questions authoritarian teacher–pupil relations and the human capital school of thought which values only those skills that have a direct bearing on the labour market. In the more effective experiments, education and development projects can broaden the concept of 'skills' – often seen in international agency reports as limited to developing technical and commercial abilities – to something which comprehends the cultural, social and political aspects of education. This could form part of a process which could help to introduce more flexibility into formal education, difficult though this is likely to be.
>
> (Graham-Brown, 1991, p. 277)

This critique takes us back nicely to Chapter 5's macro-level analysis of the reasons for current authoritarian schooling and its selective curriculum emphases. Our conclusion about curriculum is that the future effective school lowers its sights in terms of the actual amount of current knowledge to be packed into a child, and raises its sights in terms of the conceptual skills and social literacy it fosters.

PEDAGOGY

The acceptance of boring and stultifying teaching for schools is an interesting one. Ranaweera's (1989) analysis for UNESCO of *Non-conventional Approaches to Education at the Primary Level* has revealing statements (p. 29):

138

The rigid, teacher-dominated oppressive atmosphere that often prevails in the formal classroom and the didactic teaching methods have to be changed to suit the more flexible teaching/learning situations that are desirable in nonformal settings . . . Acting on the realization that the didactic approach centred on the teacher and the textbook which is usually adopted in the formal school is not suitable for the learners in a nonformal setting, many countries have accepted certain general principles on which the learning/teaching methodology and strategies should be based. In general, they realize that a learner-centred approach should be adopted with the teacher as facilitator of learning, and with the emphasis on learning rather than teaching . . .

Yet why should we have accepted didacticism for the formal school? Why should learner-centred methods be reserved for NFE settings? The answers go partly back to the control function of mass schooling, but also to a complacency and inertia in formal schooling. It is ironic that only when confronted with those who have rejected or never had the opportunity of being socialized in formal schools do planners cite the importance of learner-centredness and flexibility.

It is worth quoting the guidelines for 'nonformal and alternative' programmes in full (ibid., p. 31):

- Methods of teaching and learning should conform to the needs of the learner and his environment and not be based on what is dictated by outside authorities. It is incumbent on the teachers and the supervisors to know the culture and the aspirations of the people, and to develop methods and materials accordingly.

- In the case of learners who work to earn a living or supplement the income of the family, learning/teaching sessions must be made flexible and timed in such a way as not to deprive them of their source of income. Community assemblies held after work or during non-working days could be an alternative.

- Indigenous learning materials and methods should be suitably adapted.

- An informal atmosphere in which learning can take place free from anxiety, fear and failure is desirable.

- The learners should be allowed to progress at their own pace and not according to a rigid grade structure.

- Communication in the language of the learner is also necessary. It brings us to the need for teachers to speak in the dialect of the place and gradually to introduce the language used for administrative and commercial purposes, as needed.

- The settings for learning should be selected to suit the circumstances of the learner, e.g. the homes of children, community centres, places of religious workshop, homes of teachers, temporary shelters etc.

All the above would seem to be prerequisites for *any* learning, yet it is instructive that it is felt necessary to spell them out in a book on NFE. The clear and extraordinary implication is that such things do *not* happen in formal education, and are somewhat innovative or radical. The hidden message of the above is that formal schools have a curriculum dictated by outside; have rigid timings to the day; use imported and unadapted materials and teaching methods; are full of fear and anxiety; have breakdowns in communication; and are built in the wrong place. That is probably a very good description; but it is not a recipe for effective schooling.

A flexible pedagogy is not one that is arbitrary and swings from brutality to client counselling. (We argued in the last chapter that the more effective schools are characterized by coherence of scripts across teachers and between teachers and students.) A flexible pedagogy is one that is consistent in the principles of valuation and respect for the student, but is able to differentiate in terms of needs. The Black *et al.* (1993) report on *School Improvement in the Developing World* came down firmly on the side of 'child-centredness', while not underestimating the problems of implementation (p. 74):

> The evidence is that, for example, children have to be taught how to learn in the context of interactive group work and teachers have to be trained to use it to advantage. There are equal if not greater problems in supporting teachers who choose to differentiate their teaching according to individual or group need.

Flexible pedagogy does not always come naturally, and requires rethinking of relationships and support among teachers as well as towards children. Properly student-centred teacher training is a prerequisite.

ASSESSMENT

In making schools effective for the majority, not the minority, it is clear that a wide and flexible range of assessment must be used. If something like a secondary school leaving examination is designed for only the 'top' 20 per cent, in order to screen for the next level, then parallel and equally valued forms of assessment must be found for the 80 per cent who will 'fail' or not take such an examination. This was one of the strong conclusions from Chapter 2.

In coherent schools, the nature of student assessment links clearly to the overall evaluation of what the school is for. In the UK, for example, the recently established Flexi College is closely linked to local business and industry, commerce and public service, with many activities of the College happening in these sites. The assessment, logically, involves written reports which demonstrate the relationship between the academic subject and the world of work. This is side by side with externally accredited academic and vocational qualifications, Records of Experience, and modular credits transferable to higher education (Toogood, 1992b). Although a developed country context, this example is mentioned here for two reasons: firstly, flexischooling and the Flexi College had to go through considerable resistance and scepticism by powerful adherents to conventional schooling who said it would not work; and, secondly, because such flexible learning has been established on a shoestring, and not with vast injections of cash. It is more a question of persuading existing institutions that it is not the end of Western civilization if learners put together their own learning packages and elect to negotiate an arrangement whereby they can come in and out of such institutions for particular days or even lessons as fits their programme. In spite of cries that it could not be done, this is how further education colleges work, as do those primarily home-based educators who negotiate with local schools for access for particular blocks of time (Meighan, 1992). They also negotiate relevant assessment – where desired – of competencies gained. Papua New Guinea, too, managed to achieve a balance between academic and social assessment in its Secondary Schools Community Extension Project by making the assessment of school work conditional on demonstration of how such learning had been applied in the service of the community (Vulliamy, 1981). While that project no longer continues in that shape, the quest for relevance and innovation live on in radically new ways of teacher training (Burke, 1996).

The varied assessment or evaluation practices cited in Ranaweera's survey are:

- In Colombia, techniques of self-evaluation and group evaluation are used for assessing the performance of the learners. A participation model taking into consideration ethnological principles has been developed in which the 'togetherness' of education, participation and organization is recognized.

- In an Indian project in Pune, pupils' self-evaluation during group work is a key feature. Also, the project has evolved an innovative device of cumulative evaluation by organizing a children's fair (Bal Jatra) every five and a half months. During this fair, the pupils' progress in each area of learning is assessed in a relaxed, non-examination atmosphere. The programme of the fair consists of competition in games, story-telling, elocution, singing, drawing and painting, and testing of achievement in literacy, numeracy and general information. Specially devised graded education tools are used. The performance of each pupil in different activities is observed and recorded by a pair of 'external' teachers. 'Since there is no fear of failure or repeating a class and since each child can show good skills in some activity or other, examination stress is absent.'

- The Indian Open School does have more formal examinations, but has greater flexibility in the combination of subjects and the timing of the examinations. Students are not obliged to sit all subjects at once; they accumulate credits towards the final Secondary School Leaving Certificate and can proceed at their own pace.

It is, of course, a gross anachronism and highly cost-ineffective to still have the prime emphasis on one-off examinations in schools. These will probably die out as modular systems and graded assessment take hold, but schools and learning as places of continual fear and anxiety are not effective sites for learning. Building up credits with acceptance of easy retries if necessary are ways which put meat on rhetorics of 'success for all'. In the Indonesian Kejar project, the learning materials were staggered in 22 levels of difficulty, moving step by step from easy to more difficult stages.

With younger children, the emphasis on examinations is even more debatable. The Child-to-Child initiative discussed the implications for transferring its ideas to formal schooling, as follows (Hawes, 1988, p. 83):

Conventionally education defers its objectives. We learn something. We are tested upon it at the end of a term or a year. We pass or fail such tests.

Objectives are to a greater or lesser extent determined by the real needs of children. The best education carefully links objectives with needs but tends almost invariably to concentrate on the needs which children will experience at the end of the school cycle – in other words 'needs later' rather than 'needs now'.

The Child-to-Child approach refocuses objectives to include 'needs now'. We teach children to learn ideas and skills which they may apply *now, at home, this evening.*

Such a refocusing has profound implications for the status and purpose of testing, since not only does it link knowledge with doing but doing with 'wanting to do'. It forces us to contrast, for instance, the educational worth of a child who can readily answer a multiple choice test on child development but ignores her baby sister, with another who has developed a real desire to play creatively with a younger child and has the skills to do so.

Effective schools research will also therefore have to find ways to accommodate profiling and credit accumulation in both longitudinal and cross-country research. International comparisons of, say, maths achievement at present tell us little about the proportion of time children have spent on maths, nor how that fits in their individual profiles, nor what maths is necessary for their future lives and work. The fact that a country comes ninth in an international league table for geometry tells us none of these things.

RULES

Much of the effective schools research demonstrates the importance of treading a fine line between a clear disciplinary framework and a set of imposed rules. The more successful schools appear to be those where rules are minimal and agreed by all parties (as will be discussed further in the next chapter). This sounds uncontroversial until we hit areas such as uniform and punctuality. Arguments for flexibility, particularly in time and space, would appear to preclude harsh judgements about being punctual, or leaving school at different times of the day or week. Yet many teachers and heads feel threatened by such apparent disdain for time. As we have seen in the last section, Western schools do not sit easily with informal cultural expectations about time usage, whether in Africa or the Solomon Islands. Negotiation and contextual applicability appear to be the key:

Rather than trying to convince students to adopt highly accurate approaches to time and measurement in all parts of their lives, a more culture sensitive approach involves openly discussing with them the merits of accuracy in particular contexts, such as science and mathematics classrooms, and the advantages in terms of maintaining relationships of a more flexible approach in social contexts.

(Ninnes, 1995, p. 25)

Similarly, non-negotiable uniform is seen in many countries as a way of both inducing loyalty to the organization and breaking down differences in wealth among children. Conformity seems a crucial concern. However, it is worth considering on an ongoing review basis whether the mental and material effort expended on insistence on externals such as uniform is worth it. In Pakistan, the *mohalla* school project reduced the cost of education by holding classes in homes and 'abandoning the requirement that students wear uniforms and even shoes; the enrolment of girls and rural children increased dramatically' (Lockheed and Verspoor, 1991, p. 162).

As has been pointed out by one of the authors before (Davies, 1990), reducing the number of rules by which children are labelled as deviants can solve a number of problems. If children miss school for two days, and then fear to return because they will be punished for 'truancy', then such rules are counterproductive. If, as with all the projects described above which are *designed* to be flexible in time, there is no concept of truancy, then this category of child – and punishment – becomes redundant. Flexibility in rules does not refer to an anarchy, or relativism, where any behaviour is acceptable. It refers to distinctions being made between those fundamentals of behaviour which must be adhered to by both teachers and learners (such as respect for others, non-racism, non-sexism, non-violence) and those traditional rules which are a product of colonialism, bureaucracy or even more ancient power cultures, and which may now have a questionable place in a post-bureaucratic organization.

FINANCING

As was discussed in the first chapter of this book, government money to finance full-scale conventional basic education is unlikely to be found in the near future. It would seem inevitable that varied and flexible means of paying for education must be found. Yet more than any of the other features discussed in this chapter, flexible financing presents the greatest dilemmas and presents some of the starkest management choices for governments or schools. Mixtures of private and public funding have always exacerbated differences in wealth, in that affluent parents can buy an education which is more likely to ensure maintenance or improvement of the child's social position. It would seem a truism, also, that a school with wealthy parents is more easily able to afford some of the material features associated with effectiveness. Market ideologies permeating education have meant that heads of schools the world over are being pressured to find ways to create additional – or even core – funding for their schools.

The discourse of 'cost-sharing' is a powerful one, and would certainly fit with our theme of flexibility, in that it would lead to varied ways in which the (sometimes unforeseeable) costs of education could be met and varied ways in which people could take ownership of learning for their family or community. Yet the inequalities and conflict this causes should not be overlooked in favour of a romanticized view of 'partnerships' with community or business. Here we explore some of the dilemmas associated with just two current strategies: community financing and income-generating schemes.

Community financing of education as a solution to the inability of governments to meet full costs has been on the agenda for quite some time (Bray with Lillis, 1988). Self-help initiatives are seen to give communities more control and ownership over their schools, and more involvement in the actual education of their children. Contributions can be considerable: Opolot (1994) reports that in Uganda, the gap between government provision and what was needed for schools during the 1970s and 1980s was met by parents, who contributed approximately 80 per cent of the running costs at the primary level and 60 per cent at secondary level. In Zimbabwe, Graham-Brown (1991, p. 196) recounts the community – mainly women – mobilizing themselves into a collective to sponsor needy pupils into schools. The harambee movement in Kenya is probably one of the best known examples of self-help, with harambee secondary schools comprising nearly three-quarters of the total (Bray, 1995). Here parents and community would contribute money and labour to build the school construction and later to maintain it. Parts of Nigeria used competition in the community to see who would donate the highest amount, building community finance into existing cultures with the use of launching ceremonies: 'By the general spirit of the people, it is better to be dead than to be alive and not be able to contribute to the development of one's village or clan' (Igwe, 1988, p. 111).

Yet community financing strategies are not always as 'democratic' as would appear. Maravanyika (1995) provides a synopsis of the strategies employed by the Zimbabwe government to mobilize community resources since independence in 1980. He concludes that too many responsibilities have been given to local communities for construction of schools. District Councils have limited sources of revenue and yet are expected to meet the total building costs of primary schools and 95 per cent of secondary schools. Evidence suggests the burden has been to all intents and purposes pushed onto peasant farmers. 'District Council officials appear to lack management skills, misuse per capita grants from the Ministry of Education and there have been allegations that some of them are wasteful and corrupt' (Maravanyika, 1995, p. 24). While increasing access to schools, self-reliance exacerbated wealth differences; rural peasants still pay more to build schools than their urban counterparts, who are assisted by local councils, municipalities and even government itself. In rural areas, pupils walk long distances to school and many heads have established illegal boarding establishments 'which are in appalling conditions as teachers may not supervise them. Where government has strategically built boarding schools, the intended beneficiaries cannot afford the fees, so the schools benefit the richer families' (ibid., p. 21).

Bray (1995), in an excellent overview of community financing, outlines very clearly some of the tensions associated with these initiatives. Firstly, community financing raises issues of inequality because some communities are in a better position to help themselves than others. (This parallels Maravanyika's discussion of the divergences between urban/rural as well as between former white or middle-class schools and former black ones.) When disparities become excessive, they threaten national stability, so that government planners in Kenya, for example, have made periodic efforts to control and even dampen harambee schemes. This takes us back to the discussions in Part 2 of this book of the pre-eminence of the goals of nation-building. If communities are too weak to help themselves, should governments step in? If they do not, inequalities perpetuate; if they do, the aid undermines any self-help because communities see that resources are forthcoming despite their community's inertia.

Secondly, inequalities arise within self-help projects, with leaders not always fully representative of the communities they serve, and with PTA executives coming from the most powerful or economically advantaged groups. Meetings are not conducted in free or fair ways, and financial or other irregularities not allowed to be challenged. The balance between contributions of labour and contributions of cash is difficult to measure, and poorer members of the community are discriminated against or pressurized. Societies may be torn by suspicions of embezzlement or other abuse of community resources. Self-help may look like a 'community' venture, but its success or failure may depend largely on the initiative and drive of enterprising or energetic individuals. In some circumstances this means the influence of particular personalities and parochial interests, leading to divides rather than solidarity in and across communities.

Thirdly, there are questions of inefficiency. Projects can be ill-conceived and poorly managed, with some in Kenya and Nigeria based more on a desire to upstage rivals than on more substantial developmental justifications. Headteachers embark on fund-raising without even estimating the cost of the facility. In Bhutan, buildings had been left unfinished because of loss of enthusiasm or divided loyalties (Bray, 1995). For micropolitical reasons, schools may be sited in inappropriate places, and the establishment of excessive numbers of small schools stretches scarce teacher and other resources. This mismatch with overall planning was also the experience of one of the authors in Pakistan, where the establishment of a new school could be agreed to literally in 24 hours, to promote the interests of a politician in his area, but bearing no relation to any previous attempts at school mapping or a needs survey (Davies and Kurshed, 1995).

Bray (1995, p. 17) comments: 'Given the importance of cultural factors in community financing, it is perhaps surprising that the matter has not been a stronger focus of research.' We would underscore this, and add that it should also be a stronger focus for management training. The prismatic society (see Chapter 6) provides an analytic framework to understand the tensions arising from the intersection between 'traditional' community power interests and 'modern' educational requirements, which are well demonstrated in the problems of whether this is 'ownership' of, or simply 'contribution' to, school financing. A key comment from Graham-Brown is:

> If communities are to participate in the processes of education, they
> should have the opportunity to contribute more than money and labour
> power. The World Declaration on Education for All talks of the need for
> communities to act in 'partnership' with government. Whether this is
> feasible depends very much on the relationship between government and
> society. The question of democracy in education cannot be addressed in
> isolation from the broader question of democracy in society. In an
> authoritarian state, this 'partnership' is likely to be highly unequal.
>
> (1991, p. 271)

A second – and apparently more democratic – strategy for non-governmental financing comes under the heading of *income-generation*. Schools in Tanzania were supposed to reflect the 'self-reliance' ideology of the country, and there are indeed many examples of schools not only growing food or keeping livestock for their own consumption, but also selling produce to raise funds for the school. Schools may also buy grain or stationery in bulk and sell in smaller amounts for a small profit. Vocational schools where students learn crafts or skills may also market these in terms of selling products or providing services in motor maintenance or furniture repair. All this seems a very logical way of combining learning and work, but of course comes up against local markets and possible resistance from existing business interests.

A fascinating account by Kwong (1996) of *chuang shou* (creating income) describes activity across the whole range of educational institutions in China. Schools in China have embraced business on a scale 'unthinkable' in the West. Universities, at the urging of central government, ran factories, farms, consulting/research companies and businesses. 'In the Maoist era, these provisions were to allow students and teachers to integrate theory with practice, study with labour, and to become "red", and "expert"; now their purpose was to bring in money.' In the mid-1980s, factory production brought in over half the income made by the vocational schools and a quarter of that earned by the universities. Our interest in this book is more in the school sector, where extremely 'innovative' practices have occurred.

> They rented out their premises, ran cafeterias, 'salons' or bars, or turned their premises into discos and other such places of entertainment . . . Schools with few resources did what they could. Space being a premium in crowded cities, some schools turned classrooms into hotel rooms to cater to the growing tourist trade. Others had their teachers sell bread and confectioneries to students after class; and still others knocked down the playgrounds' outer walls and built storefronts to be rented to retailers.
>
> (Kwong, 1996, p. 189)

More direct cash income came from parents in terms of making them donate or pay the schools to enrol their children, the amount varying according to demand and how prestigious the school was. As well as fees for lunch, tutorials, 'hygiene', health insurance and examinations, some schools even charged parents for heat and deposits for tables and chairs. In case this is being read as a prescription for good management, we should point out that in 1995, *China Education Daily* documented 1117 such items levied by schools, and in 1994 schools across the country were forced to reimburse their students 120 million yuan for wrongful charges (*China Education Daily*, 18 February, p. 1).

The lateral thinking in China that we praised in the discussion of time is perhaps less enviable with regard to extortion. The same issues of inequality between parents arise as with community financing, with questionable means used to extract money from them. There was inequality, too, between teachers: 'Teachers in the less successful schools were envious of those in the more successful ones. Even within the same school, the staff in some departments made more money than others, making the rest unhappy' (ibid., p. 192). (This will strike chords with those in higher education sectors in developed countries, who experience pressure to attract research funding.) One of the most telling statements was (p. 192):

These developments and the resulting attitudes among the faculty would not have facilitated pedagogy. Teachers complained of the pragmatic, materialistic, and egocentric attitudes among the young. They lamented student dropout and the latter's lack of interest in study. They did not realize that a similar problem was endemic among the staff, and they were part of the problem. Their attitudes could only reinforce the students' materialistic orientation.

Education's role in accumulation has therefore to be considered very carefully. Flexibility in financing is not about simply finding any means to extract money from surrounding interests. Nor is it simply about sending headteachers on courses on budgeting or marketing. Any attempts at extending finance must be considered in the light of overall school goals, and if these goals include equity and co-operation, then financial schemes which increase inequality or competition should be very carefully monitored. Heads and teachers may need to analyse their own strategic and status roles within the politics of communities and local business interests. Financing should certainly be on the agenda for teacher training and management training; but within a context of a full political and social understanding of economics and power.

TEACHER EDUCATION AND MANAGEMENT EDUCATION

To achieve all the above areas of flexibility for the post-bureaucratic school requires a fundamental rethink of conventional ways of organizing schools and classrooms. It will have been seen that the areas all interlink. Flexibility in time and place require sets of available resources for greater self-instructional pedagogy. A broader concept of school goals than examination success requires varied forms of learner co-operation and assessment. The features of flexible effective schools are not lists of 'factors' which can be worked through in sequence, or selected from. They form an integrated philosophy of education which needs awareness of how goals, pedagogy, climate and assessment all cohere. Such integration and awareness will not be achieved unless initial, in-service and inspector training is also fundamentally rethought. The Colombian New Schools Programme (see Chapter 9) had simultaneously to recast its teacher training programme so that the prospective teachers learned in the same way, through self-instructional materials and co-operative group work (as opposed to lectures and individualized assessments). There is little point in telling teachers and heads that they will need to be flexible; they must experience adaptability for themselves.

The Child-to-Child project raised all sorts of dilemmas for teachers. We have mentioned threats to expertise and to assessment; there are also basic organizational threats, such as timetabling:

Once children become engaged in school-based surveys and health campaigns they overrun conventional period times. If children become engaged in helping each other across grade levels or become, as in Botswana, involved in school-based work with pre-school children, then considerable reorganization becomes necessary. Once co-operation is sought with health personnel a considerable amount of flexibility will be

147

necessary from the school. Health workers are not captive and amenable in the same ways teachers are . . . None of this reorganization is very difficult . . . but to depart from the norm a teacher or a head requires support, particularly from education officers and inspectors at local level. Unless these are in sympathy with the new approaches such support may not be given.

(Hawes, 1988, p. 85)

Hawes (p. 92) raised the question 'Why is it . . . that in the face of the challenge of large classes, falling standards and shrinking budgets, practically no colleges are examining the use of alternative methodologies making more constructive use of interlearning?' Starts are in fact being made, as in the Papua New Guinea and Colombian examples mentioned above; but unless a government (or consortium of teacher training colleges) embraces fully the need for radical ways of enabling teachers to experience flexibility and autonomy in their own learning, teacher training is likely to be locked permanently in outdated, expensive and individualistic models.

Integration and coherence are also key management questions. Flexible schools present particular management challenges, to be explored more fully in the final chapter. They do not suit autocratic, non-transparent styles of managing institutions. Any management training should permeate all staff, and not be confined to heads or to the buttressing of 'strong leadership'. To arrive at a workable yet dynamic way of achieving flexibility and effectiveness in time, space, teacher/learner roles and relationships, assessment, rules and finance can only be a collaborative task. It may sound an impossible one; but schools and their managers have done it, and schools and their managers will have to do it to survive.

RESEARCHING FLEXIBILITY

Both here and in Chapter 2 we have raised concerns about the conventional effective schools research methodology, particularly the focus on tests and examinations as the really only important outcome of schooling. However, this does not mean that research should be abandoned, nor that schools should never be compared. In arguing for flexible schools, it will be important to convince policymakers that they are indeed cost-effective and do provide alternative ways both to generate new goals for education and to achieve these goals. Research must be built in from the outset of any project. As Cummings (1986) revealed, there was confusion about the research goals for the IMPACT project. The original team said it was conducting an experiment, whereas what was in fact involved was a delivery system. It was not, as is conventional in research terms, an experiment which compared success with a control group, or had before–after experimental designs. Not until the project had been in operation for a year did discussions begin on ways to evaluate its success. Project researchers evidenced a 'disturbing naivety' in presenting their experiments to policy-makers:

> . . . it is clear that the project leaders had not anticipated the need to build a case for their system. Rather, they saw themselves carrying out an interesting experiment. They somehow assumed that the experiment would speak for itself. They were not attuned to the problem of

advocacy, and, in general, handled this rather poorly. Thus the success of projects in moving towards institutionalization was based more on political factors than scientific evidence.

(Cummings, 1986, p. 95)

Effective schools research in the quantitative tradition is perhaps at its most useful and revealing when it compares conventional with unconventional, rather than attempts to fine tune and elevate minutely different factors within schools which are essentially the same. Even more care must be taken, however, as in any quantitative research, that like is indeed being compared with like. The Liberian attempt at IMPACT was indeed evaluated, but not always rigorously.

> The increased attendance at IEL schools, possibly reflecting their attractiveness, placed them at a disadvantage. While at the conventional schools low performers tended to drop out, IEL schools kept most of their original students and, moreover, attracted new students who entered at the middle grades. Thus, the academic performance of the relatively few presumably exceptional students who stayed in the conventional schools was compared with the performance of the much larger and more representative group at the IEL schools, some of whom had only been partially exposed to the IEL approach. The initial evaluations of the IEL experiment made no reference to these violations of the experimental design deriving from the developmental character of the project.
>
> (Cummings, 1986, p. 84)

The suggestion is that for innovations, the better design is likely to be a before–after approach, as strictly comparable control schools are unlikely to be found. Simple control group designs do not look into classrooms and find what is behind the differential performance; nor can they cope with divergence towards new aims.

As we have argued repeatedly, conventional cognitive outcomes must be put in the context of a school's professed wider goals. As early as 1977, the IMPACT experimenters in Indonesia, Philippines, Jamaica and Bangladesh were emphasizing the effective gains of leadership, initiative, self-confidence and co-operation. A tracer study of Philippine IMPACT students two years after graduation indicated that IMPACT graduates did as well as non-IMPACT graduates in all subjects. IMPACT graduates were also found to have a stronger self-concept (Mante, 1981).

As Kelley (1984) argued, in looking at the experimental schools in Liberia, less emphasis should be placed on the 'horse-race' design evaluating academic achievement and more on student attendance and school climate. In the Indonesian PAMONG experiment, the studies of cognitive outcome were inconclusive: 'With hindsight it is apparent that the tests used in many of these studies, being based on the conventional curriculum, did not adequately test the material taught in the PAMONG schools. Also, teachers in both PAMONG and non-PAMONG schools were known to manipulate test scores' (Cummings, 1986, p. 90).

The audience for research and evaluation will drive the focus for that evaluation. Parents may need different sorts of evidence than do policy-makers. Chen Shao-Min (1989, p. 79) reports:

Some parents ask their children to drop out of school to seek employment while others, influenced by feudal ideology, pull their daughters out of school. We must patiently persuade them to give up their old ideas . . . In a small county in Heilungjiang, for example, the local government carried out an investigation which shows that 90 per cent of the children have acquired skills in the nonformal classes and, in return, the living standards of the families have been greatly improved. Despite a natural disaster, each farmer made an income of about 41 yuan in 1985. The farmers highly praised the achievements of nonformal education, and they got rid of their old ideas.

Effective schools research has the challenge of combining formal and non-formal schooling, conventional and non-conventional goals, flexible and inflexible management, in its attempt to promote realistic models of education which will convince stakeholders for the need to 'get rid of old ideas'.

CONCLUSION

This chapter has argued for a coherent discourse of flexibility in school processes. This may sound like a contradiction in terms, but deliberate flexibility is not the same as anarchy or chaos. It is a philosophy which places value on learners and teachers to generate and tolerate a diversity of ways to 'achieve', albeit within a mutually agreed framework of roles, of rules, and of allocation of resources.

The outmoded bureaucratic school that we have described has a whole raft of overt and covert goals, but has rigid and inflexible means of trying to achieve them. The post-bureaucratic school on the other hand has a consensus on goals, but flexibility and diversity in attaining them. Effectiveness research and management training should not generate an increasingly narrow range of management processes, the 'ringbinder' approach to school improvement. Those expecting a one-page Easy Guide ticklist of 'features of the successful school' will be disappointed by this chapter and this book. The flexibility will have to be quite culture-specific, and the research and training equally grounded in sensitivity to local goals and local economies. We have merely tried to provide examples of working alternatives.

Where there *can* be international frameworks are in the surrounding principles of human rights. Decisions have to be taken on when to be flexible and when to adhere to rules and routines. Social justice in a school may need quite tight regulation around equality of opportunity, children's rights, staff promotions and uses of finance and resources. One does not get flexible on child abuse, nepotism, discrimination and embezzlement. The international conventions on rights and freedoms provide a solid non-negotiable scaffolding upon which agreed diversity can be built. The next chapter argues that the most viable and disciplined process for filling in that scaffolding is democracy.

Chapter 9

Democracy and the Post-Bureaucratic School

INTRODUCTION

The British politician Winston Churchill once described democracy as the worst system of government apart from all the others. In this chapter we argue that what applies to macro-political systems also applies to micro-political systems such as schools. As the quotation from Churchill suggests, democracy is not a perfect system (none is) and is not a panacea for all the problems facing schools in developing countries. Moreover, democratic forms and structures need to be relevant to local needs and circumstances. However, it is our general contention that school organization and management must look beyond the bureaucratic present to more democratic forms of school management that can ease the burden of such problems, enhance the internal search for solutions and coping mechanisms and improve school effectiveness/decrease school ineffectiveness.

In the Introduction to this book we expressed serious reservations about the automatic and uncritical transfer of Western management tools or techniques to the context of developing countries, both in terms of their relevance and their feasibility, and in Chapter 8 we discussed more flexible approaches that could be considered appropriate for discussion in developing countries. Yet while the particular, substantive models, tools, techniques or processes that happen to be dominant in Western educational management at any one time may well not be applicable in whole or in part, there is nevertheless a need to consider whether there are general procedural values that can best facilitate effective school management in developing countries both in terms of their response to the political context of schools and in terms of schools' need to cope with the severe issues outlined in Chapter 1. We would suggest that there are and that such values – for example, inclusion, participation and transparency – are basically democratic rather than bureaucratic and can improve school effectiveness in both developing and developed contexts. This is because, while these values in themselves do not provide 'answers' for developing countries in the same way that Western management techniques often purport to do, they both allow for the free discussion among key participants of a possible range of locally relevant answers and, in educating for a democratic political system, encourage a macro-political context where such free and peaceful debate is possible.

EDUCATION FOR A DEMOCRATIC SOCIETY

A discussion of school management in relation to school effectiveness cannot skate over the question of goals: effective at what? What sort of individual person and what sort of state and society should the effective school aim to help to produce? What management structures and practices are congruent with these goals?

The United Nations defines development as a process of enlarging people's choices. A key element of this emphasis on choice is political freedom and guaranteed human rights. In 1992 the UNDP in their human development report of that year (p. 26) put it that

> The purpose of human development is to increase people's range of choices. If they are not free to make those choices, the entire process becomes a mockery. So, freedom is more than an idealistic goal – it is a vital component of human development. People who are politically free can take part in planning and decision-making. And they can ensure that society is organised through consensus and consultation rather than dictated by an autocratic elite.

By 1995 the UNDP claimed as part of its record of human progress that two-thirds of the population in developing countries was now living under relatively pluralistic and democratic regimes, though for many this was a very new experience (UNDP, 1995, pp. 13, 16). Increasingly, Western governments and their aid agencies have come to define 'good', 'better' or effective government as democratic government because it is more likely to produce greater stability and peaceful development. They have therefore attached political strings to their loans and grants: no moves towards democracy, no money (see, for example, British Council, 1993). Moreover, it has become patently clear to most of the citizens of developing countries that one-party and military authoritarian regimes have been no more successful at delivering economic growth and social welfare than democratic regimes. Thus the argument that it is necessary to suspend democracy and respect for human rights in order to achieve economic and social development is no longer credible. Indeed, democracy and human rights are part of that development. *The Economist* magazine has even argued that on the whole the evidence suggests that democracy actually improves economic performance. The argument against this is the experience of the so-called 'Asian tigers' of the Pacific rim who have prospered economically despite having authoritarian governments. However, as *The Economist* (27 August 1994) notes:

> The claim that authoritarian government works best for development is a claim about history – but it draws mainly on evidence from one region, east Asia, over a comparatively short period. The evidence is anyway unpersuasive: east Asia may well be special but not because it has had authoritarian rulers.

The most important point is that democracy provides the best environment for the peaceful solution of disputes and conflicts. We saw in Chapter 1 how pervasive war and violence has been in developing countries. Authoritarian regimes have been marked by civil unrest, violent repression and wars against neighbours. This has caused enormous damage to the economies of developing countries, severely affected their social fabric and seriously undermined the provision of education. While democracies are not perfect, accountable and representative government minimizes internal violence and the abuse of human rights and greatly decreases the possibility of going to war without good reason. In other words, it can help to provide a peaceful context in which schools can at least function safely. Education for peace and democracy therefore is of fundamental importance in judging school effectiveness in developing countries. Good accounting, registration and assessment systems are all meaningless if the school is being shelled from the nearest hill and there are landmines under the paths to the school. As the Director-General of UNESCO has put it:

> 'Wars will not cease, either on the ground or in people's minds, unless each and every one of us resolutely embarks on the struggle against intolerance and violence by attacking the evil at its roots. Education offers us the means to do this. It also holds the key to development, to receptiveness to others, to population control and to the preservation of the environment. Education is what will enable us to move from a culture of war, which we unhappily know only too well, to a culture of peace, whose benefits we are only just beginning to sense.'

> (Tedesco, 1994, p. 1)

Schools in developing countries must contribute to the development of the skills, values and behaviours associated with peaceful conflict management if they are to be judged effective. This means that instead of the predominantly authoritarian schools of today efforts at school improvement must be directed at more democratic forms of curriculum and management. This point is brought home dramatically in the following change of mind described by Stephen Heyneman, an American economist working at the World Bank. He is writing about Eastern Europe, though what he says is every bit as applicable to developing countries.

> Wherever I have worked over the last decade I have recommended the use of educational vouchers and other measures to maximize user choice. But after working on the educational problems of Central and Eastern Europe and the Russian Federation, I have changed my opinion. My view has changed not because educational efficiency is no longer important but because I have discovered that the importance of educational efficiency has a limit. In the case of Russia, I have been working in an ethnically heterogeneous, federal system much like our own, but falling apart. More than 100 ethnic groups now may control schools and, not having the traditional restraints, may now be able – if they choose – to teach disrespect for the rights of their neighbours. Schools can contribute to armaggedon and I have been forced to learn that there are things in life – such as civil unrest and civil war – which are more expensive and important than an inefficient and cumbersome public education system. But let me begin at the beginning. What is there that makes an education system essential for a consensus of democratic values and for the creation of a democratic society?

> (Heyneman, 1995, p. 1)

Democratic political institutions do not exist in a vacuum. In order to survive in the long run they must be embedded in a civil society whose political culture is supportive of democracy. As the UNDP put it, 'But democracy is more than drawing up constitutions, designing new election procedures or holding elections as one-time events. Democracy is a way of life' (UNDP, 1993, p. iii). The values, skills and behaviours that form a political culture that is supportive of democracy are not inherited genetically, they have to be learned socially. Countries which are determined to move away from authoritarianism and violence to sustainable democratic systems must therefore reform their education system in a democratic direction. This point is well made in a book published by the Ministry of Education and Culture in Namibia, which has a supporting foreword from both the President and the Minister of Education,

> To develop education for democracy we must develop democratic education . . . Our learners must study how democratic societies operate and the obligations and rights of their citizens. Our learners must understand that democracy means more than voting . . . (and) . . . that they cannot simply receive democracy from those who rule the society. Instead, they must build, nurture and protect it. And they must learn that they can never take it for granted. In the past we were fooled by an authoritarian government that preached to us about democracy. Nor will learners today be deceived by an education system that talks about democracy and says it is for someone else at some other time. To teach about democracy our teachers and our education system as a whole must practise democracy.
>
> (Namibia, Ministry of Education and Culture, 1993a, p. 41)

Democratic political systems are based on the idea of representative and account-able government which protect human rights and the rule of law. This includes a choice of political parties, the freedom of speech, freedom of association and a free and diverse mass media. In terms of education this implies not only a certain minimum level of knowledge of the political system but also the development of political skills such as detecting bias, arguing a case and participating in group decision-making. However, it is important to remember that democracy is not just about participation but, more importantly, about *how* participation takes place. Participation rates were high in Nazi Germany and the Soviet Union, but this did not make them democracies. There are important procedural values underlying democracy, which education must foster and encourage, such as tolerance of diversity and mutual respect between individuals and groups, a respect for evidence in forming opinions, a willingness to be open to the possibility of changing one's mind in the light of such evidence and regarding all people as having equal social and political rights as human beings:

> The long-term survival of democracy in Latin America relies heavily on an educated citizenry . . . Education can provide the majority of the population with a basic framework of values and attitudes, which is essential for participatory forms of government and the proper functioning of democratic institutions. Among those values is the understanding that all people have equal dignity and therefore the right to participate in decisions affecting their lives. Promoting this common framework of values requires providing each person with opportunities to develop self-esteem and to appreciate the value of others and their points

of view, including those of people from different sociocultural backgrounds.

(Reimers, 1993, p. 4)

The post-bureaucratic, democratic school that promotes such values must involve a shift of power and authority away from staff to students, both in terms of decisions about how the institution is run and in terms of what is learned in the classroom and how. While some early work has been done on identifying specific indicators of democratic schools internationally, i.e. observable characteristics of schools that suggest democratic practice (Davies, 1995), there are certainly broad features of school organization and curriculum which will be present in any democratic school. In terms of school organization there will be some sort of elected school council which represents staff, students and parents. The powers of such a council will vary according to the ages of the students but must include matters which are of significance to them. In terms of curriculum and classroom method, the democratic school is one where students can have some real power over curriculum because there is some genuine choice and student initiative involved. Teaching and learning in such a situation will be characterized by a variety of teaching methods which regularly include those such as discussions and projects where the students themselves are influential in shaping the direction the work takes, though it will also include more traditional teacher-led instruction. This is because, as Almond and Verba (1963) argued in their classic book on the 'civic culture', democracy requires a mixture of passive and active behaviours and capabilities. It needs individuals with the abilities to participate actively and to learn independently but also to sit and listen quietly to teachers and other students and to obey democratically agreed rules.

DEMOCRACY AS EFFECTIVE SCHOOL MANAGEMENT

A research proposal on leadership devolution in schools in Trinidad and Tobago (Joseph, 1991) described the situation there as follows:

> The national, regional and global economic recession has impacted
> heavily on schools. Teacher shortages, salary cuts, loss of increments,
> scarcity of necessary teaching/learning resources, have added to the
> already existing lack of material incentives in the form of remuneration
> for professional and extra academic qualifications and promotion systems
> based largely on seniority. Decreasing benefits accompanied by
> increasing demands upon expertise thus place teachers under pressure
> . . . In addition to which, many parents in all social groups (although the
> spread has the usual inequitable impact) have been hard hit by economic
> hardships to the extent that some cannot provide the necessities for their
> children . . . the general societal perception appears to be that expansion
> of provision has led to reduction in quality. Like many generally held
> views these may be very narrow in their focus, thus providing distorted
> views. But that does not lessen the strain these notions place on teachers
> and the feelings of despair they incur, since the obvious conclusion is
> that they are not even fulfilling their basic role as academic instructors.
> Schools, then, are currently locked into a vicious cycle of helplessness.

As a way of both coping with these circumstances and improving the situation in Trinidad and Tobago, this document argues strongly for a different form of school organization where the overwhelming power concentrated in the hands of school principals is devolved and shared with others in the school, including students. Instead of the present hierarchical and authoritarian structures Joseph proposes a more democratic style of school management which could facilitate its transformation into a community. She quotes a number of local studies arguing in the same manner:

> Firstly a democratic school structure is needed in which principal, staff and pupils determine, within the broader guidelines laid down by the Ministry of Education, the aims and objectives of their schools. Secondly, schools should encourage initiative and the exercise of responsibility from an early age by giving students a greater say in school government ... They must therefore provide them with the opportunity to share power and influence.
>
> (Newton, 1975, pp. 10–11)

> The structure of relations should be the loop rather than the ladder.
>
> (Beddoe, undated, p. 2)

> Since effective leadership is more broad-based and involves greater participation, serious consideration should be given to the reorganization of the structure of our schools.
>
> (Gowrie, 1989, p. 166)

Why is this the case? Why might more democratic schools be more effective schools than bureaucratic/authoritarian ones? Why might they be better able to cope with contexts in which schools in developing countries find themselves? In respect of school organization, there are four main reasons:

1. Rules are better kept by staff and students if democratically agreed to in the first place.
2. Communications in the school are improved through regular discussion.
3. There is an increased sense of responsibility as staff and students have more control over their organization.
4. Decision-making is improved as a range of internal and external interests and opinions is considered.

One of the two writers (Harber, 1993) interviewed staff and students in two schools in Tanzania with active elected students' councils about their advantages and disadvantages. At the first school the following advantages were noted by the interviewees:

- The council enables problems to be discussed before they get out of hand. In this way it improves communication and increases understanding and therefore, as the headteacher put it, avoids strikes. The students supported this and used the example of how they had recently got the use of Saturdays changed from working in the fields to individual academic work unless a crash programme of harvesting was needed.

- It is a good way of pre-testing or piloting a new policy. The Second Master used the example of when there was a proposal to change the school uniform to long trousers. This was put to the school council after discussion in the dormitories but was rejected by the majority of students because of the extra expense involved.

- It reduces the workload on teachers as they are helped, especially in their non-teaching functions, by the students.

- Discipline problems are reduced because, as the discipline master put it, 'Staff are closer to students'.

- It provides quite a number of students with experience of leadership and increases confidence and discussion skills generally.

The main disadvantage noted, especially by the teachers, was that it was time-consuming. It was also pointed out that it did not work perfectly all the time, that occasionally there were still communication problems and that sometimes the election of unsuitable representatives caused problems. However, the balance of the argument was strongly in favour of school councils and was summed up by one teacher, who had been working in secondary schools for 25 years, when he said that when they were first introduced in the late 1960s there was considerable mistrust and hostility among teachers, but now he felt that teachers would be unhappy if councils did not exist.

In the second school the teachers and students saw the following advantages to student involvement in school management through school councils:

- It trains the students to be self-disciplined, responsible and self-reliant. It becomes routine to look after yourself and to keep the school clean and well organized.

- The school works more smoothly: 'We live like a family', 'You learn to solve problems by discussion'.

- It eases the work of the teacher and allows them to concentrate more on the academic development of the students.

- It improves communication – 'There are no secrets', 'We have no riots because pressure does not build', as the staff put it or, as one of the students who had been to another school said, 'They don't just ignore you and tell you to go away'.

- Those who take leadership roles in the school often go on to become quite prominent.

- The students become quite creative, e.g. a visitor is coming at very short notice and they will organize an excellent reception because they know each other's talents.

- There is a friendlier relationship all round. 'This is the first school I have worked in where the pupils are proud of their teachers. It is very different from elsewhere.' Neither staff nor students, despite being pressed by the interviewer, could think of any disadvantages in this school.

These findings are supported by Lwehabura (1993), who did research in four schools in Tanzania. All faced severe financial problems, resource shortages and low teacher morale. He found, both in terms of the ability to deal with practical problems of stringency and in terms of examination success, that the more democratically organized the school the more effective it was.

We have argued above that in developing countries an effective school is essentially one that educates for peace. As was suggested in Chapter 4, schools in Africa have been prone to violence, stemming from the authoritarian nature of their management structures. It is worth noting, therefore, that in the above interviews in Tanzania an interviewee in the first school argued that the presence of a school council and the resulting openness and improved communications had prevented strikes, and another, in the second school, that it had prevented riots. Similarly, in Ghana one headteacher in Dadey's study (1990, pp. 316–18) listed the ways in which he averted violence through participatory structures:

1. Formal meetings: school durbars at which all students are present; student council meetings in which each form is represented on the council; committee meetings e.g. food committee, entertainment committee.
2. Informal meetings: on the school compound, at the head's office or residence.
3. Regular reports from student leaders: weekly report from the senior prefect, weekly report from the dining hall prefect.

In terms of classrooms, sole reliance on authoritarian teaching styles is also ineffective in that they promote dependence, rigidity, passivity, a false certainty about knowledge and a uniform approach to a diverse group of people. A main thrust of the argument for democratizing education in Namibia since independence in 1990, for example, has been that in the new context of education for all, teacher-centred education is ineffective:

> As we make the transition from educating an elite to education for all we are also making another shift, from teacher-centred to learner-centred education. That, too, will seem troubling at first and will take us some time to accomplish successfully. We are accustomed to classrooms where attention and activities are focused on the teacher. Indeed, we have probably all encountered teachers set in their ways that pay little attention to the backgrounds, interests and orientations of their students ... Few people learn easily or well in that setting. Much of the significant learning that does take place is accomplished despite, not because of, the teacher. Teacher-centred instruction is inefficient and frustrating to most learners and certainly is inconsistent with education for all.
> (Namibia Ministry of Education and Culture, 1993a, p. 10)

The often difficult economic and social conditions of developing countries requires people who are flexible, creative, active, confident and self-reliant. Reimers (1993) describes two examples of educational projects from Latin America which aim at providing such an education. Fe y Alegría is a non-governmental organization which provides education in twelve countries in South and Central America. By 1992 it was reaching 512,796 students in 509 centres. Its motto is 'Where the asphalt ends, where there is no water, electricity or services; there begins Fe y Alegría'. In their schools they aim to provide education emphasizing learning processes and content that originate in the reality of daily life; an active and critical pedagogy; education in participation and education committed to a new model of humanity and society which also emphasizes the development of the students' self-esteem. Although no systematic evaluation is available that compares Fe y Alegría schools to other schools, anecdotal evidence suggests that the schools are generally recognized by parents as providing better education than the normal state schools and that the students leaving these schools have better mastery of basic skills in reading, writing and mathematics.

In 1989 democratic elections ended 16 years of military rule in Chile. In 1990 the new government launched a programme to improve the quality of primary education in the 900 poorest schools, supported by aid from Sweden and Denmark. Many of the activities introduced into the schools emphasize developing social skills and thus the self-esteem and confidence of the students. For example, at the beginning of the school year all students collaboratively develop the basic rules of the school and thereafter all members share responsibility for those rules. In language lessons the emphasis is on allowing children to express themselves and then on grammar and rules. Teachers are sensitized to promote student participation and the creative use of language. Several guides have been prepared for the teachers covering subjects such as listening to and respecting children's views and the physical and emotional development of children.

ISLANDS OF EDUCATIONAL DEMOCRATIZATION

As was argued in Chapter 3, schools in developing countries are still predominantly authoritarian in terms of both their organizational structure and their classroom teaching. However, as will already be clear from the above, there are exceptions to this general rule, though they are not widespread. This section will examine a number of examples of educational democratization at different levels of scale and implementation.

1. Rhetoric – South Korea

This is the level reached by many educational systems and individual schools. Government aims espouse democracy but the reality is sharply different. For example, in South Korea the 1968 Charter of National Education poses for education the task of fostering a sense of national identity that prepares youths for the eventual reunification of the nation in accordance with democratic principles (Sah-Myung, 1983, pp. 209–10). Although South Korea changed from a military government to a democratically elected government in 1992, it has yet to establish a democratic civil society and education is still very authoritarian. Students at many schools in South Korea regularly face physical punishment and verbal abuse from their teachers. They are taught in groups of 40–60 in a highly didactic manner in which questioning and discussion is strongly discouraged and competing for the formal examinations is strongly encouraged (Kang, 1995).

2. Partial efforts – Malawi

Fuller (1981, pp. 92–3) describes how in Malawi, with an education system that is overwhelmingly concerned with authoritarian and bureaucratic forms of school and classroom management, it is nevertheless possible to come across serious efforts in the opposite direction. In the mid-1980s the Ministry of Education began to discuss how teachers could receive better guidance and ongoing feedback on their pedagogical practices. The Malawi Institute of Education received donor support from UNICEF to draft a modest handbook on alternative teaching methods. This urged teachers to move away from the old colonial 'chalk and talk' and described simple innovations in teaching methods such as asking children more questions, using demonstration and role play and employing co-operative learning groups. The handbook has become a best-seller and 'Occasionally one can even see teachers experimenting with these new pedagogical techniques'. The Ministry of Education and the Institute also developed a training programme for District Education Officers, inspectors and headteachers that would get these local managers to encourage better teaching practices in the classroom. Fuller notes that many inspectors still assume the role of regulator and controller and are also still mostly concerned with whether the teacher has well-written lesson plans than with whether the teacher is motivating children,

> Yet, my cursory review of reports written by recent graduates of the school management training programme reveals that a new role is being assumed. These younger inspectors spend less time on aspects of organizational maintenance and more time in classrooms providing feedback about pedagogy. A sampling of comments to teachers:
> Discourage pupils from giving echo (choral) answers to your questions.
> Pupils should use new words in a sentence of their own.
> Continue to give special assistance to backward pupils.
> Break topics into more teachable units.
> Pupils should be actively involved in the lesson through questions or other activities.

Fuller notes that, although the new methods are far from widespread, the state is at least illustrating how this new set of behaviours can improve the quality of pedagogy and that this is done through careful (re)training, simple tools and recruitment of younger inspectors and headteachers who are open to new forms of management and school improvement.

3. Individual schools as models – India

In the district of Ajmer in the desert area of Rajasthan 60 night schools have been set up for children aged 6 to 14, who work all day as shepherds and farm labourers and go to school at night. Each school has an elected student parliament, which has the power to help govern the school, fire teachers who are not up to scratch, push for village improvements such as water pumps and solar-powered lighting and generally make sure that children have a say in every aspect of village life. They are also in the process of launching their own magazine to keep children informed about their rights and local politics. In what in many ways could be seen as a 'traditional' and patriarchal society parents, teachers and local officials have relinquished much of their power to children, many of them girls. The parliament is designed to teach children that democracy should be above gender, caste and creed. Despite some opposition from teachers and parents the project organizer has commented that 'Through working with children for the past twenty years we know that they are capable of taking their own decisions. We hope that adults will come to understand and accept this.' Indeed, both parents and outside observers note the maturity of the children that have been given 'adult' roles. One measure of the project's success is that it has inspired similar ventures in nine other states across India (Hughes, 1996).

4. Whole-system policy reform – Namibia

Namibia achieved independence in 1990 after one hundred years of colonization and a thirty-year war of liberation from the South African apartheid regime. The new government has not only set about ensuring greater access to education for black students but has also began to introduce a new and democratic philosophy of what it terms 'learner-centred education'. Soon after independence, at an important conference on basic education held in Etosha in 1991, the new Namibian President, Sam Nujoma, spoke of the need for learner-centred education to develop the skills necessary for responsible democratic citizenship:

> The special emphasis that I believe is guiding this conference is that education must be child- or learner-centred. The Namibian basic education must support the actual processes of individual learning, rather than continue the colonial teacher-centred Bantu education, with its emphasis on control, rigid discipline, parrot-like learning and negative assessment principles.
>
> (Snyder, 1991, p. 5)

As a result of the Etosha conference the Ministry of Education noted in its annual report in December 1991 that,

> . . . a continuous, multi-dimensional process has been directed toward the transformation of Namibian primary and junior secondary education. From the social and pedagogical limitations characteristic of the inherited South African system, a wider range of measures have been applied to implementing the letter and spirit of the Constitution as well as transforming the Namibian classroom into an accessible, learner-centred and effective learning environment.
>
> (Namibia Ministry of Education and Culture, 1991, p. 10)

The Namibian government has therefore embarked on a programme of democratic reform across all aspects of education. One of its first acts, for example, was to ban the use of corporal punishment in schools. Here we will deal briefly with two aspects of democratic change – curriculum and assessment and school management.

The school curriculum has traditionally often been seen solely in technical terms of, for example, improving literacy and numeracy, as though these are unproblematically value-free and good things in their own right. The Namibian educational reforms, however, are informed by a philosophy which has asked more basic questions about the purposes of education. As a result, literacy and numeracy are seen as necessary but not sufficient. The reasons for literacy and numeracy are part of more fundamental questions about the sort of human beings and the sort of society that are the purposes of education. 'Effectiveness' and 'quality' in relation to schooling can only be judged in these terms. In Namibia the answer to these questions is clearly in terms of a democratic and egalitarian society and individuals who share these values. Therefore,

> We must understand quality even more broadly . . . consider a primary
> school where children master basic reading and writing but do not learn
> about citizenship in a democratic society or respect for others' cultures
> and values. That is not high quality education.
> (Namibia Ministry of Education and Culture, 1993a, p. 39)

A Ministry-sponsored workshop on learner-centred education identified 29 key features. The following are some of them (Namibia Ministry of Education and Culture, 1993b, pp. 81–6):

- active student participation in learning
- a willingness by teachers to let go of some of the old ideas – an emphasis on problem-solving
- continuous assessment of learning
- systematic use of valuable life experiences
- sufficient time for teacher- and student-initiated activities
- encouragement of creativity on the part of the learner
- encouragement of trial and error learning
- encouragement of choice
- encouragement of both flexibility and balance (the teacher as guide or coach)
- stress on the joy of teaching and learning
- mutual respect and co-operation of all teachers and learners
- all teachers and learners are both learners and teachers
- every student can be successful; there are no required failures

If learner-centred education is to be successfully implemented then assessment is an issue that must be confronted. In practice teachers often start with assessment and work backwards i.e. their teaching is based on what they think will be assessed rather than their assessment being based on what they have decided to teach. Changing assessment is therefore a vital aspect of changing teaching and learning. The Ministry of Education has started to introduce criterion-based assessment at all levels. Existing South African examinations will be replaced by the International General Certificate of Education and the Higher General Certificate of Education. The principle behind these examinations is that students are rewarded for positive achievement – what they know, understand and can do – rather than being penalized for an accumulation of errors. IGCSE and HGCSE use a wide range of assessment techniques appropriate for different skills and attributes in different subjects. These include oral and listening tests, practicals, project work, perform-ance and course work as well as various types of written examination, which can involve skills such as comprehension, analysis, synthesis and application as well as memorization (Namibia Ministry of Education and Culture, 1993a, pp. 123–8; 1993c, pp. 1, 7).

The nature of school management will also be a crucial factor in introducing and facilitating learner-centred education. The Deputy Minister for Education and Culture, for example, said the following to a course for school inspectors:

> Most of us in this room share a common background of school
> management and educational administration. Whether in the most
> privileged schools or the most neglected schools, a common feature was
> the tight control, a sometimes rigid and inflexible dependence on top-
> down authority, the rigid authoritarianism of South African educational
> philosophy. The net results of all this was that in the classrooms, the
> learners were clients and hostages to authoritarian, teacher-centred
> education and in the schools the teachers and principals were clients and
> hostages to the detailed control and attention of inspectors and subject
> advisers, who in turn were hostages and clients of the director who,
> whether knowingly or not, promoted the programmes of the authorities
> south of the Orange River. It was a perfect system for preventing change,
> for exercising a negative and punishing type of authority – a perfect
> system for telling people exactly what to do to stay out of trouble, how to
> be passive and avoid responsibility.
>
> (Ministry of Education and Culture, 1992, Annexe 4.5)

Indeed, a report for USAID on Namibia noted that one of the accomplishments of the Namibia government since independence had been widespread access to, and participation in, various decision-making processes. It commented that field visits had indicated that this was a common conclusion with respect to inspectors, subject advisers and heads (USAID, 1993, p. 7). The same report (p. 54) also noted the important role that headteachers will play in creating an environment for instilling democratic values into both learners and teachers, and there is no doubt that headteachers have been one of the key groups involved in the early stages of the reform of the education system. For example, at a workshop held for those who would go on to train primary schools heads there was agreement that principals should no longer be unaccountable despots but that rather the principal's respons-ibility was to be an example of well-mannered treatment of all persons without dominance or subservience, to set an example of willingness to listen to others, to resolve differences of opinion amiably, to show fairness to all learners without favouritism and to show proper professional conduct towards teachers and learners (Namibia Ministry of Education and Culture, 1993b, pp. 164–5).

The role of students in school management has been agreed by both student and teacher organizations and is set out in the *User's Guide to the Education Code of Conduct* (1993). At sixth-form level students are directly represented through democratic election to school boards along with parents and teachers. School boards have responsibility for such important matters as discipline, budgets, appointing teachers, the use of school facilities and school fees. At this level, therefore, students are fully involved in the democratic organization of schools. Below this level, however, their role is consultative rather than democratic, as they have the right to have their opinions considered on matters regarding discipline, rules and punishment but seem to have no formal role in actual decision-making.

5. Large-scale implementation of democratic education – Colombia

The Escuela Nueva or New School Programme was launched in 1975 to improve the quality and effectiveness of primary-level education in rural areas of Colombia. By 1991 some 20,000 of the 27,000 rural schools in the country were involved in the programme (Torres, 1992, p. 511). This reform is very much rooted in the contextual realities of rural Colombia. For example, each teacher involved in the project must write a monograph on the area in which she or he describes the community organizations, cultural and sporting traits, nutritional habits, health conditions, employment situation and agricultural products. This monograph helps the teacher to plan school activities based on the characteristics of the region. Also, the teacher must elaborate the agricultural calendar of the region jointly with the community and include the products and dates when the different agricultural tasks are performed. This is an essential element for the planning of educational activities (Rojas, 1994, p. 49).

The New School Programme's slogan 'More and better primary education for children in rural areas' sums up its attempt to reconcile quantity with quality:

> It is a matter not just of providing children in rural areas with greater access to education, but of offering them a better education. The endeavour to depart from conventional teaching and learning practice – top-down, authoritarian, rote and passive learning – and the attainment of higher levels of achievement than in conventional schools have been crucial, constant elements in EN's development.
>
> (Torres, 1992, p. 514)

In terms of curriculum the New Schools Programme promotes active and reflective learning, the ability to think, analyse, investigate, create, apply knowledge and improve children's self-esteem. It incorporates a flexible promotion system and seeks the development of co-operation, comradeship, solidarity, civic, participatory and democratic attitudes. In order to facilitate this approach the programme has introduced a number of self-instructional elements such as teaching corners, which are areas of curriculum interest such as science, mathematics, social sciences and languages, which contain material the students can study by themselves. Emphasis is also placed on individual use of the library and the production of self-study guides. In-service teacher training is provided which is based on the conviction that if teachers are to develop the classrooms in which children's learning is active, discovery-oriented, co-operative and creative then the processes of teacher training must have the same characteristics. School government is organized to provide an introduction to a democratic way of life. Children are organized into committees where they learn group decision-making and responsibility. The school committees can be linked to community groups and projects and are seen as facilitating social-affective and moral development as well as linking the school with family and community (Colbert *et al.*, 1993; Rojas, 1994). It is not surprising that one researcher on Latin America commented that 'Colombia is doing wonderful things in terms of education for democracy' (Villegas-Reimers, 1993, p. 76).

In one evaluation of twelve case-study schools it was found that in almost all the schools there has been an improved relationship between teachers and students. Teachers felt that they had become more accessible to students and, in some cases, recognized that they could learn from the children. In almost all of the schools, the teachers acted as facilitators for the children, as suggested in the guides and training workshops. In the classrooms students were observed to approach teachers with questions and challenge them in both large- and small-group situations (Rojas, 1994, p. 63).

Moreover, other recent evaluations have found that New Schools students have higher achievement scores than their counterparts in conventional rural schools as well as significant achievements in terms of self-esteem, creativity and civic behaviour (co-operation, responsibility and solidarity). It has increased community participation in school-related activities and has reduced the expected drop-out rate. It has also been found to have had a significant impact on adult education, agricultural extension, athletic competitions, health campaigns and community celebrations (Torres, 1992, p. 515). '

In an article which describes some of the difficulties faced by the New Schools programme as well as its strengths and achievements the author concludes by stating:

Transforming formal education is, without a doubt, *the* great challenge.
Schooling must be made less formal and more flexible, relevant, useful,
creative, enjoyable, responsive to pupils' intelligence and personal
inquiry, respectful of diversity, attentive to children's needs, responsive
to teachers' needs, open to participation by parents and the community
and accountable to society for the results achieved. This is precisely what
EN is endeavouring to do. And this is why it is worth supporting the
programme, understanding it better and learning from it.

(Torres, 1992, p. 519)

CONCLUSION

This chapter has argued that effective schooling will not be achieved without democracy and that school improvement is a process of democratization. This is not a message that will be popular with those who see schools in apolitical or technical terms or who believe that they have 'right' answers to school management and school effectiveness. This is because the paradox of democracy is that it rejects the idea of right answers for all times, all contexts and all people. It celebrates diversity within a system of rules agreed to through participation. Schools in developing countries are not currently democratic institutions in the main and do not contribute to the development of a wider democratic political culture. However, that they can be more democratic and that this can bring benefits is evident from the examples cited in this chapter. Achieving more democratic schools is as much a matter of political will as of money. It is therefore more than time for democratic education to stop being perceived as a minority, alternative interest within 'conventional' or 'mainstream' debates on school management and school effectiveness. For, inasmuch as such debates influence policy-makers, it should be at their core. If it is not, the academic literature on school management and school effectiveness is itself actually contributing to school ineffectiveness.

Conclusion

School Management and Development: Goals and Own Goals

The argument of this book is that conventional school effectiveness literature – whether from North or South – has failed to grasp or to transform the nature of school management in developing countries. This is because the research has neither a proper empirical or theoretical base. What this book has tried to show is that to attempt any improvement of schools we need a proper socio-political understanding of school *ineffectiveness*.

Our approach is new on two grounds. One is in the demonstration of the realities of school life and contexts: if schools in developing countries are ineffective, they may display problems and dysfunctions very different from schools in industrialized settings. In the book we have provided a great deal of evidence supporting this hypothesis. The second is that the reasons why they appear ineffective have a different base. Schools are not ineffective just because they 'lack' something (resources, management training, and so on). They are ineffective because the logic of schools in fragile states is a different logic. Ineffective schools are usually effective for someone or for some interest.

There are similarities here with the work on satisfiers and dissatisfiers. It has been shown that the 'dissatisfiers' of teaching (poor conditions of work, low pay, inefficient management) are not the direct opposite of satisfiers (which are feelings of self-worth, recognition, helping children develop or interacting with young people). Removal of dissatisfiers does not automatically make teachers more satisfied or motivated (Nias, 1981). Similarly, removal of some of the factors associated with ineffectiveness (lack of textbooks, little teacher training) will not automatically make schools or teachers more effective. They are ineffective – and would become effective – for different reasons, reasons concerned with the nature and purposes of schooling itself.

Our theoretical section tried to demonstrate some of the analyses of why this is. Macro theories of development (whether from right or left, capitalist or socialist) all came together to explain why schools in developing countries continue to exhibit features of inefficient bureaucracy. It is not just colonial heritage. Mass schooling organized in a pyramidal, hierarchical and selective way is able, at best, to maintain a system of natural selection and survival of the fittest, so that a society roughly allocates and prepares 'appropriate' people for appropriate slots. At worst, such schooling merely legitimates the existing elite and props up a fragile state by the promise of mass opportunity. For those theorists and governments espousing versions of modernization theory, the streamlined selective school is a deliberate choice; but even those governments attempting socialist transformation and genuine mass education appear to have been unable to divert systems away from bureaucratic forms. The poorer the country, the more inefficient the bureaucracy becomes. Ironically, the poorer the country and the more fragile its government, the more important it is to retain the myths and to retain the inefficiencies. Drop-outs, wastage, absenteeism, examination failure – they are all there for the reason that the country cannot cope with too much success.

In moving on to examine meso levels of national culture and micro levels of schools and individuals, we were able to plot these political logics against the needs and logics of the people who make up the institutions. Schools in developing countries operate in a prismatic way, occupying a range of contrasting discursive fields. One of the potential tensions is between the apparent rationality of Western forms of mass schooling and localized cultures of, for example, particularism, family, patriarchy and religion. We tried to show how institutions and individuals select their scripts for action on a daily basis from a great array of possibilities. In linking the macro analysis with the micro analysis we took the notion of agency and structure to show the interplay between script and social reproduction, between, for example, individual actors choosing scripts for stagnation, or resignation, or domination and those choices cumulatively acting to support existing regimes. Individuals have a vested interest in the scripts they choose and prefer, and draw on local national or international discourses as it suits them. To an outsider, their behaviour may appear irrational or outmoded. But to understand the outwardly ineffective or contradictory school, we have to understand the internal logics and script choices of all the actors.

We have laid great emphasis on the goals of schooling as a key starting-point for any discussion of whether a school is effective, and for whom. The image is a simple one of a dialogue box on the computer. If we take a goal such as *maximum achievement for all*, we can look at the motivations of all the actors concerned to establish whether they desire this, to see whether that box is 'switched on':

[   ] International agencies
[   ] Government
[   ] Local community/culture
[   ] The school/principal
[   ] Teachers
[   ] Students
[   ] Parents

While it might seem that everyone would want maximum achievement, we would argue from our research that it is not necessarily the case. Governments, as we have shown, may not genuinely welcome a mass increase in achievement and qualifications. Local communities might; but individual students and their parents rarely want success for all. In a competitive system they want their own success, bought at the price of someone else's failure. Introducing co-operative learning in a system designed to select only some for future advancement, is doomed to failure. It is not in their interests. Even some teachers may not actually want – or expect – mass achievement. At the classroom level, there are enormous vested interests in preserving the notions of differential ability (which is code for permanent failure for some).

If we take another goal such as gender equity, then this might have a different set of on–off combinations. Governments and international conditionalities certainly espouse this; but patriarchal interests in the community and local culture provide an important source of scripts for power for individual actors (students and teachers) in the school. The intersection between achievement and gender means that the less easily that students – or teachers – can draw on scripts for achievement, the more they may resort to scripts for dominance in other fields – such as masculinity.

Our interest, as has been clear, is in the consistency around goals for democracy. Many governments now contain such phrases in their constitutions or statements. Yet not only will the term democracy be interpreted in very different ways across all actors, the practice of democracy will not necessarily be in the interests of those concerned to preserve authoritarian power at various levels of education. Are the rhetorics of government White Papers and school mission statements actually translated into recognizable indicators of participation, respect for human rights, and legitimate authority? Do fragile states, fragile heads and even more fragile teachers genuinely want students to challenge and question?

In attempting change, we not only have to provide new scripts, but also new logics and new rewards. If governments, schools, teachers and students have vested interests in ineffectiveness for different reasons, then piecemeal injections or ringbinder training is going to make very little difference.

It will have become clear that we have little interest in making schools in developing countries (or elsewhere) simply more efficient selective bureaucracies. We have tried to show that finding more efficient ways of getting marginally more children through examinations is not in the country's interest in the long term. This will not help the problems of world peace, poverty or inequality. We were nonetheless able to find examples of what we would call genuinely effective, post-bureaucratic schools or systems, in schools or countries which have been prepared to take risks. For us, what characterizes those initiatives is three things: a degree of consistency in the goals of all the participants; flexibility in organization to maximize current learning and enable lifelong adaptability and lifelong ability to learn skills; and a democratic ethos and structure, which not only enhances such learning but prepares children for future political participation in a more sane world.

Our emphasis throughout has been on the match between goals and processes. Bureaucratic façade schools are characterized by elastic goals and rigid processes; the post-bureaucratic school by relatively firm goals and flexible processes. Bureaucratic schools in the end become driven only by their processes; management is seen as having a life of its own. The post-bureaucratic school on the other hand is driven by its goals and principles; management is there only to achieve those ends. We have argued that the failure of conventional (or even bureaucratic) effectiveness research is the emphasis on changing processes before – or instead of – changing goals. Post-bureaucratic effectiveness research and school improvement policy focuses first of all on the goals of all actors in the game in a particular country or culture and only then looks at processes (including management processes) which may be able to meet or reconcile those goals.

If governments or heads want to improve schools, they not only have to establish achievable goals, they have to surface those schools' scripts and discourses. This requires examination of

169

- what the discourses are
- where they are from
- whether they are deeply embedded or experimental
- whether they are agreed or contested

This will start to explain and reveal goals and own goals. Chapter 7 explored what was called 'footshooting' or 'own goal' schools and teachers: those behaviours which appeared actually to prevent or hinder learning. Various layers of meaning have to be unravelled, like peeling back an onion. If a teacher abuses a child's rights through violence (mental or physical), they will have a script to underpin this. They may genuinely believe (or have been told in teacher training) that this is efficient; or they may believe that children and parents will respect them; or they may be concerned to project an 'I'm in charge' script; or they may actually enjoy it. They may use an efficiency script to mask a sado-masochistic one. We need to discover *why* teachers act in ways that mean that in the long term their role and status is ineffective. Providing 100 textbooks (according to the World Bank-type improvement factors) will not alter these scripts, nor get inside the onion. In a context where teachers turn up irregularly, extra resource provision will not address the question of how or whether these books are used, and why, and according to whose logic.

There is a four-prong strategy in establishing effective school management for the post-bureaucratic school or society:

1. To establish a range of goals *achievable by the majority of learners*, which match national goals for development. Democracy is now currently one of these national goals.
2. To establish a number of indicators for those goals at the level of the school. For example if the national goal is health, then the school-level indicators may be health knowledge and application of related health skills; if it is citizenship, then the indicators may be participation in decision-making and knowledge of the political system; if it is mass literacy and communication skills, then the indicators may be students talking with each other to solve problems and ensuring that all can read.
3. To experiment with and to trace through a flexible range of processes which may achieve particular goals, and to cost out their implications. This part includes ethnographic research to establish how and whether participants come to share the same discourses; what rewards or costs are experienced.
4. To engage in parallel work on footshooters, the logics explaining why teachers remain ineffective and why schools retain cost-ineffective ways of operating. Are these own goals kicked in by the government, by the head, by individual teachers, by the students themselves?

The islands of effectiveness that we have highlighted appear to have engaged in at least some of this process. The goal may remain mass academic achievement, but this has percolated down the system so that students take responsibility for their own and others' learning, and are not afraid to work co-operatively. They are less fearful, because the competitive element is reduced through flexible ways of organizing the time and location of learning, and using criterion-, not norm-, referenced assessment. Teachers gain satisfiers, or rewards, in participating in curriculum and organizational decisions and seeing greater numbers of students enjoying learning. Democracy is not just a rhetoric at the mission statement level, but operationalized in the acknowledgement of dialogue and debate, and of a management which is open to challenge and change. If people do not get the rewards they seek, they can voice their concerns, instead of disguising or side-stepping them into legitimizing scripts for dominance or for hidden material gain.

One of the key reasons why schools operate ineffectively is fear. At individual and institutional level, it is easier to maintain the current system than to take risks and experiment with challenges to orthodoxy. Conventional effectiveness research and school improvement programmes present no such challenges. That is why they are so popular. They do not tackle the fundamental principles of what a mass education system might be *for*. The primary focus on internal process and factor side-steps uncomfortable but vital questions of purpose, in favour of attempts at 'neutral' or 'technical' mechanisms to enhance effectiveness.

However, our view is that the colossal expenditure on mass education is prone to equally colossal wastage unless governments take the risk of designing open systems, and attempt some honesty and realism about goals. In the absence of such attempts at what we would label democracy, then it is left to school managers to determine educational purposes – explicitly or by default. Sometimes this is positive subversion of authoritarian government; more often it is the survival of their particular school. Our argument has been that competitive and individualized systems are not effective for the mass of learners, still less for national goals of development and peace.

As stated in the Introduction, we are not relativist about educational values. This book has traced the sources of many competing discourses within schools. This does not mean that we subscribe to the position that all are equally valid for education in the future. If a country genuinely wants to achieve harmony, equity and economic stability, then its schools must move into the next century, and not remain anachronisms rooted in times when work patterns or food supplies were more predictable, and territories could be contested without global and massive warfare. Moving into the next century, however, does not automatically mean today's latest technology and surfing the Internet. It refers to more fundamental issues of educating people for co-operation, adaptability and the uncertainty of the unknown world of whatever technology or global weather conditions will bring. This is why our two key values are flexibility and democracy, and our conclusion is that these should be inseparable.

Our own prescriptive theory of the relationship between education and development is that the democratization of schools can – or should – go hand-in-hand with economic and political democracy. We do not subscribe to the view of some commentators (for example Monshipouri, 1995) that economic liberalism must precede any attempts to democratize government or society. Schools cannot of course transform society on their own. But they – and the individuals within them – can help and they can make a start. The failure of some previous socialist experiments in democratizing schools lay in the contradictions of the context of a one-party state, in top-down measures, and in not acknowledging the agency of heads, teachers and parents in subverting these and seeking alternative rewards. Democratic initiatives will succeed only with some realism about what material and psychological gains people will accrue from them. Yet our examination of more successful islands of effectiveness shows that the mix of pragmatism and idealism can be achieved. Our conclusion is that the democratic, post-bureaucratic school is in fact the only hope for the future.

REFERENCES

Abbey, E. (1989) 'The realities of school management in Ghana'. Unpublished MEd essay, University of Birmingham.

Achebe, C. (1960) *No Longer At Ease*. London: Heinemann.

Agnelli, S. (1986) *Street Children: A Growing Urban Tragedy*. London: Weidenfeld & Nicolson.

Albrow, M. (1970) *Bureaucracy*. London: Macmillan.

Almond, G. and Verba, S. (1963) *The Civic Culture*. Princeton, NJ: Princeton University Press.

Alverson, H. (1978) *Mind in the Heart of Darkness*. New Haven, CT: Yale University Press.

Anderson, L., Ryan, D. and Shapiro, J. (1987) *The Classroom Environment Study: Teaching for Learning*. Columbia: University of South Carolina.

Angus, L. (1993) 'The sociology of school effectiveness', *British Journal of Sociology of Education*, **14** (3), 327–39.

Armah, A. K. (1969) *The Beautyful Ones Are Not Yet Born*. London: Heinemann.

Avalos, B. (1980) 'Teacher effectiveness: research in the Third World, highlights of a review', *Comparative Education*, **16** (1), 45–54.

Avalos-Bevan, B. (1996) 'Schooling and the state: a review of current issues', in J. Turner (ed.) *The State and the School: An International Perspective*. London: Falmer.

Ba, M. (1986) *Scarlet Song*. Harlow: Longman.

Ba, M. (1987) *So Long a Letter*. London: Virago.

Bala, H. (1994) 'Effective schooling? the case of Catholic schools in northern Kenya'. Unpublished MEd dissertation, University of Birmingham.

Ball, S. (1987) *The Micro-Politics of the School*. London: Methuen.

Ball, S. (1990) *Politics and Policy-Making in Education*. London: Routledge.

Banya, K. (1991) 'Economic decline and the education system: the case of Sierra Leone', *Compare*, **21** (2), 127–41.

Barley, N. (1986) *The Innocent Anthropologist*. Harmondsworth: Penguin.

Barley, N. (1988) *Not a Dangerous Sport*. Harmondsworth: Penguin.

Beddoe, I. (undated) 'Public relations in educational institutions'. Unpublished and undated paper, School of Education, University of the West Indies, St Augustine, Trinidad.

Bennett, N. (1993) 'How can schooling help improve the lives of the poorest? The need for radical reform', in Levin and Lockheed (1993).

Berger, M. (1957) *Bureaucracy and Society in Modern Egypt*. Princeton, NJ: Princeton University Press.

Biddlecombe, P. (1993) *French Lessons in Africa*. London: Abacus.

Black, H., Govinda, R., Kiragu, F. and Devine, M. (1993) *School Improvement in the Developing World: An Evaluation of the Aga Khan Foundation Programme*. Edinburgh: Scottish Council for Research in Education.

Bowles, S. (1976) 'Cuban education and revolutionary ideology', in P. and G. Figueroa (eds) *Sociology of Education: A Caribbean Reader*. Oxford: Oxford University Press.

Bowles, S. and Gintis, H. (1976) *Schooling in Capitalist America*. New York: Basic Books.

Bray, M. (1995) 'Community financing of education: cultural variations and policy tensions in developing countries'. Paper presented at the 1995 DICE conference, 'Partnerships in Education and Development: Tensions between Economics and Culture', London.

Bray, M. with Lillis, K. (eds) (1988) *Community Financing of Education: Issues and Policy Implications in Less Developed Countries*. Oxford: Pergamon Press.

British Council (1993) *Development Priorities: Guidelines*. Manchester: British Council.

Brittain, V. (1994) 'Hope constantly deferred is Africa's lot under the West's economic reform', *Guardian* (London: 14 March 1994).

Brown, P. and Lauder, H. (1996) 'Education, globalization and economic development', *Journal of Education Policy*, **11** (1), 1–26.

Burgess, R. (1986) *Sociology, Education and Schools*. London: Batsford.

Burke, C. (1996) 'The changing agenda of teacher education in Papua New Guinea', *International Journal of Educational Development*, **16** (1), 41–52.

Bush, T. (1995) *Theories of Educational Management*. London: Paul Chapman.

Caillods, F. and Postlethwaite, N. (1989) 'Teaching/learning conditions in developing countries', *Prospects*, **19** (2), 169–90.

Carnoy, M. and Samoff, J. (1990) *Education and Social Transition in the Third World*. Princeton, NJ: Princeton University Press.

Carr, W. and Hartnett, A. (1995) *Education and the Struggle for Democracy*. London: Cassell.

Chantavanich, A., Chantavanich, S. and Fry, G. (1990) *Evaluating Primary Education*. Ottawa: International Development Research Centre.

Chapman, J., Froumin, I. and Aspin, D. (1995) *Creating and Managing the Democratic School*. London: Falmer.

Chaturvedi, Y. (1989) 'A case study from India', in Ranaweera (1989)

Chen Shao-Min (1989) 'A case study from China', in Ranaweera (1989).

Chew, D. (1990) 'Internal adjustments to falling civil service salaries: insights from Uganda', *World Development*, **18** (7), 1003–14.

Christie, P. (1991) *The Right to Learn*. Johannesburg: SACHED/Ravan.

Colbert, V., Chiappe, C. and Arboleda, J. (1993) 'The New School Programme: more and better primary education for children in rural areas in Colombia', in Levin and Lockheed (1993).

Colclough, C. with Lewin, K. (1993) *Educating All the Children*. Oxford: Clarendon Press.

Creemers, B. (1992) 'School effectiveness, effective instruction and school improvement in the Netherlands', in Reynolds and Cuttance (1992).

Crowder, M. (ed.) (1984) *Education for Development*. Gaborone: Macmillan for the Botswana Society.

Cummings, W. (1986) *Low-Cost Primary Education: Implementing an Innovation in Six Nations*. Ottawa: International Development Research Centre.

Dadey, A. (1990) 'The role of the headmaster in the administration of secondary schools in Ghana'. Doctoral thesis, University of Birmingham.

Dadey, A. and Harber, C. (1991) *Training and Professional Support for Headship in Africa*. London: Commonwealth Secretariat.

Danish Union of Teachers (1994) 'Waiting for peace – Liberia's tragedy', *Education International*, **1** (3), 2–3.

Da Silva, T. (1984) 'Pedagogy and social class in a Brazilian urban setting'. Doctoral thesis, Stanford University, California.

Datta, A. (1984) *Education and Society: A Sociology of African Education*. London: Macmillan.

Davies, L. (1984) *Pupil Power: Deviance and Gender in Schools*. Lewes: Falmer.

Davies, L. (1986) 'Policies on inequality in the Third World', *British Journal of Sociology of Education*, **7** (2), 191–204.

Davies, L. (1988) 'Contradictions of control: lessons from exploring teachers' work in Botswana', *International Journal of Educational Development*, **8** (4), 293–304.

Davies, L. (1990) *Equity and Efficiency? School Management in an International Context*. Lewes: Falmer.

Davies, L. (1992) 'School power cultures under economic constraint', *Educational Review*, **43** (2), 127–36.

Davies, L. (1993) 'Teachers as implementers or subversives', *International Journal of Educational Development*, **13** (2), 161–70.

Davies, L. (1994) *Beyond Authoritarian School Management: The Challenge for Transparency*. Ticknall: Education Now.

Davies, L. (1995a) 'International indicators of democratic development', in Harber (1995).

Davies, L. (1995b) *Performance Indicators in the Zimbabwe Education Service*. Report to Zimbabwe Government.

Davies, L. and Iqbal, Z. (1997) 'Tensions in teacher training for school effectiveness: the case of Pakistan', *School Effectiveness and School Improvement*, **8** (2), 254–66.

Davies, L. and Kurshed, T. (1995) *The Restructuring of Secondary and Intermediate Education*. Study 14 of the Government of Pakistan/World Bank Secondary Educational Reform Programme. Islamabad.

Departemen Pendidikan Dan Kebudayaan (1987) *The Cianjur Project* (video). Jakarta.

Donors to African Education (1994) *Newsletter*, **6** (2).

Dore, R. (1976) *The Diploma Disease*. Berkeley: University of California Press.

DuBey, D., Edem, D. and Thakur, A. (1979) *The Sociology of Nigerian Education*. London: Macmillan.

Dzvimbo, K. (1995) 'Didactics or educational sciences: curriculum, and instruction and the search for an alternative paradigm for effective schools in a new South Africa', *Zimbabwe Journal of Educational Research*, **7** (1), 1–22.

Edem, D. (1982) *Introduction to Educational Administration in Nigeria.* Chichester: John Wiley.

Edwards, G. and Fisher, J. (1995) 'Effective and ineffective secondary schools in Zimbabwe: a preliminary study', *International Studies in Educational Administration,* **23** (1), 27–37.

Ferguson, F. (1993) 'Huni Valley', *Focus on Africa,* **4** (4), 42–3.

Focus on Africa (London: BBC).

Foucault, M. (1977) *Discipline and Punish.* London: Allen Lane.

Freire, P. (1970) *The Pedagogy of the Oppressed.* New York: Herder & Herder.

Fullan, M. (1991) *The New Meaning of Educational Change.* London: Cassell.

Fuller, B. (1987) 'What school factors raise achievement in the Third World?', *Review of Educational Research,* **57** (3), 255–92.

Fuller, B. (1991) *Growing Up Modern.* London: Routledge.

Fuller, B. and Clarke, P. (1994) 'Raising school effects while ignoring culture? Local conditions and the influence of classroom rules, tools and pegagogy', *Review of Educational Research,* **64**, 119–57.

Fuller, B. and Heyneman, S. (1989) 'Third World school quality: current collapse, future potential', *Educational Researcher,* **18** (2), 12–19.

Fuller, B. and Holsinger, D. (1992) *Secondary Education in Developing Countries: Issues Review.* Draft Issues Review Paper. Washington, DC: World Bank.

Fuller, B. and Snyder, A. (1992) 'Teacher productivity in sticky institutions: curricular and gender variations', in D. Chapman and H. Walberg (eds) *International Perspectives in Educational Productivity.* Greenwich, CT: JAI Press.

Giddens, A. (1976) *New Rules of Sociological Method: A Positive Critique of Interpretive Sociologies.* London: Hutchinson.

Giddens, A. (1977) *Studies in Social and Political Theory.* London: Hutchinson.

Giddens, A. (1979) *Central Problems in Social Theory.* London: Macmillan.

Giorgiades, W. and Jones, H. (1989) *A Review of Research on Headmaster and School Principalship in Developing Countries.* Washington: World Bank.

Giroux, H. (1981) *Ideology, Culture and the Process of Schooling.* Philadelphia: Temple University Press.

Gordon, R. (1994) 'Education policy and gender in Zimbabwe', *Gender and Education,* **6** (2), 131–9.

Gowrie, G. (1989) 'The relationship between principal–teacher interaction and primary school climate in the Saint George East Division of Trinidad and Tobago'. MA thesis, University of the West Indies, St Augustine, Trinidad.

Graham-Brown, S. (1991) *Education in the Developing World: Conflict and Crisis.* Harlow: Longman.

Hallak, J. (1990) *Investing in the Future.* Oxford: Pergamon.

Handy, C. (1984) *Taken for Granted? Understanding Schools as Organizations.* York: Longman.

Handy, C. and Aitken, R. (1986) *Understanding Schools as Organizations.* Harmondsworth: Penguin.

Hanson, E. (1986) *Educational Reform and Administrative Development: The Cases of Colombia and Venezuela.* Stanford, CA: Hoover Press.

Harber, C. (1989) *Politics in African Education*. London: Macmillan.

Harber, C. (1992) *Democratic Learning and Learning Democracy*. Ticknall: Education Now.

Harber, C. (1993) 'Democratic management and school effectiveness in Africa: learning from Tanzania', *Compare*, **23** (3), 289–300.

Harber, C. (ed.) (1995) *Developing Democratic Education*. Ticknall: Education Now.

Harber, C. (1996) *Small Schools and Democratic Practice*. Nottingham: Educational Heretics Press.

Harber, C. and Meighan, R. (1989) *The Democratic School*. Ticknall: Education Now.

Harbison, R. and Hanushek, E. (1992) *Educational Performance of the Poor: Lessons from North-East Brazil*. Washington: World Bank.

Harris, G. (1989) *The Sociology of Development*. Harlow: Longman.

Hayter, T. (1971) *Aid as Imperialism*. Harmondsworth: Penguin.

Hawes, H. (1988) *Child-to-Child: Another Path to Learning*. Hamburg: UNESCO Institute for Education.

Hawes, H. and Stephens, D. (1990) *Questions of Quality: Primary Education and Development*. Harlow: Longman.

Hawkridge, D., Jaworski, J. and McMahon, H. (1990) *Computers in Third World Schools: Examples, Experience and Issues*. London: Macmillan.

Heneveld, W. (1993) *Research into Practice: Guidelines for Planning and Monitoring the Quality of Primary Education in Sub-Saharan Africa*. Washington, DC: World Bank.

Heyneman, S. (1990) 'Economic crisis and the quality of education', *International Journal of Educational Development*, **10** (2), 115–30.

Heyneman, S. (1995) 'Good educational governance: an American export', *The American School Board Journal*, **6**, 22–6.

Heyneman, S. and Loxley, W. (1985) 'The effects of primary school quality on academic achievement across twenty-nine high and low income countries', *American Journal of Sociology*, **88**, 1162–94.

Holmes, M. and Wynne, E. (1989) *Making the School an Effective Community*. Lewes: Falmer.

Hoogvelt, A. (1976) *The Sociology of Developing Societies*. London: Macmillan.

Hopper, E. (1971) 'Educational systems and selected consequences of patterns of mobility and non-mobility in industrial societies: a theoretical discussion', in E. Hopper (ed.) *Readings in the Theory of Educational Systems*. London: Hutchinson.

Hough, J. (1989) 'Inefficiency in education – the case of Mali', *Comparative Education*, **25** (1), 77–85.

House, E. and Lapan, S. (1978) *Survival in the Classroom*. Boston: Allyn & Bacon.

Hughes, L. (1996) 'A far cry from Westminster', *The Independent Magazine*, January.

Hughes, M. (1987) 'Theory and practice in educational management', in M. Hughes, P. Ribbins and H. Thomas (eds) *Managing Education: The System and the Institution*. London: Cassell.

Hughes, M. (1990) 'Improving education and training for educational administrators and managers: urgent needs'. Paper presented to UNESCO International Congress 'Planning and Management of Educational Development', Mexico.

Hunt, F. (1987) *The Incorporation of Education*. London: Routledge.

Ianello, K. (1992) *Decisions Without Hierarchy: Feminist Interventions in Organization Theory and Practice*. New York: Routledge.

Igwe, S. (1988) 'Community financing of schools in Eastern Nigeria', in Bray with Lillis (1988).

IIEP (1983) *Intensive Training Course in Microplanning and Mapping*. Jamaica: IIEP.

Ishumi, A. and Cooksey, B. (1985) 'Policy and practice in Tanzanian secondary education since 1967'. Seminar paper, University of Dar Es Salaam. (A revised and shortened version of this was published as B. Cooksey (1986), 'Policy and practice in Tanzanian secondary education since 1967', *International Journal of Educational Development*, **6** (3), 183–202.)

Jansen, J. (1995) 'Effective schools?' *Comparative Education*, **31** (2), 181–200.

Jeffs, T. (1988) 'Preparing young children for participatory democracy', in B. Carrington and B. Troyna (eds) *Children and Controversial Issues*. Lewes: Falmer Press.

Jeng, M. (1995) 'The better schools modules in the Gambia: an evaluation'. Unpublished MEd paper, University of Birmingham.

Jensen, K. and Walker, S. (1989) *Towards Democratic Schooling: European Experiences*. Milton Keynes: Open University Press.

Joseph, S. (1991) *Developing the School as a Caring Community through the Devolution of Leadership*. Research proposal, Department of Educational Research and Development, Faculty of Education, University of the West Indies, St Augustine, Trinidad.

Kang, S. W. (1995) 'Education and democratisation in Korea'. Paper presented at a seminar, University of Birmingham.

Kann, U. (1984) 'Problems of equity in the educational system: the provision of basic education in Botswana', in Crowder (1984).

Kelley, E. (1984) *Horse Races, Time Trials and Evaluation Designs: Implications for Future Evaluations of the Improved Efficiency of Learning Project*. Albany, NY: Center for Educational Evaluation, SUNY-Albany.

Kinyanjui, R. (1990) 'A study of parental involvement in education with special reference to Kenya'. MEd dissertation, University of Birmingham.

Kwong, J. (1996) 'The new educational mandate in China: running schools running businesses', *International Journal of Educational Development*, **16** (2), 185–94.

Leonardos, A. (1993) 'CIEP: a democratic school model for educating economically disadvantaged students in Brazil?', in Levin and Lockheed (1993).

Levin, H. and Lockheed, M. (eds) (1993) *Effective Schools in Developing Countries*. London: Falmer.

Levine, D. and Lezotte, L. (1990) *Unusually Effective Schools: A Review and Analysis of Research and Practice*. Madison, WI: National Center for Effective Schools Research and Development.

Leys, C. (1996) *The Rise and Fall of Development Theory*. London: James Currey.

Lockheed, M. (1993) 'The condition of primary education in developing countries', in Levin and Lockheed (1993).

Lockheed, M. and Komenar, A. (1989) 'Teaching quality and student achievement in Africa: the case of Nigeria and Swaziland', *Teaching and Teacher Education*, **5**, 93–113.

Lockheed, M. and Verspoor, A. (1991) *Improving Primary Education in Developing Countries*. Oxford: World Bank/Oxford University Press.

Lulat, Y. (1988) 'Education and national development: the continuing problem of misdiagnosis and irrelevant prescriptions', *International Journal of Educational Development*, **8** (4), 315–28.

Lungu, G. (1983) 'Some critical issues in the training of educational administrators for developing countries of Africa', *International Journal of Educational Development*, **3** (1), 85–97.

Lutanjuka, S. and Mutembei, J. (1993) 'Management challenges in provision of basic educational needs/services in secondary schools'. Paper presented to the Heads of Secondary Schools Conference, Arusha, Tanzania.

Lwehabura, J. (1993) 'Effective schooling? Education for self-reliance and school effectiveness in Tanzanian secondary schools'. Doctoral thesis, University of Birmingham.

Ma, W. and Hawkridge, D. (1995) 'China's changing policy and practice in television education, 1978–1993', *International Journal of Educational Development*, **15**, 127–36.

Maclure, M. (1994) 'Language and discourse: the embrace of uncertainty', *British Journal of Sociology of Education*, **15** (2), 283–300.

McNie, B., White, R. and Wight, J. (1991) *Headteacher Management Training and the Development of Support Materials: A Planning Overview*. London: Commonwealth Secretariat.

Mannathoko, C. (1995) 'Gender, ideology and the state in Botswana's teacher education'. Doctoral thesis, University of Birmingham.

Mante, R. (1981) *Multiple Outcomes and Multiple Client Perspectives in the Evaluation of Project IMPACT: A Two-year Tracer Study*. Cebu City, Philippines: INNOTECH.

Maravanyika, O. (1995) 'Community financing strategies and resources within the context of educational democratization: the case of Zimbabwe'. Paper presented at the DICE Conference 24–26 May 1995: 'Partnerships in Education and Development: Tensions between Economics and Culture'.

Marcelino, E. (1992) 'The Philippines: methodology and practice in community education', in Poster and Zimmer (1992).

Martin, C. (1994) '"Let the young birds fly": schooling, work and emancipation in rural west Mexico', *Compare*, **24** (3), 259–76.

Mbilinyi, M. (1979) 'Secondary education', in H. Hinzen and V. Hundsdorfer (eds) *The Tanzanian Experience*. London: Evans.

Meighan, R. (1992) 'Home-based education', in Meighan and Toogood (1992).

Meighan, R. (1995) *The Freethinkers' Guide to the Educational Universe*. Nottingham: Educational Heretics Press.

Meighan, R. and Toogood, P. (1992) *Anatomy of Choice in Education*. Ticknall: Education Now.

Meyer, J. (1988) 'Moral education in Taiwan', *Comparative Education Review*, **32**, 20–38.

Moll, I. (1995) 'For the sake of form: managing a rural South African school'. Unpublished paper.

Molutsi, P. (1991) 'Continuity and change in African value systems in the face of modern Western technology', in Kwesi Kwaa Prah (ed.) *Culture, Gender, Science and Technology in Africa*. Windhoek: Harp Publications.

Monshipouri, M. (1995) *Democratization, Liberation and Human Rights in the Third World*. London: Lynne Rienner.

Morgan, G. (1986) *Images of Organization*. Beverly Hills: Sage.

Musaazi, J. (1982) *The Theory and Practice of Educational Administration*. London: Macmillan.

Musgrove, F. (1971) *Power and Authority in English Education*. London: Methuen.

Myrdal, G. (1968) *Asian Drama*, Vol. 1. New York: Twentieth Century Fund.

Nagel, T. (1992) *Quality Between Tradition and Modernity: Patterns of Cognition in Zimbabwe*. Oslo: Pedagogisk Forskningsinstitutt, University of Oslo.

Namibia Ministry of Education and Culture (1991) *Annual Report for the Year Ending 31 December 1991*. Windhoek.

Namibia Ministry of Education and Culture (1992) *A Report on a Course in Educational Management for Inspectors of Education*. Windhoek.

Namibia Ministry of Education and Culture (1993a) *Toward Education for All*. Windhoek: Gamsberg Macmillan.

Namibia Ministry of Education and Culture (1993b) *A Report on the Training of Trainers*. Windhoek.

Namibia Ministry of Education and Culture (1993c) *An Introduction to IGCSE and HGCSE*. Windhoek: University of Cambridge Local Examinations Syndicate/ Ministry of Education and Culture.

Newton, E. (1975) 'School organization in a changing society'. Paper presented at the Inauguration of the Trinidad and Tobago Council of Educational Administration.

Ngegba, S. (1993) 'School management, effectiveness and educational standards in Sierra Leone: a study of primary schooling'. Doctoral thesis, University of Birmingham.

Ngugi Wa Thiongo (1986) *Petals of Blood*. Oxford: Heinemann.

Nias, J. (1981) 'Teacher satisfaction and dissatisfaction: Herzberg's "two-factor" hypothesis revisited', *British Journal of Sociology of Education*, **2**, 235–46.

Ninnes, P. (1995) 'Informal learning contexts in Solomon Islands and their implications for the cross-cultural classroom', *International Journal of Educational Development*, **15** (1), 15–26.

NIR (National Institute of Development Research and Documentation) (1988) *Teenage Pregnancies in Botswana*. Gaborone: University of Botswana.

Olembo, J. and Cameron, J. (1986) *Practical Primary School Administration*. London: Edward Arnold.

Omokhodian, J. (1989) 'Classroom observed: the hidden curriculum of Lagos schools', *International Journal of Educational Development*, **9** (2), 99–110.

Opolot, J. (1994) *Study on Costs and Cost-effective Approaches to Primary Education in Uganda*. Kampala: UNICEF.

Oppong, C. and Abu, K. (1987) *Seven Roles of Women: Impact of Education, Migration and Employment on Ghanaian Women*. Geneva: ILO.

Ousmane, S. (1976) *Xala*. Oxford: Heinemann.

Ozigi, A. (1984) *A Handbook on School Administration*. Harare: The College Press/Macmillan.

Pinkompee, P. (1979) 'An investigation of perceived in-service needs and techniques to meet these needs for secondary school principals in Thailand' (doctoral dissertation, University of Missouri-Columbia), *Dissertation Abstracts International*, **40**.

Poster, C. and Zimmer, J. (eds) (1992) *Community Education in the Third World*. London: Routledge.

Prophet, R. (1987) 'Rhetoric and reality in science curriculum development in Botswana'. Paper presented to the British Educational Research Association Annual Conference, Manchester.

Prophet, R. (1995) 'Views from the junior secondary classroom: case study of a curriculum intervention', *International Journal of Educational Development*, **15** (2), 127–40.

Ramatebele, B. (1984) 'Education for development in the 1980s: problems and prospects', in Crowder (1984).

Ranaweera, A. (ed.) (1989) *Non-Conventional Approaches to Education at the Primary Level*. Hamburg: UNESCO Institute for Education.

Reid, K., Hopkins, D. and Holly, P. (1987) *Towards the Effective School*. Oxford: Blackwell.

Reilly, W. (1987) 'Management and training for development: the Hombe thesis', *Public Administration and Development*, **2**, 25–42.

Reimers, F. (1993) *Education and Consolidation of Democracy in Latin America*. Washington: USAID.

Reimers, F. (1994) 'Education and structural adjustment in Latin America and sub-Saharan Africa', *International Journal of Educational Development*, **14** (2), 119–29.

Reynolds, D. (1992) 'School effectiveness and school improvement: an updated review of the British literature', in Reynolds and Cuttance (1992).

Reynolds, D. (1993) 'School effectiveness: the international perspective'. Unpublished paper.

Reynolds, D. and Cuttance, P. (eds) (1992) *School Effectiveness: Research, Policy and Practice*. London: Cassell.

Reynolds, D., Sullivan, M. and Murgatroyd, S. (1987) *The Comprehensive Experiment*. Lewes: Falmer.

Rideout, W. M. (1987) 'Rights of access and equal opportunity', in N. B. Tarrow (ed.) *Human Rights and Education*. Oxford: Pergamon Press.

Riggs, F. (1964) *Administration in Developing Countries: The Theory of Prismatic Society*. Boston: Houghton Mifflin.

Rodwell, S. and Hurst, P. (1985) 'Learning resources for the professional development of educational administrators in the Third World', in D. Marshall and E. Newton (eds), *The Professional Preparation of Educational Adminis-*

trators in Developing Areas: The Caribbean. Ontario: Nipissing University College.

Rojas, C. (1994) 'The Escuela Nueva school programme in Colombia', in P. Dalin (ed.) *How Schools Improve*. London: Cassell.

Sah-Myung, H. (1983) 'The Republic of South Korea', in R. Murray Thomas and T. Neville Postlethwaite (eds) *Schooling in East Asia*. Oxford: Pergamon Press.

Saunders, M. (1984) 'Implementing a practical action curriculum policy: a case study of education for self-reliance Tanzania'. Doctoral thesis, University of Lancaster.

Schatzberg, M. (1979) 'Conflict and culture in African education: authority patterns in a Cameroonian Lycée', *Comparative Educational Review*, **23** (1), 52–65.

Scheerens, J. (1992) *Effective Schooling: Research, Theory and Practice*. London: Cassell.

Scott, B. (1995) 'Malawi – teachers helping teachers', *Educational International*, double issue, **1** (4) and **2** (1), 39–41.

Scott, J. (1995) *Gender and Development. Rethinking Modernization and Dependency Theory*. London: Lynne Rienner.

Sealy, G. (1992) 'The task of the primary school principal in Barbados'. Unpublished MEd dissertation, University of Birmingham.

Shipman, M. (1971) *Education and Modernization*. London: Faber.

Simon, M. (1984) 'Equity in secondary education in Botswana', in Crowder (1984).

Singhal, R. (1988) *Indian Schools: A Study of Teacher–Pupil Ratio*. New Delhi: Vikas.

Smith, W. and Andrews, R. (1989) *Instructional Leadership: How Principals Make a Difference*. Alexandria, VA: Association for Supervision and Curriculum Development.

Snyder, W. (1991) *Consultation on Change: Proceedings of the Etosha Conference*. Tallahassee, FL: Florida State University.

Stephens, D. (1993) 'Putting children first: an alternative approach to health education in India and Uganda. Research in progress'. Paper presented at conference 'The Changing Role of the State in Educational Development', Oxford, September.

Tedesco, J. (1994) 'Knowledge versus values', *Educational Innovation*, **78**, 1.

Thaman, K. (1995) 'Different eyes: indigenous educational ideas and their relevance to modern education, the case of Tonga'. Paper presented at the DICE International Conference, London, May.

Toogood, P. (1992a) 'Minischooling', in Meighan and Toogood (1992).

Toogood, P. (1992b) 'Work as an educational resource: the flexi college initiative', in Meighan and Toogood (1992).

Torres, R. (1992) 'Alternatives in formal education: Colombia's Escuela Nueva programme', *Prospects*, **22** (4), 510–20.

Trafford, B. (1993) *Sharing Power in Schools: Raising Standards*. Ticknall: Education Now.

Tsang, M. and Wheeler, C. (1993) 'Local initiatives and their implications for a multi-level approach to school improvement in Thailand', in Levin and Lockheed (1993).

Tsukudu, P. and Taylor, P. (1995) 'Management development support for head teachers of secondary schools', in D. Johnson (ed.) *Educational Management and Policy: Research, Theory and Practice in South Africa*. Bristol: Centre for International Studies in Education, University of Bristol.

UNDP (1992) *Human Development Report*. New York: UNDP.

UNDP (1993, 1994 and 1995) *Human Development Report*. Oxford: Oxford University Press.

UNESCO (1994) *Education for All: Status and Trends*. Paris: UNESCO.

UNESCO (1995) *Education, Population and Development*. Paris: UNESCO.

UNICEF (1989) *The State of the World's Children*. New York: UNICEF.

UNICEF (1994a) *The Progress of Nations*. New York: UNICEF.

UNICEF (1994b) *The State of the World's Children*. New York: UNICEF.

USAID (1993) *Namibia Basic Education Reform Program*. Windhoek: Creative Associates International.

User's Guide to the Education Code of Conduct (1993). Windhoek: Ministry of Education and Culture.

Van Mierlo, J. (1984) 'The economic theory of the political process and representative democracy', *Maandschrift Economie*, **48**, 256–85.

Van Rensburg, P. (1978) *The Serowe Brigades*. London: Macmillan.

Villegas-Reimers, E. (1993) 'Where do we go from here?', in *Colloquium on Education for Democracy: Proceedings of a Workshop*. Washington: USAID.

Vulliamy, G. (1981) 'The Secondary Schools Extension Project in Papua New Guinea', *Journal of Curriculum Studies*, **13**, 93–102.

Vulliamy, G. (1987) 'School effectiveness research in Papua New Guinea', *Comparative Education*, **23**, 209–33.

Walberg, H. (1991) 'Improving school science in advanced and developing countries', *Review of Educational Research*, **61** (1), 25–69.

Walker, R. (1974) 'Classroom research: a view from SAFARI', in B. Macdonald *et al.* (eds) *SAFARI: Innovation Evaluation Research and the Problem of Control*. Norwich: CARE, University of East Anglia.

Warwick, D., Reimers, F. and McGinn, N. (1992) 'The implementation of educational innovations: lessons from Pakistan', *International Journal of Educational Development*, **12** (4), 297–308.

Williams, C. (1992) 'Curriculum relevance for street children', *Curriculum Journal*, **3** (3), 279–90.

Women's College (1996) *Prospectus*. Cape Town: South Africa.

Woodard, D. (1985) 'A descriptive study of the South Thailand elementary principalship' (doctoral dissertation, University of Missouri-Columbia), *Dissertation Abstracts International*, **45**.

World Bank (1986) *Financing Education in Developing Countries*. Washington: World Bank.

World Bank (1989) *World Development Report*. Washington: World Bank.

World Bank (1990) *Primary Education: A World Bank Policy Paper*. Washington: World Bank.

World University Service (1994) *Education in Mozambique: Addressing the Approaching Crisis*. London: WUS.

Zimmer, J. (1992) 'Asia: diary of a community educator', in Poster and Zimmer (1992).

Name Index

Subject Index